Ray Guns, Robots and Rocket Ships

Science-Fiction Serials 1930-1953

Love's Labor Press

Ray Guns, Robots and Rocket Ships

Science Fiction Serials 1930-1953

Ken Weiss

Love's Labor Press

Distributed by Cummington Company

Dedicated to the unbilled bit players
and stunt men and women
—the real stars of serials.

ACKNOWLEDGEMENTS

The serial synopses in this book are revised and adapted versions of those that appeared in *To Be Continued... American Sound Serials 1929-1956*, Second Edition (2000), a two-volume limited edition of 250 copies. Most stills came from my collection, but I was aided mightily by Robert Brosch and most especially by serial historian Jim Stringham, who came through when all else failed, and to Gerald Haber. For new cast and credit information I'm indebted to *Serial Report* and the work of Boyd Magers, James Stringham, Hal Polk, Ed Billings and Joel Wise. Robert Brosch (14845 Anne St., Allen Park, MI, 48101)has a lot of serial stills available at reasonable prices.

Anyone who loves serials should have a subscription to *Serial Report*, a fact-filled quarterly that keeps the spirit of the old cliffhangers alive. They're at 1312 Stagecoach Rd., SE, Albuquerque, NM 87123 . Good serial information and terrific pictures show up regularly in *Filmfax* (1320 Oakton St., Evanston, IL 60202), well worth a subscription.

Softcover ISBN 0-9724631-1-9
Hardcover ISBN 0-9724631-2-7

Cummington Company
17 Old Orchard Road
New Rochelle, NY 10804

CONTENTS

INTRODUCTION

A science-fiction serial is not just science, and not just fiction. A love story about two scientists wouldn't qualify. And it takes more than just a scientific gizmo. There has to be a variety of gizmos, as well as a certain ambience, a sci-fi feel, that crowds out other genre factors. Take *Dick Tracy* (Republic-37) for example, which features a microwave device that can destroy a bridge and a "flying-wing" bomber of advanced design, both science-fiction elements. But no matter how you slice it, *Dick Tracy* is essentially a detective-adventure serial and won't show up in this book. *The Phantom Empire* (Mascot-35), on the other hand, at first appears to be a Western, with Gene Autry, Frankie Darro and Betsy King Ross doing a lot of galloping. But as soon as they hit the underground city of Murania everything changes. In Murania, as you'll learn, robots do all the work, people live long, healthy lives and want no exposure to the corrupting influences of the outside world, which its queen can observe through a special "television." The "Western" elements, while still important, more or less fade into the background as the science-fiction wonders take over: the glistening city of Murania, with its towering structures, uranium-powered generators and factories, ray guns, robots, and a weapon "capable of destroying the universe." *The Phantom Empire*, which receives considerable attention in this book, emerges as the fourth science-fiction sound serial, and the first to feature an advanced civilization.

Three serials, *The Lost City*, *The Mysterious Dr. Satan* and *The Monster and the Ape* were strictly judgement calls: *The Lost City* (35) could just as easily have been considered a jungle serial. It takes place in a jungle, has native tribes including Arab slave traders and pygmies, and occasional wild animals. But it also has a futuristic lost city, a scientist madman who is causing havoc throughout the planet by disrupting the weather and who plans on conquering the world using black Africans he has turned into giants, television, death rays, and a resident scientific genius who's being forced to do the evil one's bidding. *The Lost City*, the reader should be warned, is easily the most racist sound serial ever made. The heroes respond to a cry for help because "that sounds like a white woman screaming," and among the scientific genius's achievments is a formula for turning black people white. We watch him do it for a pygmy who has begged him for this privilege. "This is the greatest scientific discovery yet," the hero tells the scientist. The serial abounds with similar abuses, each one carefully described in the synopsis. *The Mysterious Dr. Satan* (40) is here on less secure footing. The main villain utilizes closed circuit television, remote-control devices that can kill people and another that can "revolutionize warfare." Which by themselves would be pretty weak science-fiction soup. But Dr. Satan also has a robot, which was the deciding factor. The rationale for including *The Monster and the Ape* (45) is even more tenuous. It boils down to a robot (the "monster") being an essential part of the plot. Anyone who insists that the latter two serials are not really science fiction will get no rebuttal from me.

Serials, no less than feature films, reflected the racism and sexism of their times. There's plenty of both within this book. I'd guess very little of it was conscious. Racism and sexism were so ingrained they were simply taken for granted. Sometimes stereotypes were contradicted: sometimes the heroine rescued the hero and sometimes people of color were treated as rational human beings. These rare occasions are also detailed when found. Happily, ageism is often absent as middle-aged, or older, characters slug it out with good guys or bad guys and pretty much beat them to a pulp. (See Pierre Watkin in *Jack Armstrong*, and Charles Middleton in the latter chapters of that serial, or George Eldredge in *Captain Video*.)

As a genre, science-fiction serials developed their own required ingredients. There's almost always a scientific genius involved, either as the main antagonist or as a prisoner/pawn of the evil one. There are usually secret weapons or fabulous inventions as the objects of desire, the key to which is generally a secret formula, map or blueprints, or all three. Miraculously, nearly all the serials in this book are available on videotape and/or DVD. Only *Voice from the Sky* is among the missing. The reader is encouraged to buy the tapes or DVDs and see for him or herself the wonders—deliberate and unintentional—that can unfold.

Although the sound ones start in 1930 with the totally-lost *Voice from the Sky*, science-fiction serials really blast off in 1936, with Universal's *Flash Gordon*, the studio's second largest money maker that year, right behind *Three Smart Girls* (which introduced Deanna Durbin). Pretty good for a serial. Arguably, *Flash Gordon* might be the best sound serial ever made. Its qualities seem to become more endearing with age and even today's youngsters are seduced by its charms. No science fiction serials were produced in 1941-1944 during the World War II years. Too many other dangers seemed far more real, and Germans and Japanese became the enemy of choice. (Although many Western serials continued in the timeless manner.) The end of the war saw an increase in serials (not all of them sci-fi) about atom bombs and atom power (*Lost City of the Jungle, The Crimson Ghost, Jack Armstrong*) and reports of flying saucer sightings were quickly converted into serial fodder by appreciative writers (*The Purple Monster Strikes, Flying Disc Man from Mars, Radar Men from the Moon, Zombies from the Stratosphere*). Flying Saucers from outer space were a natural for serials, especially when the war's end resulted in a dearth of suitable bad guys: after Nazis and kamikaze Japanese, the conventional smugglers, racketeers and ambitious businessmen seemed pretty tame. It's easy to see 1945's *The Purple Monster Strikes* as being the progenitor of the latter three serials, all produced in the 1950s. What's also obvious is Cold War influence. Some serials seemed to reflect then-current concerns. In *Radar Men from the Moon* the moon guys have a nuclear advantage because their ray guns are fueled by lunarium, far more potent than Earth's uranium. The hero's mission is to steal lunarium from the moon so America can build its own even deadlier ray guns—a mirror image of the U.S.-Russian arms race at the time.

All the serials in this book were made at a time when kids across the country would line up in front of their local movie theaters on Saturday mornings for "kiddy shows" (that's what they called them), a melange of cartoons, a B movie, short subjects and, most importantly, the serial, whose cliffhanger endings kept us coming back week after week. We sat in awe of the huge images on the silver screen, completely engaged in the terrible dangers and deadly weapons that imperilled our heroes and heroines. We were young and innocent then, and the world was still a mysterious, magic place full of all sorts of possibilities.

Not a bad frame of mind for the world you're about to enter.

The Voice from the Sky

(G.Y.B. Productions-1930) Supervised and directed by Ben Wilson. Story and dialogue: Robert Dillon. Photography: William Nobles. Editor: Eddie Roskams. Foreign rights controlled by E. S. Manheimer

Cast:

Jack Deering . . . . Wally Wales
Jean Lovell . . . . Jean Dolores
Edgar Ballin . . . . Robert Walker
Geoffrey Mentor . . . . . . J. P. Lockney
Patch Eye . . . . Al Haskell
Humpy . . . . Cliff Lyons
Man From Nowhere. . John McCallum
Mrs. Deering . . . . Merle Farris

10 Chapters:

1. Doomed   2. The Cave of Horror
3. The Man From Nowhere   4. Danger Ahead   5. Desperate Deeds   6. Trail of Vengeance   7. The Scarlet Scourge 8. Trapped by Fate   9. The Pit of Peril 10. Hearts of Steel

This is a genuinely lost serial. The only information that exists so far comes from press books (from which the following is derived) or the memories of others. Although there has been some question as to whether it was actually produced, evidence strongly suggests that the serial was released to theaters.

A mysterious voice, known only as "The Voice From the Sky," booms out on the airwaves at periodic intervals warning the nations of the world that unless they disarm he will nullify all electrical energy and bring the universe to a standstill. Some of his messages: "All wars must stop!" "I'll shatter the White House itself!" "I'll turn day into night!" "I bring chaos, destruction, annihilation!" ""There shall be peace or I'll destroy the world." Same old stuff, another crackpot ready to destroy the universe in order to save it. [In the audience, young Edward Teller is inspired.] At first ignored as the raving of a pacifist fanatic, The Voice demonstrates his power by changing night into day, as threatened. "This feat," a promotional synopsis says, "commands the attention of the U.S. Government." And well it might. John Deering, a Secret Service operator, is sent West to investigate.

The trail leads to electrical wizard Geoffrey Mentor, in a small town in Arizona. Mentor has discovered the secret of controlling all electrical energy. Jack learns that enemies in the employ of an ambitious group of "proletarins" in Russia are seeking to get Mentor's secret formula through his niece, Jean Lovell, who has it imprinted

Electrical wizard J. P. Lockney (left) confronts the mysterious Man From Nowhere.

on her back. The girl is relentlessly pursued and Jack has his hands full protecting her. She begs her uncle to give up his reckless work, but he refuses.

The Russian agents are led by Edgar Ballin, the main bad guy. A mys-

BEN WILSON presents
The Startling Mystery Serial
The VOICE FROM THE SKY
with WALLY WALES and JEAN DOLORES
DIRECTED BY BEN WILSON

terious character, "The Man From Nowhere," befriends Jean and helps her escape on a few occasions. Eventually, he's killed and a friend of his, Amos Gates, takes his place. The trail leads Jack and Jean from Arizona to Los Angeles, where we meet F. Suey Wing, whom Ballin believes is a Russian sympathizer but who's really a SS Agent) and then to Washington, DC and Canada. En route they "face death under the grinding wheels of the Transcontinental Limited," are "caught in the flames of a chemical plant,

doomed to death by a fall over a precipice in a racing automobile, stricken by height sickness while walking a plane high above the ground," and pushed from a roof to the street below.

Ballin and his cohorts are never brought to justice. They quarrel among themselves, have a shoot out and succeed in killing each other. Jean and Jack are newlyweds by the final fade-out.

The Whispering Shadow

(Mascot-1933) Directed by Albert Herman, Colbert Clark. Supervising editor: Wyndham Gittens. Original story by Barney Sarecky, George Morgan, Norman Hall, Colbert Clark, Wyndham Gittens. Photography: Ernest Miller, Edgar Lyons. Editor: Ray Snyder, Gilmore Walker. Sound engineer: Homer Ackerman. [7-33]
Cast:
Prof. Strang . . . . Bela Lugosi
Bradley . . . . Henry B. Walthall
Jack Foster . . . . . Malcolm McGregor
Robert Raymond . . . Robert Warwick
Alexis Steinbeck . . . . . . Roy D'Arcy
Sparks . . . . Carl Dane

Vera Strang . . . . Viva Tattersall
Bud Foster . . . . George Lewis
Countess Helen . . . . . . Ethel Clayton
Dr. Young . . . . Lloyd Whitlock
Jasper Slade . . . . Bob Kortman
Dupont . . . . Tom London
Martin Jerome . . . . Lafe McKee
Williams . . . . Jack Perrin
Mitchell. . . . . George Magrill
Krueger . . . . Max Wagner
Jarvis . . . . Lionel Backus
12 Chapters:
1. The Master Magician   2. The Collapsing Room   3. The All-Seeing Eye   4. The Shadow Strikes 5. Wanted for Murder   6. The Man Who Was Czar   7. The Double Doom 8. The Red Circle   9. The Fatal Secret 10. The Death Warrant   11. The Trap 12. King of the World

In the House of Mystery, a waxworks, the sinister Prof. Strang makes wax figures that move and speak with lifelike precision. Each time one of the radio-directed trucks of the Empire Transport and Storage Company carries one of Strang's figures, its driver is attacked and killed. Despite the fact that Empire Transport is a huge international enterprise with offices in Berlin, Germany and Los Angeles, the company is unable to stop the attacks, which

Professor Bela Lugosi and daughter Vera Tattersall cast apprehensive looks about as they discover someone has tampered with the lock.

Strange goings on in the Strang Wax Works where wax figures abound and Viva Tattersall and Bela Lugosi decide what to do with the unconscious Malcolm McGregor.

are masterminded by someone called "The Whispering Shadow." There have been four such killings in less than a month. Each is preceded by the mysterious jamming of the broadcast towers atop the corporation's ultra-modern headquarters building.

Empire traffic manager Jack Foster is faced with truckers who refuse to transport the wax figures, and who can blame them? Jack accuses them of cowardice, to no avail. His younger brother Bud volunteers to drive. Jack isn't crazy about the idea but can't say no without conceding that the truckers are right. He checks the truck's radio and assigns a guard to accompany Bud. Shortly after the truck has left Jack is informed by Sparks, Empire's radio operator, that something is wrong with the radio. The company's communications manager, Alexis Steinbeck, tells

Bela Lugosi fiddles with his advanced radio and television surveillance equipment. Could he be the mysterious Shadow?

Malcolm McGregor listens as Bela Lugosi explains it was this accidentally-triggered robot's club that had clobbered him.

Radio operator Karl Dane, recovering from an attack by an unseen assailant, as usual.

him that the same interference preceded the other attacks.

Bud is driving along, a guard next to him, when he notices a motorcycle behind him rapidly gaining on him. The guard is ready to fire his shotgun as the bike pulls alongside, but Bud realizes that its driver is Jack, who signals them to stop and tells them about the radio. He warns them that an attack is likely. The shadow of a cloaked figure appears on the truck. "Stay where you are," a soft, mysterious voice commands. Cars loaded with thugs pull up. Jack grabs the shotgun and tells Bud to "get going." Jack provides cover fire as the truck speeds off and smashes through a barricade the Shadow's men have set up. The gangsters open fire and Bud is hit. Jack watches in horror as the truck crashes and is totally destroyed.

Jack manages to capture a thug, and brings him to the police. Elsewhere, the Shadow's men gather around a table. Each of their seats has a light above it. The Shadow, who appears only as a cloaked, slouch-hatted silhouette on a wall, scolds his men. Because of their incompetence, he tells them, "Kruger is in the hands of the police." Indeed he is. The police are giving him the third degree, demanding to know the identity of the Whispering Shadow, and Kruger is wavering.

All this is heard by the Shadow, via his advanced radio technology. "Kruger is weakening," he tells his men. "Watch this light." Kruger finally says he'll spill the beans on everything he knows. He suddenly screams and falls to the floor—dead. The light above his chair fades. "Kruger talked too much," the Shadow whispers. "His light has gone

Malcolm McGregor is about to be knocked out from behind, as he battles with the Shadow's henchmen, who have landed their autogyro on the roof of the Empire Transport Building.

Viva Tattersall cowers behind the caped Bela Lugosi, Malcolm Mcgregor has his hands up, and Robert Warwick is closest to the dread, armed, Whispering Shadow. Roy D'Arcy is on the far left and Lafe McKee is barely visible between Lugosi and McGregor.

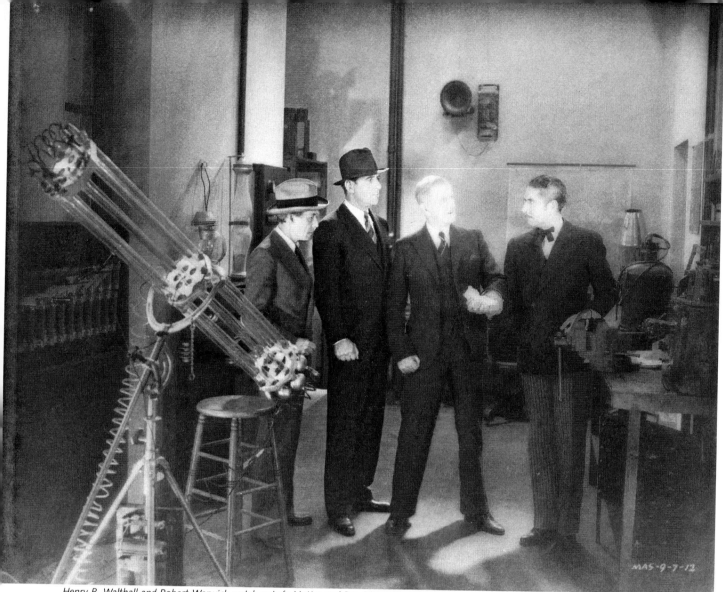

Henry B. Walthall and Robert Warwick watch as Lafe McKee and Roy D'Arcy trade accusations.

out." His men get the message.

Famed criminologist Robert Raymond enters the case and determines that Kruger was electrocuted by means of a disc (which acted as an electrode) found on the body. The diabolical murderer had no need of wires, he tells the police. "That man was killed by a radio death ray."

No one has ever seen the Shadow in the flesh; but his fiendish genius for manipulating radio and television enables him to project his voice and shadow wherever he wishes. That's how he communicates with his men, who must wear radio discs by which they can be killed whenever the Shadow is in the mood. He can see through doors, hear through walls and electrocute people by radio death ray.

We meet the suspects: Bradley, the president of Empire, who might have

his reasons; Jerome, an Empire vice president who was once in the radio business; Steinbeck, head of corporate communications, who mentions he's seen Jerome operating the radio equipment and that the attacks began when Jerome bought into the company; and Sparks, a "yumpin' yiminy" Swede who's the radio operator.

And then there's Professor Strang. When Raymond is told that only the wax figure shipments for Strang's "House of Mystery" have been attacked, he has Jack arrange a visit. It's easy because Strang has filed a claim against Empire for a damaged figure. Introducing Raymond as "Stevens," Empire's "insurance adjustor," they gain access to the Museum, where they are amazed by the incredibly lifelike wax figures which actually *move.* They meet Strang, who lives up

to his name, and his daughter Vera.

While the others discuss insurance matters, Jack snoops around the house. An electric signal warns Strang and he excuses himself. Unseen, he knocks Jack cold, then claims that Jack had triggered one of the moving wax figures, in this case a cave man with a club, which had clobbered him. Vera backs up his story and Raymond pretends to accept it. He tells Strang he'll take a damaged wax figure, have it appraised and return it the next day. When his guests leave, Strang shows Vera an envelope he removed from the "insurance adjuster's" pocket. It's addressed to Robert Raymond, a name Strang instantly recognizes.

We're introduced to "the world's richest collection" of not-so-secret jewels hidden in the wax-figure warehouse, coveted by Strang and another character, Slade, a convict who tells a cell mate he originally stole the jewels and plans to recover them, and actually escapes from prison to do just that.

Raymond settles Strang's claim and uses the returning of the wax figure as a pretext to plant Jack in the crate. From this vantage point Jack overhears Strang vow to "strike at the warehouse tonight." Strang leaves, dressed in slouch hat and cape. Jack quickly reports the news to Raymond. At the Shadow's hideout, his five men sit in their assigned chairs around the long table. The Shadow's whispering voice barks out orders and tells them they must not fail in their mission. "I will be there," he warns.

The warehouse is part of Empire Transport and Storage Co.'s huge headquarters structure, and practically everybody shows up that night. The place is surrounded by Raymond's police, who check everyone entering. While Bradley and Jerome go to their offices, Strang, disguised as a workman, sneaks in. He sees Slade emerge from a trunk and watches him rummage through the stored goods.

Sparks announces to Steinbeck that the interference has started again. Steinbeck tells him to check the roof

antennae and warns him not to lock himself out on the roof, which he had previously done. Sparks bumbles with the roof door, finally managing to prop it open. He starts to climb an aerial tower but is halted by the sight of an autogyro landing on the roof. He dashes inside and yells for help, but is knocked out by an unrecognizable figure. The autogyro lands and two of the Shadow's men get out.

In the warehouse Slade finds the package he's been searching for. In rapid succession it's stolen and possessed by Strang, who then has it taken away by the Shadow's men. Raymond sounds the alarm and the Shadow's men are chased to the roof. After a battle with Jack they hop into their autogyro and take off, with him jumping aboard and continuing the battle. The aircraft spins out of control and crashes, with Jack jumping back onto the roof just seconds before it does. The package flies from the ship and lands on the roof, where it's picked up by Slade. Not that it matters much. The package is empty.

Sparks recovers and says he didn't see who slugged him. Raymond reveals that the jewels in question are "the imperial jewels of the Czar," and practi-

cally everybody is suspected of stealing them. As he assists Raymond in the investigation Jack must survive car crashes, fist fights, electrocution via disc, shootouts, falls from windows and—a new menace—a death ray operated by the Shadow. Bradley and Jerome meet their maker. Vera, who turns out to be innocent of what's going on, is kidnapped, among other things, and rescued by Jack.

Raymond rounds up the remaining suspects and forces them to explain their suspicious behavior. In true Mascot fashion everyone has his reasons and none of it makes too much sense. Professor Strang is really a representative of the Federated Balkan States. He had brought the Czar's jewels to the United States but they had been stolen and hidden in the Empire warehouse. Jerome turns out to be the only living heir to the Czar, and has been after the jewels because he believes they belong to him.

Raymond and Jack listen to the stories. As Sparks is warming up the radio equipment Jack comes to a decision and grabs him, proclaiming that Sparks is the Whispering Shadow. He put two and two together when he'd noticed that a disc was in his pocket and Sparks was fiddling with the radio. Sparks was going to electrocute him. And besides, he says, he had suspected Sparks for some time.

Sparks doesn't deny his guilt. He's asked how he was able to project his Shadow image. "I might as well show you," he sighs. He puts on his cape and hat—and pulls two pistols from the cape. "You fools," he says, and runs to the elevator. He doesn't get very far. Jack catches up and during a fierce struggle Sparks is shot, ending forever the threat of the Whispering Shadow.

The Vanishing Shadow
(Universal-1934) Directed by Louis Friedlander. Screenplay: Basil Dickey, George Morgan, Het Manheim. Story and dialogue: Ella O'Neill. Photography: Richard Fryer. Editors: Edward Todd, Alvin Todd. Art direc-

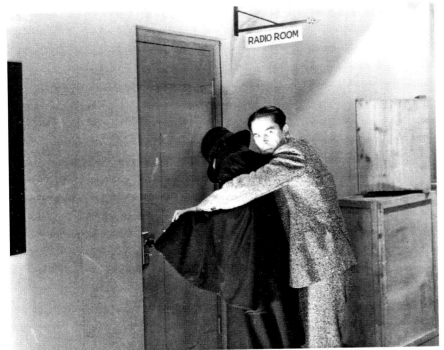

Can it be that Malcolm McGregor has actually captured the Whispering Shadow?

7

tion: Thomas F. O'Neill. Electrical effects: Kenneth Strickfaden, Raymond Lindsay, Elmer Johnson. Associate producer: Henry MacRae.

Cast:

Stanley Stanfield . . . . Onslow Stevens
Gloria Grant . . . . Ada Ince
Wade Barnett . . . . Walter Miller
Carl Van Dorn . . . . James Durkin
MacDonald . . . . . William Desmond
Dorgan . . . . Richard Cramer
Denny . . . . Sidney Bracy
Kent . . . . Edmund Cobb
John Cadwell . . . . . . J. Frank Glendon
Stark . . . . Al Ferguson
Badger . . . . Monte Montague
Gun moll . . . . Beulah Hutton
Construction foreman . . . . Lee J. Cobb

12 Chapters:

1. Accused of Murder   2. The Destroying Ray   3. The Avalanche   4. Trapped   5. Hurled from the Sky   6. Chain Lightning   7. The Tragic Crash   8. The Shadow of Death   9. Blazing Bulkheads   10. The Iron Death   11. The Juggernaut   12. Retribution

Electrical wizard Professor Carl Van Doren is working in his office-laboratory in a large city, when he's visited by a young electrical engineer who introduces himself as Stanley Stanfield. Stanfield's name is familiar: his father had been a crusading publisher, driven to death by business worries. He had once done Van Dorn a great favor, and the professor invites the young man in.

Stanley explains he needs Van Dorn's advice. He displays some blueprints and Van Dorn studies them care-fully. Stanley says his invention is almost complete, except for one undesirable effect. He hopes that Van Dorn will recognize the effect and come up with a means of eliminating it. He mentions that Van Dorn's articles, "on the disposition of atoms in space, and the osmotic pressure of dissolved substances" prove that he's the greatest authority on electrical energy.

The professor agrees to check out Stanley's plans, but warns that constructing the invention will be costly. Stanley pats a briefcase he's holding and says he's got valuable bonds he plans to sell. As soon as Stanley leaves, Van Dorn opens a sliding panel, revealing a male dummy wearing a suit and a metal control box, and compares Stanley's plans to the box's circuitry.

Below: Ada Ince is restrained while Onslow Stevens is frisked for stock certificates by Monte Montague. An invisible Van Dorn is lurking about, which is why Ed Cobb has his hands up. Richard Cramer wields the destroyer beam gun.

Ed Cobb looks on as the runaway robot grabs Ada Ince, after nearly crushing bound and unconscious Onslow Stevens.

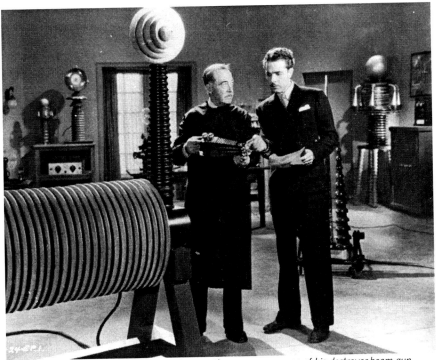

James Durkin is about to show Onslow Stevens the awesome power of his destroyer-beam gun.

He also activates a seven-foot robot, and maneuvers it clunkily around the room, via a control sleeve that fits over Van Dorn's left arm.

As Stanley walks to his car he notices a young woman, confused and dizzy, standing in the street in the path of a speeding fire engine. He rushes to a last-second rescue, carrying her out of harm's way. She's a bit shook up, and accepts Stan's offer of a lift to the Tribune, where she works.

They stop at a light. A chauffeured limousine pulls up alongside them Its prosperous-looking passenger, silver-haired and unsmiling, stares coldly at the young woman, then equally coldly at Stanley. The light changes and the cars move on. Stanley tells her that the man was Wade Barnett and asks if she knows him. She deflects the question, replying that "everybody knows Mr.

Bowler-hatted Edmund Cobb watches as Richard Cramer and Monte Montague hold Onslow Stevens while Al Ferguson removes the invisibility control box. On the right, Ada Ince is held by her father, Walter Miller.

Barnett, don't you?" Unfortunately, he says, he does know Barnett, whose business tactics he blames for his father's death.

The young woman tells Stanley that Wade Barnett is her father, but they'd become enemies and she'd changed her name to Grant, Gloria Grant. She's a reporter for the *Tribune*, and hopes to uncover evidence to incriminate her father. "My sympathy was all with your father," she says as they arrive at the Tribune Building.

In his offices, investment broker John Cadwell receives a surprise visit from Wade Barnett, whose two goons, Dorgan and Kent, wait in the reception room. Wade tells Cadwell he wants the bonds Stanfield had put up for sale, but wants them at his own price. Cadwell

says that's unlikely, that Stanfield is setting a high price. They're debating when the receptionist reports that Mr. Stanfield is there to see Cadwell.

Barnett refuses to leave, insisting that he can handle Stanfield, "who hasn't had time to forget what happened to his father for opposing me." As soon as Stanley enters he and Barnett are hurling insults at each other and nearly coming to blows. Barnett pulls a revolver and aims it at Stanley, who grabs Barnett's hand as Cadwell gets in the way. There's a struggle, a shot, and Cadwell slumps to the floor. Stanley grabs the pistol from Barnett's hand. The receptionist, Dorgan and Kent rush into the room. Barnett tells her to call the police, then tells Stanley "you'll swing for this," reminding him that four

people will swear the gun was in his hand after the shot.

Stanley recognizes a frame up when he hears it—he decks Barnett, Dorgan and Kent, and flees by car, with the two thugs after him. A moment later, Cadwell recovers, and discovers he has a mildly-grazed shoulder, but no other injury. Barnett is disgusted—there goes his case against Stanley.

Unaware of this, Stanley heads straight for Van Dorn's office and quickly explains what happened. He knows he's been followed and wants a place to hide or a way to escape—maybe through a back window. But, the professor says, there is no place to hide, and no back window. Outside the building, Dorgan and Kent have discovered Stanley's parked car.

10

Van Dorn opens the sliding panel and Stan is amazed to see the dummy and "my invisible ray. But how can you build it in such short time?" Van Dorn corrects him. "*Our* invisible ray. I also have been working on it for years." Stanley's plans had solved the final problem. He asks if Stanley has faith in its operation, and Stan says yes, "all except the shadow." "Never mind the shadow," Van Dorn urges. "Put it on, quick." He tells Stanley exactly where to stand. Dorgan and Kent are banging on the office door as Stanley works the knobs and levers of the control box—and disappears.

Van Dorn opens the doors and lets the thugs in. They see Stanley's shadow reflected in the glass segment of a door, but find the room empty. They guess the shadow was reflected through a skylight, and rush to the roof. "It worked, Stanfield, it worked," Van Dorn exalts when the thugs have gone. "We've created the greatest, most far-reaching invention of the age," its only flaw being the shadow it casts. Stanley explains what happened, and how Barnett was responsible for his dad's death. Van Dorn agrees that Barnett and his associates are a menace to society, but what is to be done?

It is Stanley who gets the idea of using the invisible ray and whatever other devices they can dream up to combat and eventually defeat Barnett. Van Dorn is an eager partner and suggests his beach laboratory as a hideout while Stan is a fugitive. It turns out to be perfect, a large cabin hidden among trees behind a remote-controlled gate.

Stanley and Prof. Van Dorn, aided and abetted by Gloria—who discovers Cadwell is still alive and notifies her friends—develop a wide array of technological gizmos, including a destroying-ray gun that extracts the life from any living thing and another gun whose ray cuts through steel effortlessly, which enable them to confront Barnett and his strongarm boys. They're often assisted by Gloria's boss, Tribune editor MacDonald. In addition to trying to steal the invisibility ray, Barnett is busy scheming to gain control of the Tribune, mostly by stealing the stock certificates

that belong to Stanley, who's the controlling stockholder.

Stanley has a number of narrow escapes from death. His car is hit by a speeding train, he's nearly fried by the destroying ray, trapped in an out of control auto, locked in an airtight steel safe and almost crushed by the robot—which had been programmed to attack Barnett but got confused. Gloria has her own narrow escapes—she's with Stan as their plane crashes and their car goes off a steep mountain, and she's nearly electrocuted by a trap Van Dorn had set for intruders—but mostly she's useful. For example, using the thermal beam gun, she cuts a hole in the airtight steel safe and saves Stanley's life. There are car chases galore and a veritable parade of early-thirties convertibles, limousines and touring cars, many of which are demolished in mountainside crashes.

Gloria often visits her dad (his office door reads "Wade Barnett, Public Utilities"), attempting to reform him. Sometimes she wavers, then regains her

determination. To him this is strictly business. He seems genuinely concerned about her, however, and is distraught when he thinks she's been killed in one of his men's attempts to assassinate Stanley. Barnett (played with ruthless conviction by Walter Miller, sporting white hair and a cigar) displays a few dimensions usually lacking in serial villains.

A shot that grazes Van Dorn's head causes him to, shall we say, become a bit over zealous in his anti-crime efforts. (It must be admitted that Van Dorn showed signs of dementia almost from the start, becoming power mad whenever he had a weapon in hand. At one point he tells Stanley he'll get needed information "in my own way." "Yes, I know your own way," Stanley smilingly tells him, "but we don't want to murder anybody." Later on he'll let the robot run amuck, as it scares local farmers and horses and nearly crushes Stanley.)

Dorgan, Barnett's right-hand man, steals the invisible ray machine from

Ada Ince looks on admiringly as the team of James Durkin, wearing his invisibility control box and holding a death-beam gun, and Onslow Stevens wielding the destroyer beam (which can cut through steel), just some of the awesome weapons they've invented.

11

Van Dorn and starts to get big ideas. He convinces other members of Barnett's gang, Stark, Badger and Kent, that they'll get a better deal from him. They capture Stanley, Gloria and Van Dorn, get the stock certificates, and Dorgan goes to Barnett's office for a showdown. He tells Barnett he wants fifty thousand dollars for the stock and the release of Gloria. Barnett is shocked to hear that Gloria is being held hostage. He says he'll bring the fifty thousand to Dorgan as quickly as he can round it up. But as soon as Dorgan leaves, Barnett decides to call the police.

Barnett shows up with the money at Dorgan's hideout ("He's alone," Badger reports), and demands that Gloria be released. Dorgan says he wants to count the money first, but as he starts, the police break in. Realizing he's been double crossed, Dorgan pulls a gun and shoots Barnett, before he himself is shot by the police.

Barnett is dying. He apologizes for everything, says he wishes things had been different, tells Gloria his will leaves his vast fortune to her, and she forgives him just before he dies. Stan and Gloria look forward to an uncomplicated life together.

The Phantom Empire

(Mascot-1935) Directed by Otto Brower, Breezy Eason. Production supervisor: Armand Shaefer. Original story: Wallace MacDonald, Gerald Geraghty, Hi Freedman. Continuity: John Rathmell, Armand Shaeffer. Photography: Ernest Miller, William Nobles. Editor: Earl Turner. Sound engineer: Terry Kellum. Music: Lee Zahler. [2-23-35] Feature titles: *Radio Ranch, Men with Steel Faces*.
Cast:
Gene . . . . Gene Autry
Frankie Baxter . . . . Frankie Darro
Betsy Baxter . . . . . Betsy King Ross
Queen Tika . . . . Dorothy Christie
Argo . . . . Wheeler Oakman
Mal . . . . Charles K. French
Rab . . . . Warner Richmond
Prof. Beetson . . . . . . Frank Glendon

Oscar . . . . Lester "Smiley" Burnette
Pete . . . . William Moore
Dr. Cooper . . . . Edward Peil
Saunders . . . . Jack Carlyle
Sheriff . . . . Bruce Mitchell
Ghaspa . . . . Stanley Blystone
Lom. . . . . Wally Wales
Featuring the Scientific City of Murania.

12 Chapters:

At two o'clock each afternoon Gene Autry broadcasts a musical show from his Radio Ranch. He's got to do this to fulfill a contract. If he misses even a single performance the contract will be cancelled and he'll lose the ranch, which he co-owns with his partner, Mr. Baxter. After a song or two Gene introduces his young friends, Baxter's children Frankie and Betty, the founders of the National Thunder Riders Club, an organization devoted to

Gene Autry finishes off two outlaws while Smiley Burnette tries to stop a sneak attack.

"ridin', ropin', real horses, real cowboys and cowgirls." Frankie explains that the club is named after the Thunder Riders, a legendary band of riders whose sound is like a "roll of thunder" and who the two children once saw galloping across the plains. "If we ever see them again we'll tell you about it," Frankie promises his listeners.

Arriving at the ranch via plane is a band of explorers, led by Professor Beetson, who has heard of a strange, fabulously rich underground city named Murania, which is supposed to exist under Gene's ranch. Gene greets them, is told they're merely doing mineral exploration, and trustingly sets them up in a guest cabin. Frankie has been getting radio signals from "straight down." Betsy wonders if there's any truth "to the story of an underground with people and cities and everything." "Why of course they're true," Gene tells her.

The friends ask Prof. Beetson about it. Beetson tells them the signals are merely static. Gene shows him a soldier-like carved doll he'd found nearby on ranch property. "Hmm," says Beetson, studying it carefully, "an interesting example of antediluvian Americana." He asks Gene to show his two associates, Drs. Cooper and Saunders, the place where the figure was found. After Gene has gone Beetson tells a henchmen what to do.

The next day, as Gene leads Cooper and Saunders to the spot, a boulder rolls from a ledge and narrowly misses Gene, who sees a figure get on a horse and gallop off. Gene rides in pursuit, but a rifle shot by Saunders hits him, knocks

Gene Autry laughs as good old Smiley Burnette digs himself out from under a bale of hay.

13

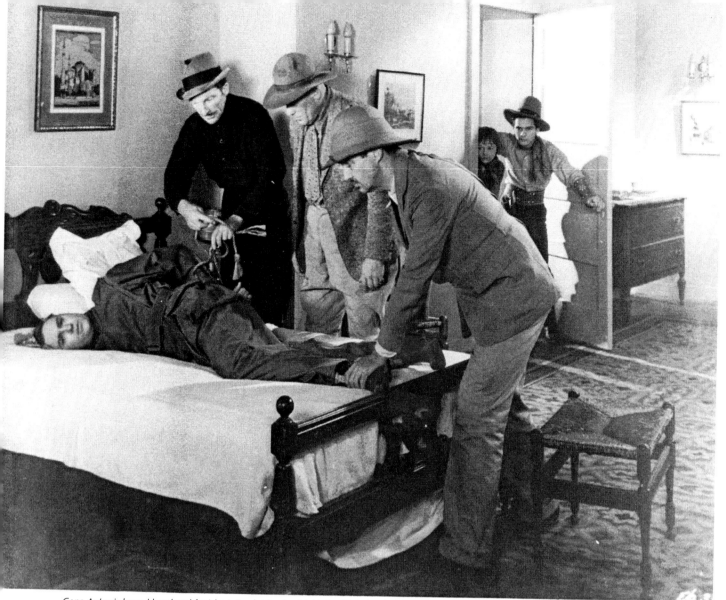

Gene Autry is bound hand and foot by J. Frank Glendon (right, in pith helmet) and a lackey, as Jack Carlyle (center) looks on. Betsy King Ross and Frankie Darro watch from a doorway. This looks like a job for the National Thunder Riders Club.

him from his horse and sends him rolling down a hill where he lies unconscious or worse. Cooper now spies a robed and masked figure riding away. "A Muranian," he declares, and the two doctors gallop after the strange rider, who dismounts and hides among brush. As the two men approach, the stranger fires a futuristic weapon, hitting Cooper in the chest with—an arrow. Saunders fires back with an old-fashioned bullet, hitting the man, who drops like a rock.

Saunders runs about, calling for Beetson, who is riding by with a few men. He tells them he's found a Muranian. When they return to the

Right: Something suspicious has caught Gene Autry's attention

scene, the Muranian is gone. But his gas-mask type helmet is on the ground—evidence of his existence. Beetson deduces that Muranians can't breath regular oxygen and that the man had been carried off by allies. He's right. A mounted band of gas-masked Muranians carrying their wounded comrade approaches the side of a mountain, which suddenly opens to allow them entrance.

They gallop past the robots that attend to the entrance door and drop their horses off at the upper stables. They rush the wounded man into the tube-shaped elevator that begins to descend 25,000 feet to Murania. The wounded Muranian begins to breath more regularly, and the others remove their gas masks. Murania is a glistening city of glass and chrome, with gleaming skyscrapers and elevated highways.

Robots do virtually all hard labor.

This veritable utopia is ruled by the beautiful Queen Tika, who is determined to keep her kingdom unknown to the upper world, fearing, justifiably, that exposure to it would hopelessly contaminate the place. She is not pleased to hear that one of her men has been seen and shot by an upper worlder. She sends the injured man to "the radium reversal chamber," where his wounds will be healed.

It seems that in Murania radium is a healer, life restorer and life prolonger, and lots of exposure to it is a good thing. She walks past rows of humming dynamos, into her laboratory where she orders an attendant to tune in "the Garden of Life." She gazes into a huge circular tv screen while the attendant pushes and pulls various levers on a master control console. Images flash

by: crowded trolley-car and auto traffic in a big city ("The fools are always in a hurry," Tika mutters); a horse race; a boxing match; an auto-race crash. Tika barks at her attendant to find the Garden of Life so she doesn't have to witness such surface-life madness.

Finally, the Garden of Life, so called because of its high radium content, comes into view. Tika sees and hears the wounded Dr. Cooper being carried away and Beetson and Saunders conspiring to get rid of Autry so they can take control of the radium-rich Radio Ranch. Tika summons her council and warns that the kingdom is in imminent danger of being discovered. "Outsiders have already invaded the Garden of Life," she informs them. She contacts her surface guards and tells them to destroy the entrance to the Garden, so it can never be found by the

Below: Two Muranian guards pin down Gene Autry as Queen Dorothy Christie and her adviser Wheeler Oakman (center) look on.

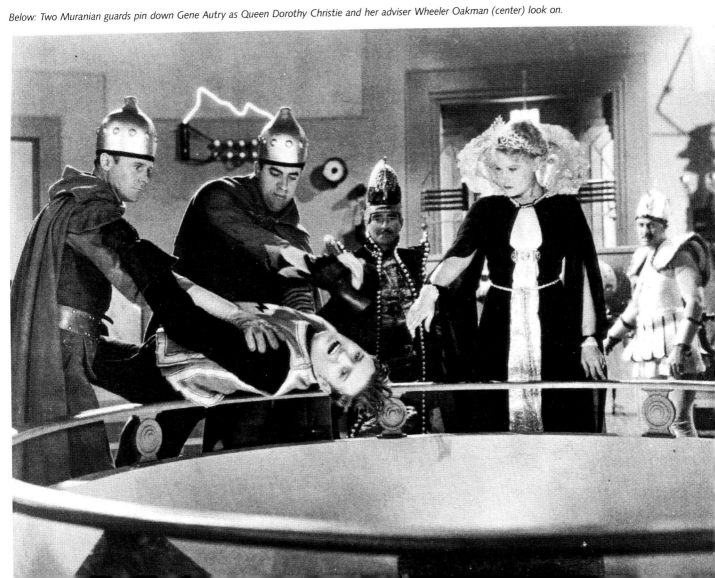

In the highly-advanced Muranian laboratory, Gene Autry gets the drop on machine-operator Stanley Blystone.

outsiders. A division of Thunder Riders soon thunders out the mountainside passageway.

Elsewhere, Gene is coming to. Unsteadily, he gets to his feet and looks around. He's horseless in the middle of nowhere. In their clubhouse, the Junior Thunder Riders are conducting a meeting. Armed with a gavel, Frankie maintains order, oversees the reading of minutes and asks for suggestions for a club motto. Suddenly a thunder-like sound is heard. "That's like the sound we heard that day," Betsy declares. They rush out to see what's causing it. All they see is a horse cantering toward them. "It's Gene's horse," Betsy says. Frankie agrees. "Maybe it's the real Thunder Riders. Maybe they've captured Gene," he exclaims. "To the rescue," he yells, and the mounted kids, about thirty of them, gallop off furiously, yelling "To the rescue!" A motto is

Dorothy Christie and Wheeler Oakman (center) study the unconscious Gene Autry.

16

born!

The kids split into groups to search for Gene, with Frankie and Betsy heading for Thunder Valley. Gene, too weak to stand, tries making a smokey fire in the grass. He passes out and is soon threatened by the spreading flames. Frankie and Betsy are riding along when they see smoke. "It must be Gene," they decide, and gallop to the scene, getting there in time to rescue the unconscious singing cowboy. A drink of water fully revives him. He suddenly remembers he has to be at Radio Ranch by two o'clock for the broadcast. "We've got to ride like the dickens," says Frankie. Off they gallop.

Queen Tika and Argo are watching all this on her tv screen. "If we can capture Gene Autry," Argo suggests,

"Radio Ranch will soon become deserted. The entrance to our underground kingdom will forever go undiscovered." This makes sense to Tika, who adds, "We must never allow Murania to become desecrated by the presence of surface people. Our lives are serene, our minds are superior, our accomplishments greater. Gene Autry must be captured." Thunder Riders are ordered to catch Autry and bring him to Murania. Gene and the kids manage to evade the Riders, getting to the ranch just in time, much to the displeasure of Beetson, who has been assured that Autry was dead.

As Beetson and his confederates watch, they, too, decide "that the only way we can keep our discoveries to ourselves is to rid this ranch of people. The

easiest way to do that is to see that Autry doesn't broadcast again." "You mean...?," asks Cooper. "Exactly," Beetson replies. Meanwhile, the Riders return to Murania and Tika demands to see their captain. He has failed in his mission and the penalty is death. Tika is merciful, however. She gives him one more chance.

Gene's broadcast continues. It is a fictional reenactment of a Thunder Rider raid on a stagecoach. Everyone on the ranch joins in the performance. Supposedly blank shots are fired. Unseen, Beetson's men fire a real shot and hit Gene's ranch partner, Mr. Baxter, Frankie and Betsy's dad. After the broadcast concludes, it's noticed that he's dead. Everyone's weapons are checked and a live shell is found in

Betsy King Ross and Frankie Darro, hiding amidst the industrial hubbub of the Phantom Empire. They're probably wondering why members of the production crew, visible top right, are in the shot.

Uh oh. Gene Autry is in the hands of the Muranians again.

Wheeler Oakman orders that the captured Frankie Darro and Betsy King Ross be separated.

Gene's saddle rifle. Gene is dumfounded. Beetson suggests things look bad for Gene. The sheriff is notified.

Later, in Gene's room, Frankie and Betsy tell him they know he didn't do it, "but everybody says you did," and that the sheriff is coming to arrest him. Gene says that if he's in jail he'll never be able to find the real murderer. The kids help him escape. The sheriff and his deputies see Gene galloping off and are going to ride off in pursuit, when Beetson suggests the sheriff take his plane, from which Autry could be easily spotted. The sheriff heads for the plane, taking some tear gas bombs along, while his deputies give chase on land. Queen Tika, watching this on her giant circular tv screen, sends her Riders to get to Gene first and capture him.

The kids, too, have seen what's happening and rush to the plane, intend-

18

Gene Autry swashbuckles valiantly and even the robots join the fray.

Queen Dorothy Christie is not pleased by Gene Autry's rebelliousness. She'll make him pay for his impertinence.

ing to sabotage it. But the pilot and sheriff get there too soon, and the kids are forced to hide in a rear compartment. Gene finds himself being chased by Thunder Riders who are followed by the posse. His horse is shot out from under him. Now the plane appears and the sheriff, seeing the strange Thunder Riders surrounding Gene, starts tossing tear gas bombs. Queen Tika orders her defense department to fire an "aerial torpedo" at the plane. The torpedo flies through the air and hits the plane.

Frankie and Betsy had long ago found parachutes and jumped to safety. Not that it mattered—the torpedo merely damages the plane and it makes a crash landing. No one is seriously injured and the posse arrives to chase off the Muranians and to pick up the sheriff and the pilot, who are weak from the crash. Two reluctant deputies,

Oscar and Pete, lamebrains who all too often provide alleged comic relief, are sidekicks of Gene's and they aid him in escaping.

In Murania, the Thunder Rider captain must once again report failure. This time there is no mercy. In her spacious, glass-domed palace with a commanding view of Murania's skyline, she explains why he must die: "Thousands of years ago our ancestors were driven here by the glaciers. They built this city, and since then my subjects and their forebearers have lived in peace. They have lived a life far more attractive than the life led in the mad world above. If the surface people discover the entrance to Murania our advanced civilization is in peril." Queen Tika orders Argo to take the captain to the "electricity chamber" for execution.

The captain and Argo enter the

electrocution chamber. Argo closes the door. "Captain, you are the thirty-seventh soldier to be executed this year," he says. "I know," the Captain replies, "many of them were my friends." Argo smiles cannily. "What if I told you they still live—every one of them?" He goes on to explain that their lives were spared because they vowed to join his rebel group and help him overthrow the Queen. After a bit of coaxing, the captain agrees to join Argo's cause. He's escorted "through the secret passage, to rebel headquarters."

This combination of forces— Beetson and his cronies, the sheriff, Queen Tika and the venomous Argo— tend to keep Gene, Frankie and Betsy hopping. They must survive cave explosions, burning cabins, assassination attempts, cars going off cliffs, death rays and more, while managing to broadcast every day at two o'clock, sometimes from remote locations while Gene is a fugitive.

During one foray, Gene dons the costume of a Rider and rides with them into Murania. But as soon as he's forced to remove his mask he's exposed and captured. Queen Tika is delighted to see him. She asks him how he likes Murania. He answers, "Well, I think the dampness and dead air of your land is more suited for rats and moles." Such sweet talk, Tika smilingly tells him, has earned him a visit to the electricity chamber, where he'll be fried to a crisp.

First she takes him to her viewing room and, via the picture screen, introduces him to life in Murania, where citizens pursue their leisure and intellectual interests while work is done by robots. A hungry beggar appears on Tika's screen—a scene from Gene's upper world, she reminds him, contempt dripping from her voice. Which is exactly why he must die, so that upper-world values don't corrupt Murania. He's placed in the electricity room, and Tika tells Argo to apply the maximum voltage. Gene darts around the room, trying to elude the bolts of electricity.

Argo, suspecting that Gene might make a useful ally, covertly pushes a lever that sends Gene through a trapdoor into a locked room, then turns the voltage on full blast. Tika smiles and leaves, believing Gene is dead. Gene overhears a conversation in the next room, where rebels are discussing rebellion. "How much longer must we await the word that will start the revolution?," a man asks. He's told to be patient, that they're not yet ready to strike because "my disintegrating atom-smashing machine is still in construction. When it is completed," the man announces triumphantly, "it will be capable of destroying the universe."

Argo announces to his rebels that he wants the surface man spared from electrocution because they can use him "for vivisection, so that we may take him to our laboratory and learn how a surface man's lungs differ from ours" as a way of improving their breathing masks. Gene breaks away, gets to the surface and returns to Murania followed by Oscar and Pete who, through sheer stupidity, actually succeed in being of some use. Argo seizes control of

Below: Gene Autry ducks a dagger tossed at him by a Muranian guard and Betsy King Ross huddles behind Frankie Darro, who's trying to hold off Wheeler Oakman.so they can all get into the elevator and escape to the upper world.

Murania and, with a common enemy, Gene and Tika team up, mostly with Gene—always a gallant gentleman—doing the rescuing. With Tika as his prisoner, Argo sentences her to die, bringing her to the weapons laboratory for execution, where he shows her the now-perfected disintegrating atom-smashing machine.

Gene comes to the rescue, bursting into the lab and aiming the machine at Argo and his officers. As they cower in a corner Gene grabs Tika and races from the room, locking the door behind him. Argo and his men can't get out. Argo orders that the disintegrating ray be used to melt the door, and the engineer complies, though warning that he can't use it at full power, lest he lose control. Tika and Gene head straight for the control room where she tunes her video to what's going on in the

He can run, but he can't hide. It looks like Gene Autry is finally catching up with Frank Glendon.

Below: With corpses littering the floor, cowed Muranian deposers, including leader Wheeler Oakman (fourth from left) are held at bay by the atom-smashing disintegrating machine. To the right: William Moore, Gene Autry wielding the awesome weapon, Dorothy Christie and Smiley Burnette.

weapons lab. Argo is impatient: the disintegrating ray is taking too long. He orders his engineer to turn it on full power. The man is reluctant to do so, but the machine is set to its highest capacity. Suddenly it spins out of control, knocking Argo and the engineer to the ground. The deadly machine spins about, melting everything it zaps, especially the unfortunate Argo and his staff.

Tika and Gene see this on the video monitor. There is no way to turn the disintegrator off (talk about bad engineering), she tells Gene, and it is just a matter of time before Murania itself is completely destroyed. Gene and, unfortunately, Oscar and Pete, rush to the elevator to escape before it's too late. They implore Tika to come with them, but she declines. She is a queen, and she prefers to die with her people. As all that is solid melts into air as the friends crowd into the elevator and shoot up the 25,000 feet in no time flat. They get out of the mountain just as the situation reaches critical mass, tons of rock come crashing down on the machine and the once-proud, ten-thousand year old kingdom of Murania vanishes forever.

The Lost City (Krellberg-1935)

Directed by Harry Revier. Story: Zelma Carroll, Geo. M. Merrick, Robert Dillon. Cinematography: Edward Linden, Roland Price. Continuity: Perly Poore Sheehan, Eddy Graneman, Leon D'Usseau. Dialogue director: Zelma Carroll. Technical director: James Altweis. Electrical effects: K. Strickfaden. Sound: Cliff Ruberg. Assistant directors: William Nolte, Dick L'Estrange. General Production Manager: Geo. M. Merrick. Producer: Sherman S. Krellberg. Distribution by Super-Serial Productions, Inc. Feature titles: *The Lost City* and *City of Lost Men*.

Cast:

Bruce Gordon . . . . . Kane Richmond
Zolok. . . . . . . William "Stage" Boyd
Natcha. . . . . Claudia Dell
Manyus . . . . Josef Swickard
Butterfield. . . . . . . George S. Hayes

Jerry . . . . Eddie Fetherstone
Gorzo . . . . William Bletcher
Andrews . . . . Milburn Moranti
Queen Rama . . . . Margo D'use
Appolyn . . . . Jerry Frank
Reynolds . . . . Ralph Lewis
Colton . . . . William Millman
Ben Ali . . . . Gino Corrado
Hugo . . . . Sam Baker
General . . . . Henry Hall

12 Chapters:

1. Living Dead Men   2. The Tunnel of Flame   3. Dagger Rock   4. Doomed   5. Tiger Prey   6. Human Beasts   7. Spider Men   8. Human Targets   9. Jungle Vengeance   10. The Lion Pit   11. The Death Ray   12. The Mad Scientist

Note: The Lost City, *as you will discover, is unquestionably the most racist sound serial ever made. That its contents were never questioned and that*

23

The world's political and military leaders (like General Henry Hall, left) watch Kane Richmond as he locates the source of Earth's disturbances. Working with him is Eddie Fetherston (center). Peering over Eddie's shoulder is William Millman.

it was deemed fit for showing around the country demonstrates the general consciousness at the time.

A series of electrical storms disrupts the world, causing floods and power shortages. Boats explode in mid-ocean, the Mississippi floods, inundating St. Louis. Dams collapse, populations panic. Scientific and political leaders of the world gather in the laboratory of electrical engineer Bruce Gordon who is demonstrating a machine he claims will trace the cause of the disasters. One jealous scientist, Reynolds, considers the whole thing a "publicity stunt." Another scientist, Colton, disagrees, insisting it's "a promotion scheme."

Working feverishly at the machine, Bruce discovers that the source is in central Africa and, although it's unexplored territory, he recommends an immediate expedition. A high-placed statesman tells him, "The resources of the entire nation are at your disposal." Bruce's loyal companion, Jerry, and the two jealous colleagues, Colton and Reynolds, accompany him.

In that part of Africa natives are terrorized by powerful black giants who carry off villagers and bring them to Magnetic Mountain. The mountain contains a beehive-type empire, a lost city ruled by a scientific wizard named

Zolok who has unleashed the electrical fury threatening civilization as part of his plan to conquer the world. The city features gleaming dynamos, futuristic laboratories and chrome tunnels. Interestingly, there are only five non-giant humans in the whole place.

Zolok (1) is unwillingly aided and abetted by Dr. Manyus (2), the elderly, captive scientific genius behind his power. The good doctor, a humanitarian at heart, is forced to do Zolok's bid-

ding because his lovely daughter, Natcha (3), is also held prisoner, and Manyus fears for her life, or worse, if Zolok is displeased. His usual cry of protest as he reveals each new death machine is, "When I created this instrument I did it for the *benefit* of mankind."

As the only woman in the lost city, Natcha is under a certain amount of pressure. Zolok's muscular right-hand man, Appolyn (4) corners her in a tunnel and proposes. "Don't talk to me of marriage again," she tells him. "You'll change your mind," he says smugly. Zolok is also aided by Gorzo (5), a hunchback pygmy who hopes that his master will someday make him strong and straight. Five people. That's it, the entire human population of the lost city. And two of them are prisoners. The master, as Zolok is sometimes referred to, has decorated everything, from microphones to t-shirts, with a lightning-bolt motif.

The evil wizard also commands a cadre of brainless native giants who are the product of a couple of Manyus's humanitarian inventions, a brain-destroying device and an enlarging machine which can turn a normal tribesman into a brain-dead behemoth capable of following orders. It is with an army of such giants that Zolok

Eddie Fetherston and Kane Richmond are greeted by scientific wizard William Boyd and his strong-arm man Jerry Frank.

24

"I need more power," William Boyd tells Josef Swickard (he's talking about electricity), who's expected to come up with it. Jerry Frank and William Bletcher watch interestedly.

intends to conquer the world.

We see the giants carrying screaming kidnapped natives through a secret cave entrance into the city. The terrified tribesmen are placed in a metal cage. Occasionally one is selected, carried kicking and screaming to Zolok's laboratory and strapped in the "brain destroyer." After the man's brain has been turned to guacamole he is placed on an operating table, an enlarging globe hovering above him. At Zolok's command the power is turned on and before our eyes the native grows into a seven-foot giant.

Bruce's African journey leads to a trading post run by Butterfield, a shrewd trader who also dabbles in slaves. Bruce sets up his machine in front of the post and finds that the disturbances emanate from an area dominated by Magnetic Mountain. Zolok is closely monitoring Bruce's progress

utilizing his own advanced television system—which seems to cover the entire surrounding jungle, including Butterfield's post.

Impressed with Bruce's machine, Zolok lures the expedition to his head-

Claudia Dell tells her father, Josef Swickard, that white men are in the area. Rescue is possible.

quarters. While Bruce and his party are heading for the mountain, Zolok forces Natcha to scream into a microphone wired to a thatched hut in the jungle. "That sounds like a white girl's voice," Jerry yells. He and Bruce dash into the hut (Bruce says "This must be the place" as they enter), fall through a trapdoor, slide down a long chute and find themselves within Zolok's lost city, facing the master himself, who's sitting behind a futuristic desk.

Bruce asks him who he is and Zolok hammily replies. "As you may know, the Ligurians were a race of master scientists. I am the last of that race, carrying on the electromagnetic traditions of my people." How did the brilliant Ligurians allow themselves to be reduced to just one? What *are* their "electromagnetic traditions"? These irresistible questions are not asked. Zolok vows he will exploit Bruce's

25

Prisoners William Millman (left) and Ralph Lewis are threatened by William Boyd.

engineering knowledge to further his schemes of world conquest or, failing that, turn him into a mindless giant, the first white one.

Meanwhile, Colton and Reynolds have been captured by Gorzo and a few giants, and are brought to the lost city. When they see what Manyus's scientific skills have produced, they start to think about the power they could command if *they* controlled him. Gaining the old scientist's confidence, they convince him to show them the way to a cave leading to the outside jungle. Then, despite his protests, they force him to escape with them.

When Natcha learns that her father has left with Colton and Reynolds, she draws Bruce and Jerry aside and leads them out of the city via the same cave route. Enraged at the escapes, Zolok sends out Appolyn, Gorzo and a few giants to recapture the escapees, and keeps track of all concerned through his vast jungle television network. Meanwhile, back at the trading post, Butterfield, via a trader whose party has been attacked by giants, hears rumors of Dr. Manyus's ability to create the giants. "With an army like that," he sighs, "I could control Africa." Summoning his trusted natives,

Butterfield goes hunting for Manyus.

As he makes his way through the brush Butterfield comes upon the camp of Ben Ali, a veteran Arab slave trader. Ben Ali, too, has heard about the giants and figures they'd be a hot item on the auction block. Butterfield does his best

to convince Ben Ali that no such giants exist. Bruce, Natcha and Jerry see the Arab camp. Bruce decides that Natcha and Jerry should enter the camp while he continues the search for Manyus. Ben Ali is delighted to see his new guests. "What's a nice girl like you doing in a jungle?" he asks Natcha. He entertains them, not realizing what's happening in the bush outside. Hugo, one of Zolok's giants, and Gorzo capture Manyus and Colton. They're heading back to the lost city when they are captured by Ben Ali's men and taken to the Arab's encampment.

Ben Ali is mightily impressed when he spies the massive Hugo. Colton, in order to save his own skin, tells the slave trader of Manyus's scientific brilliance and suggests they become partners in picking the doctor's brains. But Ben Ali doesn't see how Colton fits into the picture and has him shot. Adios, Colton. The Arab also has Butterfield imprisoned for lying about the giants.

In an adjacent tent Gorzo and Hugo are shackled to a pole. As soon as they're alone, Gorzo orders Hugo to break their bonds, which the powerful giant does. Obeying Gorzo's com-

Josef Swickard between two of the recipients of his experiments—white pygmies! Extremely impressed are Claudia Dell, Kane Richmond, William Bletcher, and Eddie Fetherston.

Claudia Dell zaps giant Sam Baker into releasing his hold on Kane Richmond's neck.

mands, Hugo then kills the Arab guarding their tent and the two flee into the jungle. Natcha, left unguarded, slips out of her tent and also heads for the jungle, where, as fate would have it, she runs into Bruce. He decides to infiltrate the Arab camp and help the others escape. He's spied by an Arab, who turns out to be Jerry, who had overpowered his guard and donned his cloak as a disguise. Together the three friends free Manyus and Butterfield and run for it, with Ben Ali's men in close pursuit.

Butterfield gets to his trading post, rounds up his obedient natives and attacks Ben Ali's men, putting them to flight. Butterfield then turns on his rescuers, ordering his natives to capture Manyus, and once again Bruce, Natcha, Jerry and Manyus find themselves running for their lives. Pursued through

the jungle, they cross a trail called the "Path of Skulls" and enter the dreaded Spidermen's village of thatch huts. Because of a local but well-known superstition Butterfield's men refuse to cross the ju-ju Path and retreat in panic when they come to it.

As Manyus and his group enter the village the doctor explains that the white, Pygmy-sized Spidermen were once black, but have been turned white by another of his remarkable formulas. After being greeted by the tribe, our heroes watch as a black Spiderman pleads with Manyus to change him into a white man. The doctor quickly obliges and performs the necessary procedure. As the pygmy turns white, Jerry, awestruck, says "Doc, you're a genius." Blushing modestly, Manyus replies, "Science can accomplish anything."

Bruce adds, "Doc, this is the greatest scientific discovery yet." Manyus mentions that Gorzo is a Spiderman whom he had turned white. Gorzo is listening from a window.

Meanwhile, the discouraged

George Hayes's plans for conquering Africa appeal to slave queen Margaret Duse.

27

Butterfield returns to his trading post to find that the tempestuous Queen Rama, queen of the slave trade, is looking for him. The Queen is smartly clad in a matching leopard-skin cap and mini-skirt combination that shows off her shapely gams. He explains what's been happening and makes a deal to share control of Africa with her once they get hold of Manyus. Then he sets out once again to capture the doctor, but this time with Rama's natives, the Wangas, who have no qualms about invading the Spidermen's village.

Their surprise attack is successful. The Spidermen are quickly routed and Butterfield returns to his base with his prisoners. Queen Rama is immediately taken by Bruce's good looks and imagines that he would be a lot more fun to share Africa with than Butterfield.

Kala, the slave girl, pours a drink for Kane Richmond, who has reached a tense moment in his touchy conversation with ardent queen Margaret D'use.

Below: Brain-fried giant Sam Baker has Josef Swickard and William Millman in his grip, but all of them, including Billy Bletcher (right), have been captured by Butterfield's natives.

Desire leads to action. Butterfield, much to his surprise, is tied to stakes in the middle of the jungle and left to be eaten by ants or something larger.

Rama invites Bruce to dinner in her room, and makes an offer of marriage, or anything that Bruce might find appealing. Bruce is flattered, but not interested. He suggests "a long friendship" instead and proposes a toast "to our lasting friendship." "You mean something *more* than friendship," Rama says intimately. "I'm sorry, " Bruce replies, "but that can never be." "I know what it is," Rama hisses. "It is this creature Natcha." "She doesn't enter into it," Bruce says curtly. "Let's leave her out of this silly discussion."

This, or course, only worsens the situation. The hot-blooded Rama, who has something decidedly less platonic in mind, is outraged and to vent her spleen orders that a clumsy servant woman, Kala, be whipped. When Bruce objects, Rama relents. But she is not to be trifled with. Still furious, she slips a potion into Bruce's wine that causes him to go blind. She also orders that Natcha, whom she is sure Bruce is sweet on, be thrown into a lion pit.

While this is going on, Dr,. Manyus escapes into the jungle and, wandering aimlessly, comes upon Butterfield spread-eagled to the ground and being snacked upon by ants. The compassionate scientist unties him. The slave trader is touched by this act of mercy and, admitting that he's been an "awful rotter," promises to make amends. At the trading post Kala, the servant whom Bruce had saved from a lashing, leads the blind engineer to the lion pit and helps him save Natcha. The trio escape

Will George Hayes's antidote cure Kane Richmond's blindness? Slave girl Kala and Claudia Dell wait for results.

into the jungle where they run into Manyus and Butterfield. The ex-villain brews up a pot of antidote tea he'd learned about from the natives. A few sips restores Bruce's vision.

Butterfield and Bruce decide to try to recapture the trading post from Rama. They leave Manyus and Natcha in a cave, which happens to contain one of Zolok's many television cameras. No sooner do Bruce and Butterfield leave, then Appolyn and a few giants capture the doctor and Natcha. At the post, Bruce frees Jerry while Butterfield searches for Rama. He finds her dead, stabbed to death. He smiles, and congratulates Kala for her work. Bruce and Jerry rush to the cave and find doctor and daughter gone. Bruce sees tracks and follows them into the jungle. He tells Jerry to get Butterfield and his natives and then to follow him. But Bruce himself is soon captured by Appolyn and, along with Manyus and Natcha, brought back to the lost city.

Jerry and Butterfield are on the their way to the lost city when they come upon Gorzo, who says he too is relenting and will help them find the cave entry to the city. Zolok has greeted his captives in typical style, deciding to kill Bruce with yet another of the Manyus's humanitarian inventions--a

destroying ray. Bruce is strapped to a chair and the ray is turned on, cutting a path toward him. Manyus and Natcha are forced to watch. Manyus has no stomach for seeing his weapon in action. "Spare us this horror," he begs Zolok. "It's no use, father," Natcha says. "He's so *cruel*."

At that moment Eddie, Butterfield and Gorzo sneak into the city. Gorzo leads them to the power-generating room, to cut off the electricity so that Zolok's video-spying system will be useless. Fortunately, the power dies just as the ray is about to destroy Bruce. Highly annoyed, Zolok sends Appolyn to the powerhouse to see what's happened. The muscular stooge is felled by the butt of Butterfield's gun.

In the laboratory Manyus announces, "Zolok, you've lost your mind." "He has no mind to lose," Bruce adds. Leaving his prisoners guarded by a zombie, Zolok goes to the powerhouse to see what's delaying the restoration of energy. He is knocked out by Butterfield, whose group then rescues Bruce, Manyus and Natcha.

Zolok is tossed into a dungeon but, using an "electronic key," escapes and returns to his vacant laboratory. The strain of recent events has taken its toll on the last of the Ligurians. He's gone

Giants stand guard while Claudia Dell and Josef Swickard recoil in horror and diabolical William Boyd watches gleefully as the death ray gets closer to helpless Kane Richmond.

completely mad, and, babbling incoherently, proceeds to turn on all of his powerful electrical equipment—the products of generations of Ligurian enterprise—full blast. Bruce and his friends escape through the cave just as a mighty explosion rips through the Lost City, destroying it completely and conclusively ending Zolok's dream of world conquest.

Flash Gordon (Universal-1936)

Directed by Frederick Stephani. Original screenplay: Frederick Stephani, Basil Dickey, George Plympton, Ella O'Neill. Director of photography: Jerry Ash, Richard Fryer. Editors: Saul Goodkind, Edward Todd, Alvin Todd, Louis Sackin. Electrical effects: Norman Dewes. Special properties: Elmer A. Johnson. Art director: Ralph Berger. Produced by Henry MacRae. [3-8-36] Feature titles: *Rocket Ship* and *Spaceship to the Unknown*.

Cast:

Flash Gordon . Larry "Buster" Crabbe
Dale Arden . . . . Jean Rogers
Emperor Ming . . . Charles Middleton
Aura . . . . Priscilla Lawson
Vultan . . . . John Lipson
Prince Barin . . . . Richard Alexander
Dr. Hans Zarkov . . . . Frank Shannon
King Kala . . . . Duke York, Jr.
Officer Torch . . . . Earl Askam
High Priest . . . . . . Theodore Lorch
King Thun . . . . James Pierce
Zona . . . . Muriel Goodspeed
Gordon, Sr. . . . . Richard Tucker
Prof. Hensley . . . . . George Cleveland

Flash's dad Richard Tucker (bottom left) relays the good news to colleagues: he's contacted Flash. Standing behind him is George Cleveland.

13 Chapters:

1. The Planet of Peril 2. The Tunnel of Terror 3. Captured by Shark Men 4. Battling the Sea Beast 5. The Destroying Ray 6. Flaming Torture 7. Shattering Doom 8. Tournament of Death 9. Fighting the Fire Dragon 10. The Unseen Peril 11. In the Claws

Below: Larry "Buster" Crabbe extends a friendly Earth greeting, rejected by metal-clad Earl Askam as Frank Shannon, Jean Rogers and Mongo guards watch.

Jean Rogers is held by two slaves while would-be universe emperor Charles Middleton, sultry daughter Priscilla Lawson and Earl Askam watch Flash battle in the arena.

of the Tigron 12. Trapped in the Turret 13. Rocketing to Earth

Note: Flash Gordon *is arguably the most entertaining sound serial ever made. It is as enjoyable today as it was almost 70 years ago. Its budget was $350,000, a lot of money for a serial. Sets and props from prior Universal films were used: the great god Tao was borrowed from* The Mummy, *Zarkov's rocket ship came from Fox, who had used it in* Just Imagine. *The serial was unexpectedly successful. Universal's top-grossing film that year was* Three Smart Girls, *which introduced Deanna Durbin. Right behind it was* Flash Gordon, *a serial!*

A strange planet called Mongo is rushing toward Earth, bombarding it with deadly radioactive meteorites. Populations around the world are in a state of frenzy, with riots and panic everywhere. From an eastern observa-

High priest Theodore Lorch smiles evilly as Charles Middleton listens to daughter Priscilla Lawson's pitch for Flash's life. Ming's court maidens seem interested, too.

31

tory, Professor Gordon and an international team of astronomers track the killer planet's progress and calculate their chances: zero. On the west coast, Gordon's son, Flash, gives up a polo match to catch a transcontinental plane so he can be with his dad when the end comes.

The plane, a single-engine six-passenger craft, has trouble getting through the meteor storm at night, and a bail out is suggested by the pilot. Flash offers a few words of encouragement to a pretty blond he's been eyeing, and helps her put on her parachute. As the ship lurches wildly, still holding on to the woman, he leaps from the plane and the two descend, landing lightly in the lower branches of a tree. "Nice trip. Must try it again," Flash quips. The woman notices a strange metal craft sitting

Jean Rogers holds her head in distress, Charles Middleton is encouraged and Priscilla Lawson anxious, each with different motives, as Flash battles three killer anthropoids in the dreaded pit.

Below: Frank Shannon is introduced to his new state of the art laboratory by sponsor-captor Charles Middleton.

Jean Rogers leans against Richard Alexander's ample protective chest as Charles Middleton samples the merchandise with a Mongoian finger.

nearby. It's a rocket ship, and its owner steps out of the darkness brandishing a gun and demanding to know who the intruders are. The woman introduces herself as Dale Arden. "Nice name," comments Flash.

When Flash states his name stranger becomes agitated, but introduces himself as Dr. Zarkov. It seems he knows Flash's dad, Prof. Gordon. "Your father thinks I'm mad. They all do," he complains. He tells Dale and Flash that if he can reach the approaching planet he "may be able to control its power" and divert it from hitting Earth. He mentions that the planet is "intensely radioactive." His rocket ship, never tested, is ready. Like most kids, Flash is sure that anyone his father thinks is mad

A rocket ship makes its circular landing among Mongo's craggy terrain.

must be brilliant. He promptly volunteers to join Zarkov on his flight.

The trip appeals to Dale, too. She insists on going along and, after a bit of grumbling and coaxing, Zarkov consents. They enter the rocketship and prepare for take off. This consists of

Dr. Zarkov sitting in front of a small control panel while Flash and Dale stand, holding on to wall straps. "Sure this thing will work?" Flash asks, a shadow of doubt creeping into what we will call his mind. "I've experimented with models," Zarkov replies. "Did they ever come back?," Flash persists. "They weren't supposed to," Zarkov declares as the rocket ship takes off.

They pass through the stratosphere. Dale suddenly grows weak and faints, gasping, "Air...air." As Flash rushes over to help, Zarkov remembers something. "I forgot to turn on the oxygen," he announces. "No need to worry." Flash's trust remains unshaken, even after the doctor's next report, that they had just passed through the "death

Showdown time? Jean Rogers (2nd from left) watches as John Lipson stares daggers at Buster Crabbe. Earl Askam (Center) keeps an eye out and Frank Shannon (2nd from right) advises Flash to cool it.

zone," the only thing he had feared. After a surprisingly short trip and just before the ship lands with a dull thud, a city is sighted not far away. The three disembark and head for it.

Flash is concerned about leaving the rocket ship unattended, but Zarkov assures him it's securely locked. Suddenly a dinosaur-sized, lizard-like creature appears and the Earth people run back to the ship. Zarkov stumbles and falls behind. Flash gets to the ship first and sure enough, it's locked and he can't get in. Fortunately, another lizard creature appears and the two monsters engage in a ferocious battle. The dazzling display of toothless-lizard ferocity is brought to a sudden conclusion by a death-ray blast from a passing rocket ship which kills both creatures instantly. As the strange craft lands, Flash, Dale and Zarkov rush to greet their rescuers.

The four men who emerge from the ship are clad in metal, and armed. Their leader announces that the Earth people are prisoners and are to be taken to Ming, Emperor of the Universe. Flash immediately attacks and is flailing away prodigiously when Zarkov restrains him. "No, no, Flash, no," he scolds, "we must be taken to the emperor. It's the only hope of saving the Earth from destruction." Flash calms down, but not before warning the soldiers to keep their hands off Dale.

The Earth people are brought before Ming, in the main hall of the emperor's sumptuous palace. They state their concern about the impending collision of the two planets. Ming tells them there will be no collision, that he controls the movement of the planet, then adds menacingly, "I will destroy

The wondrous Sky City, suspended in space.

Whatever it is, Buster Crabbe will face it with Priscilla Lawson at his side.

Earth in my own way." Zarkov sees an opening. "Why *destroy* Earth?" he asks. "Why not *conquer* it?" Apparently Ming had been planning to destroy Earth just for the heck of it. He's fascinated by Zarkov's suggestion. "Why not?" he mutters, greatly impressed with the doctor's brilliance. When Zarkov mentions that he arrived in a rocket ship of his own design, Ming orders he be put to work in the laboratory. "Give him everything he requires except his freedom," he commands.

While this is going on, Ming's sultry daughter Aura enters. She sizes up Flash and likes what she sees. Flash gives her a quick once over and notices her inviting look. Clean-cut American youth that he is, he's turned off by her boldness (although Aura is good-looking and really stacked). Ming, too, has been window shopping. He approaches Dale hungrily. "Those eyes," he oozes, "your hair. Your skin. I've never seen one like you before. Ahh...you're beautiful."

Dale is without doubt a succulent morsel but Ming's advances are more than Flash can tolerate. He charges to the throne, grabs the emperor and lifts him into the air. "You keep your slimy hands off her," he yells, and unceremoniously dumps Ming the Merciless,

Emperor of the Universe, back into his throne. None of Ming's guards move a muscle. "Grab him," Ming commands, as Flash pirouettes around the room in a half crouch, knocking Ming's men out of the way. Eventually he's subdued and thrown into "the arena," a caged-in corner of the huge room.

Flash faces three ominous doors. They slide open and three primitive, powerful-looking ape men emerge, dangling their arms monkey style. Two have long fangs jutting from the corners of their mouths (rendering them useless, if you think about it). Dashing about furiously, Flash makes short work of the brutes. "He fights well," Ming admits, then adds, "He shall not escape *the pit*." Aura, who had other things in mind for Flash, is greatly upset. By now she's so infatuated that she's willing to defy her father and risk her life for the stranger.

She dashes into the arena with Flash and scoops up a fallen ray gun. She blasts the guard who controls the pit's trapdoors. As he slumps to the floor his hand hits a lever, a trapdoor opens and Flash and Aura drop into the pit's bottomless depths. As they plunge to certain doom, Ming orders "the net" to be released. A net appears under the couple, saving them. Even more fortuitously there is a secret door in the pit's

35

Amidst the splendor of Sky City, Jean Rogers does not seem pleased with whatever it is Vultan king John Lipson is offering, while princess Priscilla Lawson finds Dale's discomfit amusing.

wall, right at net level. They slip through the door into a network of rock-walled caverns.

A platoon of Ming's metal-clad guards marches by, but Flash and Aura hide in the shadows and are not seen. She leads him out and to a nearby rocket ship and suggests that he wait in the ship while she finds out what happened to Zarkov and Dale. As soon as Flash closes the door behind him, she mutters, "You'll never seen Dale Arden again." Inside, Flash looks around, finds some clothes and puts them on.

Meanwhile, Dr. Zarkov is playing in his new laboratory, under the watchful eyes of Ming. As the doctor busily presses buttons and turns dials various fluorescent tubes glow, machines spark and sputter and Jacob's ladders light up. "This is a scientist's paradise," he tells Ming, with enough radioactive energy

to conquer the universe. "Which I intend to do with your aid," Ming reminds him. Ming's high priest enters and reports that Dale refuses to become Ming's bride. Ming orders that "the dehumanizer" be used, but only with

Jean Rogers cringes as King Vultan advances.

enough power to keep Dale in a trance until the wedding ceremony is over. "Science will overcome all things, even the human emotions," he predicts accurately.

A squadron of rocket ships is sighted on a television warning screen. The Lion Men are attacking in their gyroships, a sentry reports. Flash, too, observes the approaching gyroships, which look like flying spin tops. Without the slightest hesitation he attacks them, taking off and maneuvering the ship like an ace. Considering he is hopelessly outnumbered and this is his maiden voyage as a rocket pilot, he acquits himself well, blasting his presumed enemies from the sky with deadly accuracy. Ming, watching this performance via television, is impressed. He vows that the gallant pilot will be royally rewarded.

In the midst of his display of aerial virtuosity Flash collides with an opposing rocket ship and the two craft, locked together, fall through space and crash to the ground. A bearded Lion Man emerges from the twisted wreckage a bit shaken but otherwise unhurt. Ditto Flash. The Lion Man draws his sword but is quickly disarmed by Flash. The hirsute stranger introduces himself as Thun, Prince of the Lion Men, an enemy of Ming. He is understandably surprised when Flash reveals that he, too, is Ming's enemy. Thun is apparently too polite to point out that Flash has just shot down most of his gyroships, and Flash hardly seems capable of making such abstract connections.

Thun proves he's not a sore loser by declaring he'll help Flash rescue Dale and Zarkov. They notice that Ming's fleet has arrived and is busily destroying what's left of Thun's force. Thun leads Flash to a secret passage leading to Ming's palace.

While Dale is being put into an hypnotic spell by the dehumanizing machine, Flash and Thun get into the palace, capture a guard and force him to take them to the laboratory. Zarkov gives them the good news first: he's altered Mongo's course so it won't collide with Earth. The bad news is that Dale is about to marry Ming. Flash and Thun race to the ceremonial chamber, but to get there they must travel through underground caverns. This time they're seen by four guards and a fight ensues. Flash kayoes his two opponents, but a struggling Thun tells him to go on alone, which he does, opening two huge doors and slipping inside.

Unfortunately Flash has entered the domain of the guardian of the secret chamber, an enormous monster with the head of a dragon, the body of a dinosaur and the claws of a giant lobster. Although the creature is a slow-moving, lumbering beast Flash stumbles right into it and can't escape. He stands rooted to the spot until the monster picks him up and crushes him in its awesome claws. Thun shows up and kills the creature with a blast from his ray gun. Flash is a bit shaken, but recovers quickly. They dash to the ceremonial chamber and get there in time to disrupt the ceremony and rescue Dale.

Flash, Dale and Thun escape through another tunnel, which leads to

Below: In Vultan's atom-furnace room, a guard gets ready to crack the whip at a typically-troublesome Buster Crabbe, who's held back by Richard Alexander. Bearded Lion-Man James Pierce (center left) watches helplessly. William Desmond is the third guard from the right.

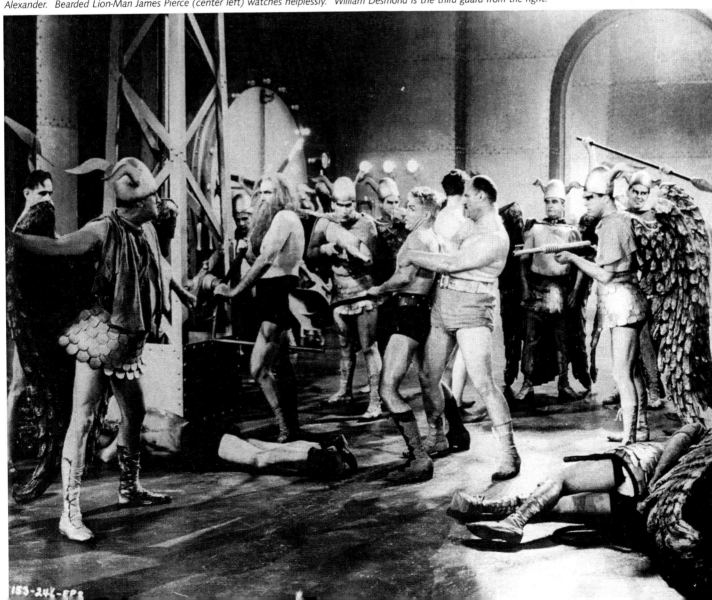

Aha! Evidence of Dale's devotion to Flash. Frank Shannon, Jean Rogers and Richard Alexander stare at the incriminating handkerchief brandished by John Lipson. Talk about beefcake!

the underwater palace of an ally, King Kala of the Shark Men, denizens of Mongo's oceans. In the underwater kingdom Flash is separated from Dale and Thun, who go to the palace's throne room to wait for him. Aura shows up and convinces Flash that Dale and Thun have left the underwater kingdom via submarine and that they are to follow in another sub. He believes her. As soon as they depart she confesses the truth to him. He tries to turn the sub around, but Aura knocks him unconscious.

Ming, learning where the escapees are heading, uses his powerful magnetic equipment to raise the Shark Men's palace to the surface of the Mongo sea. Flash regains consciousness in time to see winged Hawk Men from the Sky City (yet another kingdom on Mongo, this one led by Vultan) swoop down to the palace and carry off Dale and Thun. Aura tells him Vultan is an ally of her

father. "Then he's no friend of mine," Flash replies.

Meanwhile, in Ming's fortress, Zarkov is visited by Prince Barin, who enters through a secret passageway and reveals that he is the true ruler of Mongo, dethroned by Ming, who killed his father. Barin offers to aid the Earth people if they'll help him depose Ming. Zarkov agrees. "I've hoped for this moment since I learned of your arrival," Barin says earnestly, "My rocketship is waiting to rescue your friends." The two men take off and head to Sky City.

Upon arrival in Vultan's domain, a wondrous city of light that floats on antigravity-ray beams, Aura and Flash are seized by the winged men. The king himself is a winged, rotund, simple-minded fellow with a mean streak. Barin's approaching rocket ship is spotted and brought down by ray-beam anti-aircraft fire, but the fall is cushioned by

"the gravity-defying rays that support the sky city." Barin and Zarkov, too, are captured. Meanwhile, Vultan is entertaining Dale, trying to cheer her up by introducing her to his pet, Yurkl, a huge bear-wolverine that only terrifies her. Frustrated, Vultan lecherously advances upon Dale, who backs up against the wall, looking absolutely irresistible. He wants her to be his queen.

Vultan's romancing is interrupted by guards, who bring in Flash, Aura, Barin and Zarkov. Dale immediately rushes to Flash's side while Aura goes on the offense. "How dare you shoot down a spaceship of the Emperor Ming?," she yells at Vultan, who pleads ignorance and apologizes. He's already knows Prince Barin, and is introduced to Flash and Zarkov. Upon hearing that Zarkov is a scientist, he has him sent to one of the Sky City's laboratories. (Good scientists are always in demand.)

Flash and Barin are sent to the furnace room, "where they will be kept warm."

The atom furnace is an ultra-modern room in which prisoners continually shovel radium into roaring furnaces which supply the power that keeps the city suspended in space. Helmeted guards manually turn the dials of giant clock-like devices, much as in *Metropolis* (to which this scene pays obvious homage). In the furnace room Flash and Barin find Thun, also enslaved. The men plot their escape. In his kingdom, Ming learns that Aura and the Earth people have been captured by Vultan. "King Vultan will no doubt

Right: Prince Richard Alexander and Frank Shannon support an even more-unconscious-than-usual Buster Crabbe, while Jean Rogers pouts prettily.

Below: Buster Crabbe and Jean Rogers are glad to see one another, While Frank Shannon and Richard Alexander wait impatiently.

Buster Crabbe in the grip of a horned ape thing during the Tournament of Death.

dove," he says, holding her hand affectionately.

In the furnace room Flash comes to the aid of a fallen prisoner and, being whipped for his efforts, starts a riot. As punishment, he's sent to the "static room." Vultan wants proof that Dale really loves him. "Do you doubt my word?," she asks. He says he'll discover the truth, and leads her to the static room, where Flash hangs suspended between two electrodes. As Dale watches, electric current is sent through his body. He writhes in agony. She begs Vultan to stop. "Then you do love him," he charges. "No," Dale insists, "I just can't stand to see him tortured." Vultan is not convinced. As the shock treatment continues, Dale faints, beautifully, and is carried away by attendants.

Aura appears, ray gun in hand, and orders Flash released. She tells Vultan he can never win Dale by killing Flash. The Hawk Man thinks this over and realizes she's right. He also notices the loving care Aura gives Flash. "I'm beginning to understand," he says. Aura takes Flash to the Sky City laboratory, where Zarkov puts him in an "electro stimulator" in which he is "barraged by healing electrowaves."

Dale is a despondent guest no matter how hard Vultan tries to cheer her up. He does finger-shadow tricks, but nothing seems to work. In the meantime, Flash is comes to and Aura expresses her love, telling him how she risked her life for him. Flash says he's grateful. "I want more than your gratitude," she replies. Flash says he's an Earth man, and well, will be going back to his own planet eventually, and, well, you know. She tells him to give up Dale Arden or—she picks up a blazing electrode—she'll blind him. He remains silent. She brings the electrode close to his face, then drops it, unable to continue. She really does love the big lug.

Flash is sent back to the furnace room, only this time he's wired to the atom furnaces, so he'll be electrocuted if he tries to escape. Zarkov frees him and rewires the circuit so that a tremendous explosion occurs, destroying the atom furnaces and threatening the stability of Sky City, which starts to wob-

force the Earth girl to marry him," Ming muses. "It's a habit of his." He leaves for the Sky City.

Vultan visits Zarkov in his laboratory. The scientist has noticed very high radiation in the area. Vultan explains it's from the atom furnaces. Zarkov asks what would happen if the supply of radium ran out. "Then the city would fall," Vultan replies, and explains that Zarkov must find an alternative energy source for the city—quickly In the

meantime, Aura is having a heart to heart with Dale, blaming her for Flash's predicament, for Vultan is in love with her and jealous of Flash. She says that for Flash's sake Dale must pretend to love Vultan. Dim-witted Dale buys it.

Vultan invites Dale and Aura to dinner, and does his best to impress the Earth woman. Dale is listless, but an angry look from Aura rouses her. She smiles enchantingly at the king and pretends to find him attractive. "My little

A typical Mongo landscape.

ble. Zarkov tells Vultan that in return for their freedom he'll give Vultan a newly-invented ray that will save the city. Vultan agrees, but Ming makes an unexpected appearance and vetoes the idea. Instead he suggests they all return to his kingdom and that a tournament be held there. If Flash wins, he gains his freedom and can choose his bride. Recognizing Ming's power, Vultan is forced to agree.

"The Tournament of Death" begins and Flash faces a number of assorted monsters (including an ape-like creature with a unicorn-type horn), vanquishing them one by one. A livid Ming promises to give Flash his freedom and to allow him to choose his bride in three days. As the third day approaches, Aura slips Flash a "drug of forgetfulness," so that he doesn't recognize his Earth friends. When Ming asks Flash to name his bride, Aura answers, declaring that Flash has chosen her. To the astonishment of Dale, Zarkov and Barin, Flash offers no protest. Zarkov and Barin, suspecting foul play, bring Flash to the lab and submit him to a ray treatment which restores his memory.

Meanwhile, Ming orders troops to the lab to execute Flash. As they enter, Zarkov shoves Flash into a machine that makes him invisible and allows him to escape. While this is going on, Aura, still jealous, sends a vicious tigron, a tiger-like beast, to track down and kill Dale. It stalks her as she flees through corridors. Flash regains visibility and appears just as the tigron attacks. Flash leaps upon the giant cat. Confused, the cat attacks Aura, who had been watching the drama unfold. Prince Barin arrives and fearlessly leaps to Aura's defense, killing the tigron. Aura is drawn to Barin for his bravery, and he confesses he's been in love with her all along.

The repentant Aura goes to her father to plead for the life of her new friends, but Ming has them seized and orders Flash's execution. Before this can be carried out, Thun and his Lion Men attack the palace and break into Ming's chamber. Trying to escape, the merciless one heads through the secret tunnels but is seized by one of the dragon-monsters and presumably killed. Barin assumes his rightful place as ruler of Mongo, Aura at his side. And Flash, with Dale and Zarkov, blast off for the return to Earth.

Jean Rogers and Buster Crabbe, together again.

Undersea Kingdom (Republic-1936) Directed by B. Reeves Eason, Joseph Kane. Screenplay: John Rathmell, Maurice Geraghty, Oliver Drake. Story: John Rathmell, Tracy Knight. Production supervisor: Barney A. Sarecky. Production manager: Sol

C. Siegal. Cinematography: William Nobles, Edgar Lyons. Musical score: Arthur Kay, Leon Rosebrook, Meredith Wilson, Reginald H. Bassett, Charles Dunworth, Joseph Carl Breil. Special effects: John T. Coyle, Howard Lydecker, Theodore Lydecker. Supervising editor: Joseph H. Lewis. Sound: Terry Kellum. Executive producer: Herbert J. Yates. Producer: Nat Levine. [5-30-36]

Cast:

Crash Corrigan . Ray "Crash" Corrigan
Diana Compton . . . . Lois Wilde
Unga Khan . . . . Monte Blue
Sharad . . . . William Farnum
Ditmar . . . . Boothe Howard
Prof. Norton . . . . C. Montague Shaw
Billy Norton . . . . Lee Van Atta
Briny Deep . . Lester Smiley Burnette
Salty . . . . Frankie Marvin
Hakur . . . . Creighton Chaney

Darius . . . . Lane Chandler
Lt. Andrews . . . . Jack Mulhall
Joe . . . . John Bradford
Zogg . . . . Malcolm McGregor
Martos . . . . Ralph Holmes
Gourck . . . . Ernie Smith
Capt. Clinton . . . . . . Lloyd Whitlock
Naval Sentry . . . . David Horsley
Naval Doctor . . . . . Kenneth Lawton
Gaspon . . . . Raymond Hatton
Magna . . . . "Rube" Schaeffer
Molok . . . . John Merton

12 Chapters:
1. Beneath the Ocean Floor
2. Undersea City   3. Arena of Death
4. Revenge   5. Prisoners of Atlantis
6. The Juggernaut Strikes   7. The Submarine Trap   8. Into the Metal Tower   9. Death in the Air
10. Atlantis Destroyed   11. Flaming Death   12. Ascent to the Upperworld
Acceptance in the United States

Naval Academy at Annapolis marks the start of a brilliant naval career for Crash Corrigan. He's the school's star athlete, winning football games and wrestling matches as well as the admiration of all who know him. During one match, a young admirer, Billy Norton, brings an urgent message from his dad, the famous scientist, Professor Norton, who wants Crash to come to his laboratory as soon as possible. Crash rushes over.

Professor Norton is being interviewed by newspaper reporter Diana Compton, who finds it hard to believe that the small machine on his desk can predict earthquakes. "Not only predict, but prevent them," the professor tells her, just as Crash arrives.

The machine starts making static sounds, then subsides. "That was a signal again,'" Norton says. "They've been sending it every five minutes."

Below: Assorted officers (right over Ray's shoulder is Capt. Lloyd Whitlock—4th from right—talking to Lt. Jack Mulhall) and shipmates watch in wrapt admiration as Ray "Crash" Corrigan, with a good hold on his opponent's neck, struts his stuff. No wonder he's chosen for a special assignment.

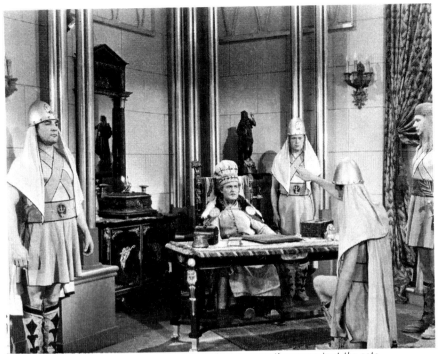

A messenger brings bad tidings to high priest William Farnum: the enemy is at the gate.

"They?," Diana asks. She's told the professor believes the signals are from humans on the bottom of the ocean, the remnants of the lost continent of Atlantis. (By the way, that's the last we'll hear of this earthquake device. It plays no further part in the serial.)

Norton shows them an artifact he claims could only have been made by Atlanteans, yet which tests show was only a few years old. He'd found it during a recent trip in his rocket-powered submarine, and indicates the general area of ocean on a map, just where Atlantis vanished thousands of years ago. "Contrary to popular belief," he tells them, "Atlantis did not sink overnight but during a period of years. During this time the people had ample opportunity to construct a roof to keep out the ocean waves." And sure enough, we see the presumably-roofed lost continent of Atlantis, where things are not going well for Sharad, high priest of the true Atlanteans, and his White Robe followers who are under attack from Unga Khan, the tyrannical ruler of the Black Robe guards. Having harnessed the atom, Unga Khan has built a disintegrating machine and is directing it at North America as part of his scheme to gain control of the upper world.

A messenger tells Sharad that Unga Khan's troops are at the gates of the secret city, and begs him to "take safety in the citadel," but Sharad declines, saying that "Poseidon, god of Atlantis, has never forsaken his people in time of need. I promise you he shall not do so now." He walks to a window and sees his guards being slain by arrows from ground troops and bombs from a double-hulled airship, a Volplane, flying above. His faith is being sorely tested.

The Volplane returns to Unga Khan's base, a launching pad in a multi-storied, glistening metallic missile-shaped tower. Through a Reflectoplate screen, he and his aide Ditmar view with great satisfaction the "upperworld" earthquakes, panics and disturbances he's created.

Professor Norton decides that he and Crash must depart for Atantis as soon as possible. His ship mechanics, Joe, Briny and Salty, are told to get the submarine ready. Billy wants to go along but is told it's too dangerous. Diana knows this is the story of a lifetime and talks her way aboard. Joe, who handles the sub's controls, panics as it descends, certain that the ship will collapse like an eggshell under the ocean's pressure. Temporarily deranged, he sends the sub into a steep dive and has to be knocked cold by Crash to prevent a disaster. During the melee it's discovered that Bobby has stowed away. When Joe comes to, he's remorseful about his behavior.

The sub's descent is tracked by Unga Khan, who has it electrically drawn to Atlantis through an inland sea cave opening in the center of the dome-covered continent. As the submarine rises to the surface the group finds itself in an inlet surrounded by woods and rocky hills. Salty and Briney, who had been sleeping in their quarters, wake up and, bringing their parrot Sinbad with them, join the others as they disembark.

Professor C. Montague Shaw and reporter Lois Wilde, in the grip of Atlantean Volkites, as Boothe Howard (right) watches. A Juggernaut is behind them.

Unga Khan and his chief aide Ditmar are watching this on the Reflectoplate screen. Khan sends out the Black Robe imperial guards to capture the intruders. A mounted patrol gallops off. Crash and the others step out of the sub. "Here we are ten thousand feet below sea level," Norton observes, "and apparently in another world." Salty and Briney wander off,

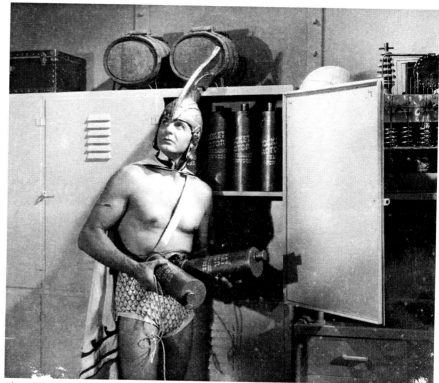

Aboard the rocket-powered submarine, Crash Corrigan gathers some high-explosive cartridges.

Loyal aide Lane Chandler and high priest William Farnum view their city under attack.

A cast of thousands (for a serial) turn out to greet their ruler, William Farnum, in a good example of Poverty Row tackiness. Note the wagon full of shields on the far right.

Below: Welcome to Atlantis! Boothe Howard (flashy helmet) pins down Crash Corrigan while another guard tries to grab his feet and berobed evil Khan Monte Blue barks orders. Note the Atlantean decor.

Crash Corrigan discards a Volkite disguise as he and C. Montague Shaw try to figure out how to escape from Unga Khan's tower.

trying to keep track of Sinbad, who immediately takes to the trees.

As a precaution the sub is submerged and its robot-control box hidden under shrubs. Crash, the professor, Billy, Diana and Joe see the imperial guards heading for them, and flee. A Juggernaut, a metallic, tank-like vehicle, rolls up and blocks their way. Four mechanical men (called Volkites) emerge. Joe, as usual, panics, and fires his revolver at them. A blast from a robot ray gun finishes him off.

Crash and Billy scramble to the top of a rocky hill, causing Khan to order that missiles be fired at them. Three rockets are launched, blasting Crash and Billy from their perch. They roll down the incline and suffer no injuries.

Things don't look good for Crash Corrigan and (to his right) John Merton, who have been sentenced to be dragged to death via chariot. Lee Van Atta (kneeling) offers words of encouragement.

While Crash Corrigan attends to a suspended Volkite, the still-mind altered C. Montague Shaw prepares to clobber him with a pipe. Despite his fancy metal helmet, Crash will be knocked cold.

The Sacred City is under attack by Black Robes. White Robe army commander Crash Corrigan gets a report from his aide, John Merton

The tyrannical would-be ruler of the world, Monte Blue (left) and his main man Boothe Howard watch the Reflectoplate screen to see how their attack is going.

They quickly find Diana and the professor and, pursued by Volkites, flee over rocks into a narrow canyon the robots can't get through. In the distance they see another kingdom, Sharad's sacred city. But at the same time, a mounted White Robe patrol spies them and they're captured. The White Robes think that Crash and company are Unga Khan agents.

All this is seen by Unga Khan on his reflectoplate, who warns his men that the upperworld people "must be captured at any cost." Black Robe riders are soon galloping to the sacred city, where they engage in mounted, sword-to-sword combat with the White Robe patrol. In the meantime, Crash, Billy, Diana and the professor, are bound and in chariots speeding toward the secret city. A Juggernaut appears and the chariot driver flees, but is cut down by a blast from the Volkite's ray gun.

Crash and Billy make a break for it and dash into the hills. They see Diana and the professor forced into the Juggernaut, which departs swiftly. Crash tells Billy to stay put, while he takes off on foot after it. He has no trouble keeping up, and is right there as the Juggernaut enters a cave in the base of the hill on top of which sits Khan's missile shaped tower.

Meanwhile, Salty and Briney have been sleeping under a tree in the woods. They're awakened by a ray-gun-wielding Volkite which indicates to them the direction to walk in.

Diana and the professor are brought immediately to Unga Khan, who is angered by Norton's bindings. "He is no prisoner," he barks to a guard. "Release him!" Once the grateful professor is untied, Unga Khan introduces himself and welcomes his guests "to my

Crash Corrigan, Lee Van Atta and C. Montague Shaw, escaping in a Volplane. What's that? Is that a missile Shaw see coming toward them?

Below: Disguised as Volkites, Crash and Moloch have rescued C. Montague Shaw who's had his memory and will power restored. Boothe Howard and Monte Blue have been locked in the alteration chamber for safe keeping.

Crash Corrigan pulls C. Montague Shaw from the wreckage of their shot-down Volplane. Lee Van Atta is on the makeshift stretcher.

underwater city of Atlantis." "Your soldiers have already welcomed us," Diana tells him, and Norton adds, "They've killed my assistant and made off with my son and Lieutenant Corrigan."

Unga Khan replies that the soldiers who attacked them were not his men, but followers of Sharad, and that his son and Corrigan "have undoubtedly been made prisoners of that tyrant." He calls out the imperial guard with orders to rescue the two upperworlders. Professor Norton is extremely grateful. He's only too happy to tell all about the rocket-powered submarine. Unga Khan is fascinated. "Do you think these rocket motors could be built powerful enough to lift this tower?" he asks. Norton assures him there's "no limit to their size or power. Given time and the necessary equipment I could construct rocket motors that could raise this tower clear to the upper world."

Unga Khan tells Norton he can

start at once. Diana is puzzled. She asks him why he wants to move the tower. He tells them the tower "contains all the machinery that has enabled me to harness the atom, the most destructive force known to science. Once I reach the surface I'll either become supreme ruler of the upper world—*or destroy it!*" Norton (with Diana's agreement) tells him he's nuts and that he will never cooperate. "We have ways of persuading people to do our bidding," Unga Khan smiles. He orders that Norton be placed in a glass "transformer" chamber, a "machine that will merely transform his mind so that he will obey me."

Crash has found his way into the city. He knocks two guards unconscious and puts on one's uniform. Avoiding Volkites, he finds the emperor's room and barges in as Norton is struggling in the glass chamber. Guards attack, Crash battles valiantly, punching

and tossing about Black Robes, and actually frees his friends for a few moments, but despite his considerable efforts Diana and the professor remain prisoners and he's forced to mount a horse and flee, followed closely by Khan's mounted troops. He heads straight for Sharad's walled palace.

Crash gets into the sacred city, but, because he's still wearing a Black Robe outfit, he's arrested by Sharad's White Robes, who assume he's a spy. He insists on being taken to Sharad, but is tossed into a dungeon while a guard delivers his message. Fortunately for Crash, Billy had been previously captured by White Robes and has since totally charmed Sharad. Now he tells the high priest that Crash is no spy. It seems, however, that a White Robe charioteer has been killed by Crash. Sharad declares that "the law is clear: only life can take a life. Corrigan shall be pitted against captive Black Robes in

mortal combat." If he wins, he'll be set free. Billy thinks that's fine because he's sure Crash will win.

Back in Unga Khan's throne room, the evil one picks up where he'd left off before being interrupted. Prof. Norton is returned to the transformation chamber and his brains properly scrambled. He is the tyrant's tool, unable to recognize Diana and eager to do his master's bidding. Through a reflectoplate Khan allows Diana to view Crash—imprisoned and waiting to do battle.

Crash is led into the arena where he pits his brawn and brains against three Black Robe captives. Two of the gladiators are quickly knocked out of the fight and play dead. The remaining Black Robe, Moloch, puts up a good fight but is finally knocked to the ground. Sharad presents a dagger to

Main-man Boothe Howard and Emperor Monte Blue are pleased by inventor C. Montague Shaw's plans for rocketing Khan's tower to the upperworld.

Below: Creighton Chaney directs two Volkites to the submarine, aided and abetted by brainwashed C. Montague Shaw.

Below: Lee Van Atta has the death ray drop on Boothe Howard (left), Mongolian-bedecked Monte Blue, a Black Robe guard and an as usual dazed-and-confused C. Montague Shaw. Ray Corrigan recovers on the floor.

Crash, the custom being to kill the vanquished opponent. Moloch girds himself for death. But Crash refuses to kill him, and breaks the dagger in half.

This takes all the fun out of the event and an offended Sharad (he's the *good* ruler, remember) orders that Crash and Moloch be tied by rope to a chariot and dragged to death. At that moment, with Crash securely bound, Magna and Gourek, the two other defeated Black Robes, attempt to escape. They tackle Sharad, throw him into the chariot and ride away, dragging Crash behind them. Magna drives the chariot through the city gates and across the Atlantean countryside toward Khan's tower.

Drawing himself hand over hand into the chariot, Crash hurls the Black Robes onto the road and, with the enemy close behind, sends Sharad back to the palace while he delays the pur-

suers. He just makes it to the palace's walls, where Moloch risks his own life by suspending himself upside down so that Crash can grab his wrists and be lifted to safety. Sharad shows his gratitude for being rescued by placing Crash in complete charge of his army.

Crash's first act is to make Moloch his assistant. And not a moment too soon, for Crash is now told that Unga Khan's entire army, led by Hakur, is advancing upon the city. During the fierce battle that follows, Juggernauts, flame throwers and catapults are brought into deadly use. Black Robe laddermen swarm over the walls. In the heat of battle Crash overpowers Hakur and, disguising himself in the officer's uniform, gives the order to retreat, thereby saving the city. But Billy is forced to hide in one of the retreating chariots, and finds himself heading for

Khan's fortress. He manages to stay hidden after arriving in the enemy city and wandering around, bumps into Diana.

Crash, still disguised as Hakur, decides to go back with the Black Robes to rescue Diana and Norton. He climbs the wall of Khan's tower, peers through a window and sees Diana about to be placed in the transformation cabinet. He breaks into the room with the best of intentions but is quickly knocked unconscious. Fortunately, Billy, armed with an atom gun, enters and holds Khan, a contingent of Black Robe guards, and the still-brainwashed Norton at bay while Diana escapes and until Crash recovers. Then they both flee and join Diana in Sharad's kingdom. Atlantis, as you've probably noticed, is a wonder of contradictory technology. Horse-driven chariots,

52

bows and arrows, spears and catapults used alongside atom guns, television reflectoplates, missiles, Volplanes and robots.

Crash learns Norton is working on a rocket motor that requires a priming powder, a supply of which is in their submarine. Immediately, he and Billy head for the inland sea in a chariot. After riding for a time, Crash sends Billy back to Sharad's palace while he sets out to the tower on foot to destroy the rocket motor. But no sooner has he sneaked into Khan's fortress than he is captured, and a diabolical scheme enters Khan's mind.

Diana and Billy are conferring with the high priest when they are interrupted by the arrival of one of Khan's Juggernauts outside the city's gates. To their horror they find Crash strapped to the nose of the vehicle. Hakur, the driver, demands the vital powder, threatening to ram Crash against the gates unless it is delivered. Stalling for time, the resourceful Billy sneaks down from the balcony and slips unseen into the Juggernaut. He frees Crash, and helps him to capture Hakur. (it's just a matter of time before Hakur escapes.) All during this time Salty, Briney and Sinbad have been Khan's prisoners, relegated to working in the stables.

Crash and Billy drive the Juggernaut to Khan's fortress, where unsuspecting guards allow them to enter the city. They make their way to Prof. Norton, but he resists their rescue attempts so vigorously that Crash has to knock him out. Finding their way back to the Juggernaut blocked, they carry Norton to one of Khan's Volplanes and succeed in taking off from the tower, a tribute to Crash's piloting skills. Missiles are fired at them and the Volplane is hit. They crash, but emerge relatively unhurt and hide among rocks as Hakur and a Black Robe patrol approaches. At the first sight of them Norton breaks away and races toward Hakur, pleading to be taken "to my master." Crash and Billy watch helplessly as they ride off.

Unga Khan, seeing on the reflectoplate that Norton is safely recaptured, vows to destroy the sacred city once and

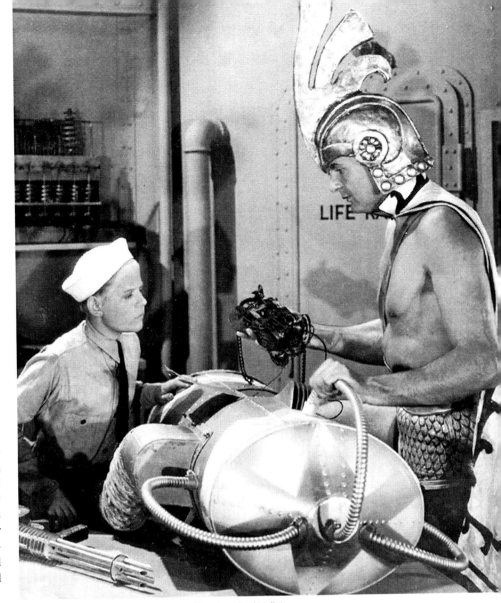

Lee Van Atta watches as Crash Corrigan dissects a dead Volkite.

for all, by using the dreaded "projector machine," so named because it hurls a barrage of deadly projectiles at its target. It's 'bombs away' and Crash, Moloch, Diana, Billy and Sharad try to find a place of safety, to no avail. The city is completely destroyed and Sharad is killed. Crash and his friends miraculously survive. They head for the submarine. Khan now prepares his final move: his metal tower is ready to serve as a huge rocket in which he'll be launched into the upper world.

Norton mentions that before the tower blasts off he needs some maps and charts which were left in the submarine. Khan sends Hakur and two Volkites along with Norton to get the papers, and they get there just moments before Crash and the others arrive.

Hakur spots them and plants the two Volkites in the sub as he and Norton steal off. Crash enters the submarine and has no trouble overcoming the robots (he has discovered they have a control button on their chests—pushing or shooting it immobilizes them). While the others stay with the sub, Crash and Moloch remove the robot interiors, get into the shells and leave for Unga Khan's tower to rescue Norton.

Joining a line of robots (all Volkites having been ordered into the tower for blast-off) Crash and Moloch penetrate Khan's conference room and, aiming ray guns at Khan and Ditmar, force the tyrant to restore Norton's memory. Then Khan and Ditmar are locked in the chamber as Crash, Norton and Moloch

Crash Corrigan puts a protective arm around C. Montague Shaw and a sword point against the stomach of Creighton Chaney, as Malcolm McGregor (far left), emperor Monte Blue (4th from right or left) and Boothe Howard watch.

flee. Hakur hears Khan rapping against the glass door and frees them. The three fugitives are approaching the tower's rocket base. Khan orders immediate departure, figuring that the heat generated by blast off will kill them. Which is nearly what happens. The engine's rockets almost do the job; Moloch is fried, but Crash and Norton fall through hole into an underground chamber and are saved. Crash discards the robot shell.

Fast-thinking Billy (who all along has proved to be the brains of Crash's group), seeing the tower blasting off, orders Salty and Briney to start engines full blast and quickly maneuvers the sub around the inland sea and through the cavernous exit that leads to the outer ocean. Billy has no trouble single-handedly working the sub's levers, dials and controls. [Salty, Briney and Sinbad, you may recall, were last seen working in the Black Robe stables. How they wound up back on the sub is anyone's guess.] Khan's tower crashes through the domed roof, sending the ocean pouring into Atlantis and making

more permanent its reputation as a lost kingdom.

Still in the tower, Crash and Norton have found Khan's radio room. They contact the U.S. Navy, describe what's happening and give their position ("latitude fifty-three degrees, longitude forty-nine degrees"). Navy armadas rush to the scene. In the meantime the tower has reached the surface, where it floats perpendicularly. Khan sees a four-masted sailing ship nearby and blasts it with a missile, just because he can. Crash and Norton are captured by Khan's men just as the Navy ships come into view. Khan immediately orders that a "wall of atom rays" be placed around the tower.

Navy battleships open fire, but their shells cannot penetrate the atom wall. While Khan and his men are diverted by events, Crash and Norton break free and jump into Khan's control room, where they begin turning off the tower's power system. The atom wall is off and howitzer shells hit the tower. Confusion reigns. Crash and Norton head for the Volplane launching pod.

They get there seconds before Khan does, and blast off just as several hits from the navy demolishes the tower, which sinks beneath the sea.

Crash and Diana make marriage plans while Professor Norton dedicates himself to perfecting the Volkite concept so the world can be forever freed from the drudgery of manual labor.

Flash Gordon's Trip to Mars (Universal-1938) Directed by Ford Beebe, Robert Hill. Original screenplay: Wyndham Gittens, Norman St, Hall, Ray Trampe, Herbert Dalmas. Director pf photography: Jerome Ash. Editors: Alvin Todd, Louis Sackin, Joe Gluck. Supervising editor: Saul Goodkind. Associate producer: Barney Sarecky. [2-8-38] Feature titles: *Mars Attacks the World*, *Deadly Rays from Mars*, *Perils from the Planet Mongo*.
Cast:

Flash Gordon . Larry "Buster" Crabbe
Dale Arden . . . . Jean Rogers
Emperor Ming . . . . Charles Middleton

54

Dr. Alexis Zarkov . . . . Frank Shannon
Queen Azura . . . . . . Beatrice Roberts
Prince Barin . . . . . Richard Alexander
Clay King . . . . C. Montague Shaw
Happy . . . . Donald Kerr
Tarnak . . . . Wheeler Oakman
King Fir . . . . Anthony Warde
Gen. Rankin . . . . Edwin Stanley
Prof. Denourd . . . . . . Hooper Atchley
Prof. Richards. . . . . James Blaine

15 Episodes:
1. New Worlds to Conquer   2. The Living Dead   3. Queen of Magic
4. Ancient Enemies   5. The Boomerang   6. Tree Men of Mars
7. The Prisoner of Mongo   8. Symbol of Death   9. Symbol of Death
10. Incense of Forgetfulness
11. Human Bait   12. Ming the Merciless   13. The Miracle of Magic
14. A Beast at Bay   15. An Eye for an Eye

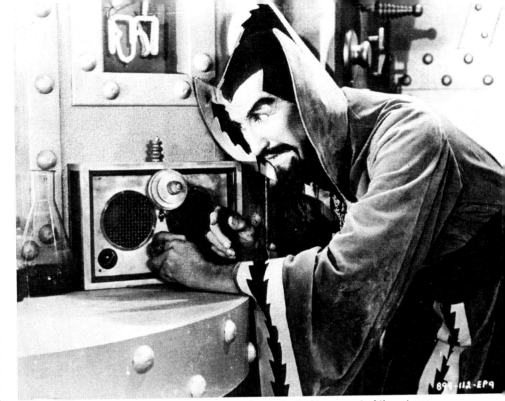

Still up to his old tricks. Charles Middleton relays the latest plan for his conquest of the universe.

Station WGAB gets a message from outer space from a rocket ship hurtling to Earth from outer space. It is confirmed by noted authority Dr. Metz that the message is authentic, and the news broadcast to a waiting world: Flash Gordon, Dr. Alexis Zarkov and Dale Arden are returning to Earth from Mongo, their rocketship traveling at the "incredible speed of at least twelve hundred miles an hour." The trio are given a hero's welcome replete with a ticker tape parade, and Dr. Zarkov speculates to a radio audience that advanced civilizations on other planets might well have methods of transportation "at the speed of light."

While the Earth celebrates, Ming the Merciless of Mongo (where he's now persona non grata), the would-be master of the universe, has allied himself with Azura "Queen of Magic," of Mars. We meet her as she sits on her throne and administers punishment, casting a spell which turns a dissenter into a Clay Person, fit only to live in caves, away from the light of day. Her subjects, and even Ming, usually address her as "your magnificence." Ming makes his entrance by walking through a wall of flames. (So *that's* how he escaped last time.) Together they admire his powerful new Nitron lamp, designed to suck the nitrogen from Earth. Mars is rich in the fuel needed to keep the Nitron beam burning. Ming promises Azura "the complete annihilation of the Earthfolk and the advancement of this planet towards its conquest of the universe." The Nitron beam is aimed at Earth and turned on.

Sudden, unexplainable atmospheric changes all over the Earth produce earthquakes, hurricanes, tidal waves, widespread flooding and a host of calamities resulting in great loss of life and property. In every country of the world, mass panic reigns. The President of the United States meets with experts to discuss probable causes, but all are stumped. Reporter Happy Hapwood, wise-cracking and persistent, wonders why Dr. Zarkov isn't at the

Big news. Deadly rays are attacking the Earth. Reporter Donald Kerr (right) is determined to get the story.

From left: Richard Alexander, Jean Rogers, Frank Shannon, Clay King C. Montague Shaw (under the make up), Donald Kerr and various Clay People watch as captured-queen Beatrice Roberts performs a spectacular trick: she disappears.

meeting. He's told that Zarkov is working on his own theory. Happy decides to track Zarkov down and get the story.

Dr. Zarkov has determined that the beam is coming from Mongo. Flash doesn't think that can be — they all saw Ming the Merciless die. Still, Zarkov insists, "someone up there is waging war on the Earth, and I intend to find out who." He plans to fly back to Mongo. Flash tells him he hasn't a chance in a million. "You're not asking me to stand by," Zarkov retorts, "without doing all one man can to prevent the destruction of the Earth, are you? Of course not, Flash." "In that case," Flash says, "the two of us will make the trip together." "You mean the three of us," Dale adds.

Once again, with Earth in peril, Flash, Zarkov and Dale blast off for Mongo, hoping to locate and destroy the mysterious force which is drawing

nitrogen from the atmosphere. "The World's Last Hope," screams the headline of the *New York Eagle* as the rocket ship departs. Flash and the others discover a stowaway — Happy. They're less than delighted, but quickly adjust to reality. When he finds out they're heading for Mongo, Happy is less than delighted too.

On Mars, Azura asks Ming how long he intends to keep the Nitro beam burning. (She'd like to use it against the Clay People.) Ming replies until every Earthman is dead. "And why not?" he muses. "An Earthman named Zarkov and his friend Flash Gordon once dared to pit themselves against me. Now let us see them save Earth, if they can."

On board his ship, Zarkov is now able to see exactly where the beam is coming from — Mars, not Mongo as he'd thought. The rocket ship is divert-

ed from its course by an unknown force, and drawn toward Mars and the beam. Watching this via television, Ming tells Azura that the enemy ship is the one Flash Gordon stole and used to return to Earth. He accurately guesses that the ship contains Flash, Zarkov and Dale. The ship hits the beam and immediately goes into a tailspin, hurtling toward Mars. Fortunately, it spins out of the beam's range and Zarkov is able to crash land. Azura and Ming see this and promptly head for the site in a Martian war ship.

Their ship is irreparably damaged but Flash, Dale, Happy and Zarkov are okay and climb out. They hide as a Martian war ship flies overhead, spots the wreck and lands. When Ming and some troops leave to examine the wreck, Flash sneaks into the Martian craft, knocks out a few guards, forces the pilot to stay on board, gets Dale,

56

Happy and Zarkov and takes off as Ming and his men do their futile best to stop him. Azura, still aboard, merely laughs at Flash's questions, snaps her fingers—and vanishes. But Flash has spotted Ming, knows he's alive and allied with Azura, and tells the others.

The Martian air force descends upon Flash's ship and, despite some fancy sharp shooting by Flash, he's forced to crash land. Azura has materialized in her palace and, when told that Flash has landed in the dread Valley of Desolation (so named because the cave-dwelling Clay People, who occupy the area, kill all of Azura's men on sight—none of whom has ever returned to tell the story), orders her troops to find the Earth people, despite their pleas that it means "certain death."

In the valley, Flash, Dale, Happy and Zarkov seek shelter in a cave, where they're captured by the Clay People—so named because that's what they're made of—who materialize out of the rock walls and who do not seem friendly—that is, until a Martian ship lands and Azura's troops enter the cave, intent on killing Flash and his friends. The troopers are disposed of by the Clay People, who are impervious to bullets and who are happy to discover that Azura is Flash's enemy, too. "Long ago we were the mightiest people on Mars," the Clay King tells the Earthlings, "but Azura became jealous and by her magic changed us from men into clay and banished us to this place." Only Azura can return them to their former human state, but because of their condition they cannot live on the outside, and so are unable to go after the evil queen.

The Clay King tells Flash and Zarkov they must capture Azura and bring her to him so she can lift the curse, and that Dale and Happy will be held hostage until they return. And that's not all. Azura's magical power is derived from a jewel she wears. He's not sure what the jewel looks like, but Flash and Zarkov must be certain to bring that, too. The Clay King gives Flash and Zarkov trooper uniforms and helmets and sends them on their way.

Pretending to be one of Azura's squadron commanders who has caught an Earthman (Zarkov) and wishes to deliver him personally to the queen, Flash bluffs his way into Azura's throne room, where he's not recognized because he's wearing a helmet and goggles. He tells Azura that the prisoner has confessed that Flash Gordon has allied himself with the Clay People, who have made him invisible and told him to steal her magic jewel. "He could be standing beside you right now," he warns Azura, who protectively grasps her necklace's white sapphire

The second she lets go, Flash grabs the jewel, pulls his ray gun and escapes with Zarkov and a struggling Azura. They cross a "bridge of light" and flee to the "landing tower," a structure held in space by a latticework of steel. Ming has seen all and, with Zarnak, Azura's ambitious adviser, decides to dispose of the Earthmen and Azura, too, by destroying the tower's underpinnings, easily accomplished by Zarnak's pushing and pulling several levers. The tower collapses but the intended victims all escape, with Flash saving Azura's

Below: Buster Crabbe tosses a drape over two Martian guards. The one on the right is Tom Steele.

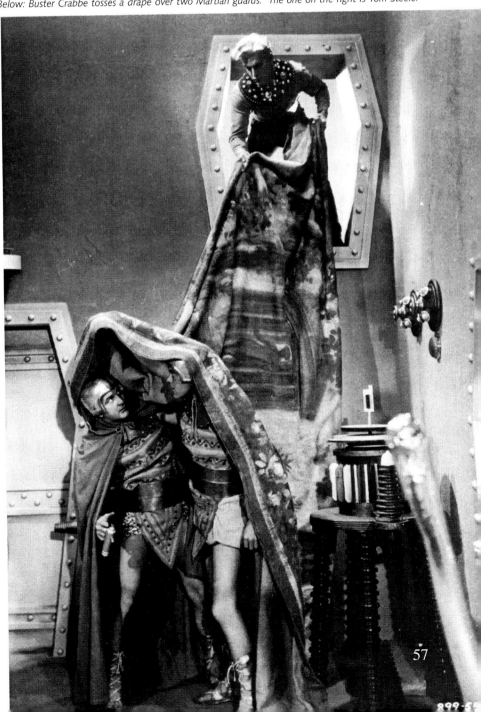

57

Amidst Mars Deco, queen Beatrice Roberts offers a supporting touch as Buster Crabbe brings merciless Charles Middleton to one knee.

life. (Ming, watching on television, is disgusted.) Azura recovers her jewel and returns to her palace.

Flash is joined by his old friend Prince Barin of Mongo, who came to Mars to enlist the aid of the Forest People in his war against Ming, "but they turned on me." He explains that the Forest People's help is essential because "they're the only nation on Mars who are immune to Azura's magic." That's because "Azura's magic power rests in a sacred white sapphire she wears about her neck. And in the forest in the temple of Kalu there's a black sapphire, and Azura is powerless to harm anyone who possesses it." They rush to the temple of Kalu.

Jean Rogers and Donald Kerr spot more trouble.

Below: Forest-People leader Anthony Warde (center) is pleased to note that Jean Rogers, under the influence of the "incense of forgetfulness," is in a trance and ready to become a temple maiden.

It's Happy who manages to steal the black sapphire from the temple, but you can bet that the stone will change hands a few times in the episodes that follow. The Forest People are particularly pesky, acting as spies for Ming and capturing Dale, giving her a whiff of "the incense of forgetfulness" ("All that you have known shall pass away, and henceforth you will be a temple maiden. You are dedicated to the service of the god Kalu") and nearly succeeding in converting her to their weird persuasion. She's rescued by Flash, who in the course of his many efforts, actually succeeds in winning the friendship of the Forest People.

Flash defies explosions, rocket crashes, electrocution, disintegrating rays, gas and the like as he takes on Ming and Azura and recovers the Black Sapphire. The Queen of Magic meets her end, the victim of a bomb dropped by one of Ming's "Death Squadron." Flash tries to rescue her, but can't get to her in time. Mortally wounded, she expresses astonishment that her own troops bombed her. "I never should have trusted Ming," she says, then gives Flash her White Sapphire and tells him that when it and the Black Sapphire are destroyed, the spell on the Clay People will vanish. Flash and the others hurry back to Clay Kingdom and give the king the good news. The jewels are destroyed and the spell lifted. The Clay People are human once again.

In Azura's throne room, Ming has gathered all of the neutral kingdom rulers of Mars. He wants them to crown him the King of Mars. But Flash, Barin, Zarkov and Dale appear and tell the group that Ming had previously illegally deposed Barin on Mongo and has just killed Queen Azura. The Frigians present are shocked, and Ming's bid for the crown is decisively rejected. Ming tries to threaten the group into submission but that tactic doesn't work.

The man who would be king slips away to escape the crowd's fury. He races to the powerhouse, where his crony, Tarnak, turns on him, locks him in "the disintegrating room" and turns on the disintegrator. Flash bursts into the powerhouse, but Tarnak holds him

off with a ray gun. "No matter what Ming's done," Flash pleads, "you can't kill him this way." Tarnak disagrees. By the time Flash gets the gun away from Tarnak, Ming has disintegrated and is gone forever. Or is he?

The Fighting Devil Dogs

(Republic-1938) Directed by William Witney, John English. Writers: Barry Shipman, Franklyn Adreon, Ronald Davidson, Sol Shor. Cinematography: William Nobles. Musical directors: Alberto Colombo, Cy Feuer. Production manager: Allen Wilson. Supervising editor: Murray Seldeen. Editors: Helene Turner, Edward Todd. Special effects: Howard Lydecker, Theodore Lydecker. Executive producer: Herbert J. Yates. Producer: Sol C. Siegel. Associate producer: Robert Beche. [5-28-38] Feature title: *The Fighting Devil Dogs*.

Cast:

Lt. Tom Grayson . . . . . . Lee Powell
Frank Corby . . . . Herman Brix
Janet Warfield . . . . . . Eleanor Stewart
Gen. White . . . . Montague Love
Ben Warfield . . . . Hugh Sothern
Col. Grayson . . . . Sam Flint
Crenshaw . . . . Perry Ivins
Benson . . . . Forrest Taylor
Prof. Gould . . . . John Picorri
Johnson . . . . Carleton Young
Lin Wing . . . . John Davidson
Sam Hedges . . . . Henry Otho
Parker . . . . Reed Howes
Wilson . . . . Tom London
Ellis . . . . Edmund Cobb
Macro . . . . Alan Gregg
Todd . . . . Allan Mathews
Jacobs . . . . Monte Montague
Jamison . . . . George Magrill
Sam . . . . Duke York
Thompson . . . . John Merton
Smith . . . . Ray Hanson
Snell . . . . Frank Baker
Dirigible captain . . . . . Lloyd Whitlock
12 Chapters:
1. The Lightning Strikes   2. The Mill of Disaster   3. The Silent Witness   4. Cargo of Mystery   5. Undersea Bandits   6. The Torpedo of Doom   7. The Phantom Killer   8. Tides of Trickery   9. Attack from the Skies

Marines Herman Brix, Montague Love (second and third from left) and Lee Powell (far right) listen as the police chief finds a lightning bolt memento on the dead body of John Davidson, who was going to give them "certain papers." Sam Flint is third from right.

10. In the Camp of the Enemy
11. The Baited Trap   12. Killer at Bay

U. S. Marine lieutenants Tom Grayson and his friend Frank Corby have been assigned to escorting stranded Americans out of Lingchuria, during the Chinese-Japanese War. Tom leads his platoon away from their regular line of duty to investigate a strange-looking fortress, and finds it strewn with the dead bodies of soldiers but with no sign of injury. "Even the flies are dead," one Marine observes.

In another part of the fortress a rat-faced hunchback, Professor Gould, speaks, via short-wave radio, with someone he calls "master." The master warns him "anyone entering the fort must be destroyed." Tom's men are searching the place when a humming, meteor-like projectile hits the fort, turning it into a crackling mass of deadly electricity. The entire platoon is elec-

Below: This must be the place, Herman Brix seems to be saying to fellow Devil Dog Lee Powell, as they arrive at the Marine base on Gehorda.

trocuted—except for Tom and Frank who had been searching the grounds outside.

Tom is called back to the United States to face censure, and a formal inquiry is begun into the loss of his men. He is convinced they were victims of a new kind of weapon, an artificial "thunderbolt." Although ridiculed at first, his opinion is confirmed when a similar weapon sinks a steamship. It turns out that this thunderbolt, an aerial torpedo, has been created by a mysterious master criminal, known only as "the Lightning."

Tom and Frank are assigned to track down the Lightning, and a group of scientists is organized to develop some means of defense against this menace and his deadly thunderbolt. This prestigious group of exemplary citizens includes Colonel Grayson, Tom's father; Warfield, a prominent

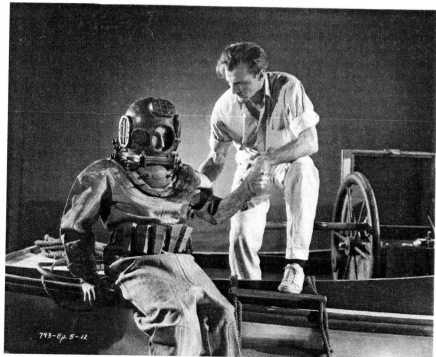

Lee Powell, about to go underwater to search for the remote unit, aided by Herman Brix, who'll be manning the air pumps on deck.

Perry Ivins, Herman Brix, Lee Powell, Sam Flint, Hugh Sothern, and an assistant are all entranced by one of Warfield's new inventions.

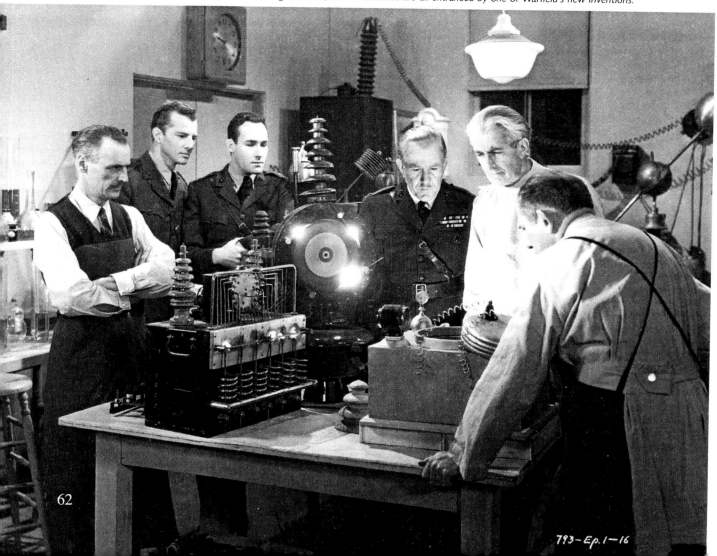

The Lightning checks out Warfield's laboratory. He'll wreck it before he's through..

793-Ep. 2-5

manufacturer of electrical machinery (hmmm); Janet, his daughter who serves as his assistant; Crenshaw, a famous electrical inventor, and several other no doubt prominent scientists. Also hanging around is Janet's gardener Sam Hedges, who is usually seen eavesdropping.

Before their work has begun, the Lightning (whose head is covered by a neat black helmet with a lightning bolt logo across the front) launches a missile from his superplane, the Wing (so-called because it looks like a flying wing, recycled from *Dick Tracy*), and electrifies the scientist's laboratory, killing Tom's father. "I destroyed the instruments and the people working them," the Lightning tells Prof. Gould. "My secret is no longer in danger of discovery." He's eagerly awaiting a shipment of torpedo cases so he can fully unleash his weapon. "There is no force on earth I can't bring to my feet. The power of electricity can rule the world, professor, *and we control that power.*"

Colonel Grayson's death adds additional motivation, and Tom redoubles his efforts to track down the Lightning. At one point, with the help of the Marines, he locates and attacks the evil one's headquarters, but the Lightning slips away. It's obvious that one of the group is the master criminal. All clues point to Crenshaw, who always manages to excuse himself just before the Lightning makes an appearance, shows up with a bandaged arm after the Lightning has injured his own and generally behaves so blatantly suspiciously you can safely bet the ranch that he isn't the bad guy.

Tom and Frank are ambushed by Jacobs, one of the Lightning's men, who succeeds only in getting himself captured by the two Marines. After questioning proves futile, a truth-telling serum (scopalimine) is applied and Jacobs loosens up a little. Just as he's about to reveal the Lightning's identity the lights go out and he's electrocuted. Tom goes back to the Atlas laboratory, finds Brown dead and his killers ransacking the place, looking for incriminating shipping records. He chases them on his motorcycle but they get away. We also get to meet the butler, Benson, who along with Hedges, the gardner, serve as additional red herrings by acting suspiciously beyond reason.

Lee Powell and a contingent of Devil Dogs open fire on the Lightning's raiders..

Janet is kidnapped and taken in the Wing to the Pacific island and village of Lehorta, where mercenary Asians and

Below: Mayhem at the laboratory. The Lightning (center), in his cool mask, and his men earnestly destroy important electronic prototypes and leave a few corpses about.

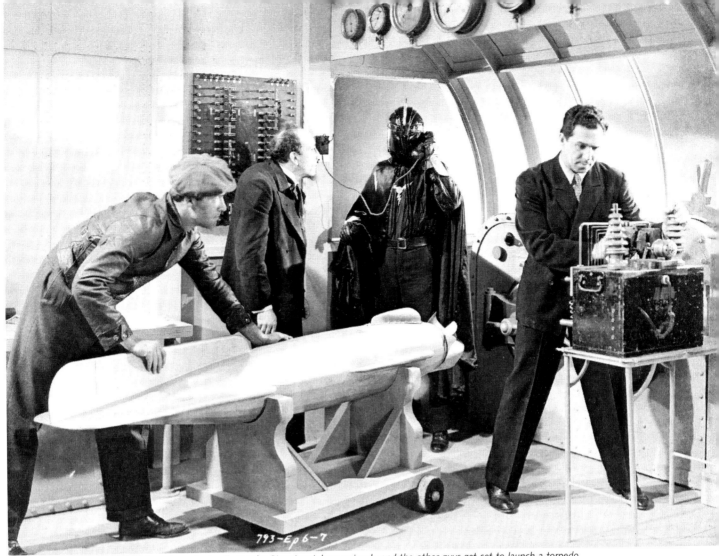

The Lightning (center) engaged in an important call as John Picorri watches anxiously and the other guys get set to launch a torpedo.

misled natives, inspired by the cunning Lightning, cause all kinds of trouble for the Marines stationed there. The island is also the Lightning's off-shore base of operations, and he has a laboratory and various rooms in a cave, which is where Janet is held prisoner.

Among the vital elements the Lightning must have is a special gyro control and to get it he lures Tom and Frank into a trap, but the Marines beat his henchmen to a pulp. During another attempt the Lightning's men only manage to sink the ship transporting the gyro device. When Tom gets into a diving suit and goes underwater to recover the control, the Lightning's men cut his air line. Frank jumps in to save him and is attacked by a shark. While Frank successfully defends himself with a knife, Tom uses the remaining air in the diving suit and walks ashore, bringing the gyro device with him.

Macro and Ellis, two of the

Below: The Lightning (right) listens to another of the sadistic John Picorri's mad schemes for prisoner Eleanor Stewart, who recoils in horror.

65

A gaggle of serial veterans. On the right Tom London (who has appeared in more films—over 2000—than any other actor) telling off Carleton Young, while Alan Gregg (left) and Ed Cobb (who has a shot all to himself in Citizen Kane) look on.

Marine base on the mainland. Ellis is cooperative and ready to talk but history repeats itself—he's electrocuted just before he can reveal his boss's name.

At one point Tom penetrates the Lightning's hideout and makes it to the laboratory, only to be kayoed from behind and left unconscious with a bomb set to go off. Frank arrives in time to defuse the bomb. Crenshaw comes up with a device that he claims can detonate the Lightning's aerial torpedo before it's fired, but his invention isn't taken seriously. The Wing is used to drop super-incendiary bombs on the Marine supply warehouses, totally destroying them in a spectacular pyrotechnic display.

In the course of his investigation Tom manages to endure as a car he's in crashes down a mountainside and as he avoids flaming death aboard a burning ship. He's also nearly gassed, battles a shark, barely misses being crushed by the hulls of two ships as his small pursuit boat gets caught between them, races from a building just before it's blown up, escapes electrocution, asphyxiation and more incineration, avoids burial under tons of steel ingots and ducks under a handy rock ledge to survive an avalanche. His adventures cover land, sea and air.

Crenshaw is captured and Janet has remained captured during all of the preceding, but now she's right next to the Lightning. With a quick move she lifts the visor covering his face. "You!," she

Lightning's men, are sent to steal the Marine seaplane. They botch the job. Macro is killed and Ellis is captured. and brought to the base. Tom and Frank are sent aloft again to intercept the Wing, the Lightning has a thunderbolt fired at their plane. Spotting the missile, the Marines aim their plane at it, then bail out, sharing a parachute. Despite attempts by the Lightning to stop them, Tom and Frank, with the gyro device and Ellis in tow, bet to the

Right: Herman Brix, Lee Powell, Sam Flint and Montague Love (center) listen to their theories of a man-made thunderbolt denounced as sheer nonsense by Frank Baker, at a military tribunal.

Montague Love, Perry Ivins, Forrest Taylor. Eleanor Stewart and Herman Brix watch the skies as Lee Powell (kneeling) aims a new weapon. Will he stop the Lightning from escaping?

exclaims. "You'll never have the opportunity to reveal my identity," the Lightning declares, and leaves her to the tender mercies of Prof. Gould.

Following a clue, Tom, Frank and a squad of Marines check out a farm. Frank finds Crenshaw tied up in the house and Tom discovers something significant (we know that from his reaction) in the barn, but we don't know what it is.

Tom succeeds in exposing the Lightning through the time-proven method of gathering all the suspects together, on this occasion in Warfield's mansion. Tom tells them the Lightning is in the room and "I am ready to have him pointed out." Dramatically, a curtain rises and there stands Janet. Tom had found her in the barn. She is about

to reveal the Lightning's identity when a lightning bolt shoots toward her but only shatters a mirror image. Warfield, caught in the act, has revealed himself. Janet explains that he isn't her real father, but her guardian.

While Janet has everyone's attention, Warfield makes a break for it through a secret panel and is gone. Col. White apologizes to Crenshaw for believing he was the Lightning, and shows renewed interest in Crenshaw's invention. Warfield heads straight for the warmed-up (by Gould) and waiting Wing, and they take off. He tells Gould to fire a thunderbolt at the mansion. As soon as they see the Wing, Tom and the others move Crenshaw's machine into position at a window and Tom aims it. Gould is just about to push the "fire"

button when the thunderbolt explodes and the Wing is blown to smithereens.

Buck Rogers (Universal-1939)

Directed by Ford Beebe, Saul Goodkind. Story and screenplay: Norman S. Hall, Ray Trampe. Based on the "Buck Rogers" newspaper feature, owned and copyrighted by John F. Dill Company. Original cartoon strip by Dick Calkins and Phil Nowlan. Cameraman: Jerry Ash. Art direction: Jack Otterson, Ralph DeLacy. Associate producer: Barney Sarecky. Feature titles: *Destination Saturn*, *Planet Outlaws*.

Cast:

Buck Rogers. . . Larry "Buster" Crabbe
Wilma. . . . . Constance Moore
George "Buddy" Wade . Jackie Moran
Capt. Rankin . . . . Jack Mulhall
Killer Kane . . . . Anthony Warde
Dr. Huer . . . . . . C. Montague Shaw
Aldar . . . . Guy Usher
Marshall Kragg . . . . . William Gould
Prince Tallen . . . . Philson Ahn
Capt. Lasca . . . . Henry Brandon
Patten . . . . Wheeler Oakman
Lt. Lacy . . . . Kenneth Duncan
Scott . . . . Carleton Young
Roberts . . . . Reed Howes
Robotman . . . . Stanley Price

12 Chapters:

1. Tomorrow's World   2. Tragedy on Saturn   3. The Enemy's Stronghold 4. The Sky Patrol   5. The Phantom Plane   6. The Unknown Command 7. Primitive Urge   8. Revolt of the Zuggs   9. Bodies without Minds 10. Broken Barriers   11. A Prince in Bondage   12. War of the Planets

A giant dirigible, piloted by airman Buck Rogers and his young friend Buddy Wade, crashes on an icy arctic mountain. An avalanche all but buries it. The gondola was carrying tanks of the newly-invented preservative, Nirvano gas, which is released during the crash and keeps the flyers in a state of suspended animation.

Five hundred years later Capt. Rankin and Lt. Lacy of the Border Patrol of the Hidden City are cruising the frozen area in their rocket ship when they notice an enormous mound of snow, indicating a large buried object. Landing, they use their disintegrator guns to blast through the snow, find the door to an ancient dirigible ("sure is an antique," says Captain Rankin) and they discover the bodies of Buck and Buddy, perfectly preserved. They take the bodies outside, where the two revive, to the astonishment of the Patrol officers, who decide to take them to the Hidden City.

Buck, thinking it's still 1938, is impressed by the rocket ship, which he estimates is traveling at the impossible speed of a thousand miles an hour. "I don't get it,' he tells Buddy, "this ship is

Border Patrol officers Kenneth Duncan (left) and Jack Mulhall discover a five-hundred-year-old wrecked dirigible, and Buster Crabbe and Jackie Moran in a state of suspended animation.

at least a hundred years ahead of any ship I ever saw." As they approach the Hidden City it appears as if they're going to crash into the side of a mountain, but giant doors slide open and the ship enters.

Accompanied by Capt. Rankin, Buck and Buddy are to go to Dr. Heur's laboratory, which they do by entering what looks like a glass telephone booth. Their bodies disappear—and reappear in a similar booth in Heur's laboratory. "What kind of elevator is that?," Buddy asks. Rankin explains, "By radioactivity it breaks down the atoms in the body into their component parts, and, reversing polarity, reassemble them wherever we desire."

Buck and Buddy are introduced to Dr. Heur, a scientific genius, and his assistant Wilma Deering, who is watching some sort of television device. Dr. Heur tells them they've been asleep for five hundred years. Buck thinks that's impossible and is about to argue the point when Wilma interrupts to report that "Killer Kane has captured another of our pilots."

All attention is turned to a television screen that shows the interior of Killer Kane's grand chamber, where the

William Gould and Larry Crabbe in the glass teleportation booth, which can scramble their atomic structure and reassemble them in any desired place.

Buster Crabbe battles with bad guy Wheeler Oakman.

newly-captured pilot is being grilled for the location of the Hidden City's entrance. When he refuses to tell he is shown a group of work men. "Those men," Killer Kane tells him, "were once pilots of Dr. Heur's ships. Now they are living robots, men robbed of all will power while they wear the helmets I had designed for them. Shall I have you measured for a robot's helmet, or will you tell me where the entrance to the Hidden City is?" The pilot refuses to answer and is led away. Wilma turns off the television.

Buck wants to know what's going on. Heur tells him that Earth has been conquered by a horde of ganglords. It

seems that hundreds of years back civilization had been too soft on racketeers and they had managed to take over the world. What Buck had just seen is Killer Kane's dynamo room, where mindless men (the "robot battalion") work incessantly, feeding the furnaces that provide Kane's power. These drones are humans who have been forced to wear the "amnesia helmet" that removes their memory and will.

Buck and Buddy agree to join the rebels and help overthrow the despotic Killer Kane. They learn that Huer has invented paralyzing pistols, spaceships, degravity belts (which enable the wearer to float in space), invisible ray

Philson Ahn (left) watches Larry Crabbe, who has just disposed of Wheeler Oakman, point out a new danger to Jackie Moran.

machines, atom chambers, ray guns and the like in his attempt to aid humanity. They meet Air Marshal Kragg, getting to his office via the teleportation booth.

From Kragg they learn that Earth's only chance is to get help from other planets, like Saturn, but Kane's rocket ships have prevented Heur's ships from getting through. Buck suggests a radio-controlled rocket be sent up as a decoy to draw Kane's ships, and that he would pilot one of Heur's rockets and try to slip through while the enemy is distract-ed. Soon Buck, Wilma and Buddy are on their way to Saturn.

They get through and although fol-lowed and attacked by Kane's men (who want their own treaty with Saturn), arrive safely. Kane's men, led by Captain Lasca, also land and contin-

ue the pursuit. There's a pitched battle between the two parties. Lasca wins, but it doesn't matter because both groups are captured by Saturnian Prince Tallen and his Zuggs (strange, silent shuffling men with faces like pop-eyed potatoes), the remnants of a "primitive race," who take them to the Great Council of the Wise for trial

At the trial Lasca convinces the council that Killer Kane is a just and kindly monarch who is battling "revolu-tionaries" like Buck. The council wants nothing to do with revolutionaries and finds the Earth people guilty. Grabbing a ray gun, Buck holds the Saturnians at bay, and he and the others return to Earth in one of Lasca's spaceships. They fly back to the hidden city where Buck and Buddy resupply, then are

flown over Kane's modern skyscraper kingdom and dropped from the rocket ship, as their anti-gravity belts enable them to float safely to the ground.

They gain access to Kane's cham-bers, where, with Prince Tallen he is arranging a treaty with the Saturnians. Buck demands that Kane show the dynamo room on a televiser screen. At gun point, Kane complies and Tallen is shocked by the sight of the mindless slaves. He says he will recommend that Saturn ally itself with the resistance fighters.

Buck, Buddy and Prince Tallen escape Kane's kingdom but are hound-ed by his guards. Tallen is wounded by a ray gun and has to be carried around by Buck. Meanwhile, in the hidden city, Wilma, Heur and Air Marshall

70

GAS BOMBS
FOR EMERGANCY USE ONLY

Larry Crabbe, Jackie Moran and Constance Moore among the technology of the future.

Although he looks like Buster Crabbe in this shot, it's really Henry Brandon (2nd from left) trying to enlist the aid of filament-ray-helmeted human robot Stanley Price, while a couple of Zugg men look on.

Kragg are worried about their friends. Wilma and some officers are sent to search for him. They find Buck, a recovered Tallen and a wounded Buddy, who has passed out.

Killer Kane is outraged by the poor performance of his men. (Film buffs will get a kick out of Anthony Warde as Kane. Warde is usually cast as the main villain's most trusted henchmen. Here, in a main role, he delivers an over-the-top performance, screaming, scolding, cajoling his flunkies and enjoying himself enormously.) He threatens to send them to the "robot battalion" in the dynamo room. Hearing of Tallen's defection, he suggests a counter-plan.

The friends head for the hidden city, get Buddy to a hospital and introduce Tallen to Krag and Huer, who tells

the prince, "you bring new hope to a beleaguered race." Buck, Tallen and Wilma take to the air again for Saturn, getting through an air blockade set up by Kane by using an invention of Heur's which makes their space ship temporarily invisible. But Lasca and cohort Patten have already arrived on Saturn (that was Kane's idea) and trap the friends when they land, knocking them out with a dose of gas.

Lasca isolates Tallen and places a certain filament, taken from a dynamo helmet, into the helmet Tallen normally wears, then puts it on Tallen's head. The prince immediately become subject to Lasca's orders. Back on Saturn, when everyone appears before the Council of the Wise, Buck and Wilma are astounded to hear Tallen denounce

Buck and suggest a treaty with Killer Kane. It's obvious that Tallen has been drugged, but only Buck seems to notice.

Buck grabs a ray gun and, holding Tallen as a shield, escapes with the Prince and Wilma. While trying to figure out what's wrong with Tallen they remove the helmet. He instantly returns to normal, and is horrified to learn that he had denounced Buck to the Council. Now he announces Buck's innocence to the Council, which signs the treaty with Earth. Buck radios the good news to Heur and Kragg.

Meanwhile, still on Saturn (they're afraid to return to Earth having failed again) Lasca and Patten discover that the primitive "Zugg Men," have discovered one of their "human robots," abandoned in the hills, and have accepted it

72

Constance Moore, Buster Crabbe and Jackie Moran plan their next move.

Kane's rocket ships and fly to the Hidden City. But Carson, one of Kane's men, has hidden himself on the ship. When they land in the city Carson knocks out a guard, opens the mountain gates, radios Kane and tells him the city's location, "Valley 100," previously unknown. Kane commands his air force to fly into the city.

Buck is with Marshal Kragg, who notices the open gates. Carson attempts to stop him from closing them, but he's overpowered. As the gates close, two of Kane's rocket ships get in, but the others are destroyed as they crash into the closing walls. The occupants of the two ships are quickly captured. After a meeting of the military council it's decided to have the Saturnians join them in an all out attack on Killer Kane's fortress. But interference prevents them from establishing radio

as a god. Lasca quickly figures out that, since the robot takes orders from him, he can get it to inspire a revolt against Prince Tallen and his Saturnians.

Soon the Zuggs are on the warpath, invading the Council of the Wise and causing all sorts of trouble. Buck surprises Lasca and his robot as they are rousing the Zuggs to continued warfare. He manages to remove the robot's helmet, and discovers that the restored human inside is a friend who hates Killer Kane and who orders the Zuggs to forget about their rebellion and go home in peace. They do.

Returning to Earth Buck and Wilma are captured by Killer Kane's men. Buck is sent to the dynamo room where an amnesia helmet is placed on his head and he becomes one of the mindless "robot battalion." Wilma is placed in a cell. Back in the Hidden City, Buddy defies orders and sneaks out to rescue his friends. Using his degravity belt he gets into Kane's fortress, meets up with Wilma (who had escaped from her cell on her own) and together they find the dynamo room and, after a battle with guards, remove Buck's helmet, instantly restoring his memory.

The three battle their way to one of

Armed with a ray gun, Larry Crabbe points out a good hiding place to Jackie Moran.

Jackie Moran (2nd from left) watches as Buster Crabbe aims a ray gun at and manhandles despotic-gangster Earth Ruler Anthony Warde.

925-68-EP.12

communication with Tallen, so Buck volunteers to use Kane's rocket ship to return to Saturn so he can deliver the message personally. Buddy stows away on the ship, not at all to Buck's surprise.

On Saturn Buck and Buddy get to the Council of the Wise and discover that Prince Tallen has been kidnapped by Kane, who demands that he and his troops be allowed to land on Saturn, or Tallen dies. The Council is about to concede when Buck reminds them of Kane's duplicity (in a five-minute playback of an earlier scene), which gives them pause. The deliberations are interrupted by bombs, falling from one of Kane's ships, commanded by Lasca and on which Tallen is held prisoner.

The bombs are wrecking the council hall, and everyone has to flee into adjoining tunnels to survive. Buck and Buddy go outside and see Kane's ship land and a party, with Tallen, emerge.

Buck leaps upon the men guarding Tallen and knocks them out. While he's doing so, Lasca, off to a side, gets set to blast Buck with a ray gun. Buddy sees him and shoots first, killing him with one shot. Tallen is returned to his people and the council now agrees to do whatever is necessary to help in the war against Killer Kane.

Buck radios Air Marshal Kragg and requests that all Hidden World ships attack Kane's headquarters as a decoy, in the hope that he and Buddy, in their captured rocket, can slip through to Kane's chamber. It works. Buck and Buddy find their way to the dynamo room, where they remove the amnesia helmets of the prisoners, who immediately join their cause. In his chamber, Kane is ordering his officers to attack the Hidden City by land and air when Buck, wielding a ray gun, and his allies barge in. He places an amnesia helmet

on Kane, and orders him to radio his troops to lay down their arms and surrender. The memoryless Kane does so, and his threat to the universe is over. He is ignominiously led away to prison.

As a reward for his bravery and ingenuity, Buck is made "Colonel in Chief" of the planet's air force. Buddy is given a "Distinguished Service Cross" and, despite his young age, is commissioned a "Flight Lieutenant." At last, Buck and Wilma have time to consider romance.

The Phantom Creeps

(Universal-1939)   Presented by Commonwealth Pictures Corp. Directed by Ford Beebe, Saul A. Goodkind.   Screenplay: George Plympton,   Basil   Dickey,   Mildred

Barish. Original story by Willis Cooper. Art director: Ralph DeLacey. Photography: Jerry Ash, William Sickner. Dialogue director: Lynn Margolies. Editors: Alvin Todd, Irving Birnbaum, Joseph Gluck. Associate producer: Henry MacRae.

Cast:

Dr. Alex Zorka . . . . Bela Lugosi
Capt. Bob West . . . . Robert Kent
Jim Daley . . . . Regis Toomey
Jean Drew . . . . Dorothy Arnold
Dr. Fred Mallory . . . . . Edwin Stanley
Monk . . . . Jack C. Smith
Spy chief Jarvis . . . Edward Van Sloan
Mac . . . . Eddie Acuff
Rankin . . . . Anthony Averill
Parker . . . . Roy Barcroft
Black . . . . Forrest Taylor
Mrs. Anna Zorka . . . . . Dora Clement
Jones . . . . Jerry Frank
Brown . . . . Karl Hackett
Perkins . . . . Hugh Huntley
Buck . . . . Charles King
First mate . . . . Al Bridge
Harlan . . . . Hooper Atchley

12 Chapters:

1. The Menacing Power 2. Death Stalks the Highway 3. Crashing Towers 4. Invisible Terror 5. Thundering Rails 6. The Iron Monster 7. The Menacing Mist 8. Trapped in the Flames 9. Speeding Doom 10. Phantom Footprints 11. The Blast 12. To Destroy the World

Dr. Alex Zorka, eccentric (to say the least) scientist, is carrying on mysterious experiments in his laboratory with the aid of Monk, an escaped convict he's befriended. Among Zorka's inventions is a terrifying eight-foot robot which obeys his commands. "What can the police or anybody do against an army like that?," he asks. "It can crush all opposition and make me the most powerful man in the world."

A warning system lets Zorka know that his wife, Anna, and former colleague, Dr. Mallory, have entered the house. She's worried about her husband's strange doings and wants to speak to him alone, Mallory being persona non grata for refusing to remain

with Zorka because "he was working along lines contrary to the good of mankind."

In the lab, Zorka tells Monk he's not going to tell anyone about the new element he's discovered, except maybe to let Mrs. Zorka know that he "accomplished what they told me was impossible." He tells Monk to get him one of "the magnetized discs." He greets Anna and assures her he's glad to see her. He tells her she'll be a witness to his "great triumph,"the ability to induce a state of suspended animation that couldn't be told from death. They called me a dreamer and a fool, but now I have it!"

As Anna (and unnoticed, Mallory) watch, Zorka demonstrates. A metal disc about the size of dollar coin is placed on the base of a large house plant.. Zorka shows Anna a metal spider and tells her not to be alarmed. "It won't come to you. It will go only to that disc. The disc is magnetized by a positive ray of my new element which is unknown to science. And this little spider carries the negative." He places

Scientist Bela Lugosi provides a robot-monster demonstration for assistant Jack C. Smith, who is appropriately awed.

Dorothy Arnold in high heels, dangling from her parachute. She's just escaped a plane crash.

the spider on the floor and it creeps to, up and into the plant base. There's a small explosion and some gaseous smoke. The plant seems to wither and die. Zorka explains that it is not dead, only in suspended animation, as would be a human under the same circumstances.

Zorka is outraged when Mallory makes his presence known and asks Zorka what he's going to do with his invention. "I shall do with it as I wish," he answers, and that does not include giving it to the government as Mallory had suggested. Mallory reminds him that it would be a terrible weapon in the hands of unscrupulous people. "Of course," Zorka smiles. "That is why they will pay me dearly." Mallory says he'll inform the authorities immediately. Zorka tells him that would be a big mistake, and leaves. Anna says she'll stay in the house overnight to see if she can "dissuade him from his mad course."

In his laboratory Zorka fiddles with his latest invention, "the devisualizer, which can conceal me from my enemies." It's a control belt he puts on and

which renders him invisible. The giant robot pushes a fireplace aside, revealing the cave entrance to Zorka's secret laboratory, under the mansion.. Here he works with his glowing new element,

"the source of all my power," and vows never to reveal its secret to anyone. He moves all of his equipment into the hidden lab and pretty much disappears from sight.

Captain Bob West and Jim Daly of Military Intelligence, alerted by Mallory, arrives at Zorka's mansion to look around. Bob's accosted by Jean Drew, a newspaper reporter, who asks if it's true that Zorka has disappeared. They tell her they can't answer questions and escort her off the mansion's grounds. In the house they meet with Anna and Mallory, who tell him of the discs and spiders. They decide to check the laboratory. Zorka, using eavesdropping equipment, hears all this. "Let them search," he scoffs. "They will find nothing." He comes up with a new plan, and shaves off his beard.

The now-beardless Zorka is in his limousine, chauffeured by Monk, when he notices a bearded hitchhiker. He orders Monk to pick the man up. The grateful hitchhiker gets into the limo, which Monk soon has to veer precariously to avoid another speeding car. Both autos crash through the railings, plunge down a mountainside and burst into flames. Only Zorka and Monk survive. Zorka smiles as he sees the hitch-

Jack C. Smith and Bela Lugosi keep track of the agents investigating them.

Robot on the rampage. Bela Lugosi is having a bit of temporary trouble controlling his creation.

Regis Toomey, Edwin Stanley and Dorothy Arnold face spy master Edward Van Sloan (seated) as his associates Jerry Frank (right) covers them with a gun.

hiker's body. "How fortunate," he gloats. "This simplifies everything." He puts his wallet and a few other articles in the man's pocket.

The police report the accident. Mrs. Zorka is asked to fly with Bob West to identify her husband's body. Although he still loves his wife, an invisible Zorka plants a disc in her purse and releases a spider. His plan is to recover Anna after the plane lands and bring her out of her state of suspension. In the meantime he'll be certain she doesn't reveal that the body found in the auto wreck isn't his. But Mrs. Zorka notices the disc, and gives it to the Jim, who's piloting the plane. It's he who gets gassed and passes out during the flight. The plane goes into a spin. Jean Drew, who had stowed away, makes an appearance and manages to

bail out. The plane crashes with Bob, Anna and Jim aboard. Bob survives and Jim is in suspended animation, but Mrs. Zorka is dead.

Jean lands in a tree. Her parachute is tangled in its branches and she is suspended in mid-air. Zorka, driving by with Monk, comes to her rescue and asks her what happened. She explains she was on a government ship that went down, that she's a reporter and has to get to the crash site. "Come. I'm a doctor," he tells her. "I will take you there." When he discovers that Anna is dead he is grief stricken, but manages to remove the disc from the pilot's pocket. As he reads the newspaper story of his wife's death, he blames "Mallory and all the so-called scientists who drove me into hiding, *they* are responsible for her death. *They shall pay!*".

When word of his death reaches them, the international spy ring Zorka had contacted as possible customers sends out an all-points alert to operatives everywhere to be on the lookout for leads on his inventions. Their leader, Jarvis, works out of the innocently-named International School of Languages, which to all outward appearances looks like a bustling organization. Jarvis uses a gang led by Rankin to do his dirty work. He tells them to go to Zorka's mansion and find the formula or, failing that, find Zorca's assistant, Monk.

Dr. Mallory, meanwhile, has been working on an antidote for Jim, who remains suspended, but each attempt fails. "Something is missing," he says. "Some essential ingredient I've failed to hit upon." He figures their best bet is to visit Zorka's laboratory to see what can be found. "Well c'mon, before someone beats us to it," Bob says.

That evening in the supposedly-deserted mansion, Zorka and Monk go through the cave entrance to do some last-minute rummaging . But they're heard by Jean, who has been snooping around, and by Bob and Mallory when they arrive. There's a shootout in the dark, with Zorka and Monk remaining unidentifiable. Trying to escape, Monk is captured by Jarvis's men, but rescued by an invisible Zorka. (Eventually Mallory finds what he's looking for and comes up with the antidote.)

Occasionally Zorka and Monk tap the energy emitting from the meteorite fragment, which is kept in a lead box.

So deadly is this energy that as they work both men must inhale special chemicals to offset the normally-fatal effects. Zorka tells Monk he had discovered the meteorite fragment in Africa. Aided only by "ignorant natives" he had mined it, risking his life, sacrificed his career. Now that he has the power, he asks, why shouldn't he use it any way he wishes?

Bob, and co-agent Jim Daly are also on the trail of the meteorite fragment, lest it get into hands less responsible than military intelligence. Jean, too, is constantly snooping around for a story. She isn't a helpless female who stands around while the men fight. Whenever possible, she does her bit. The Chief tells his men to find Monk,

Reporter Dorothy Arnold. She's not as tough as she looks.

who might know where the meteorite fragment is.

This combination tends to keep the DMI boys busy. Fortunately for them, Monk bungles every assignment he's given, thus sparing them a lot of wear

The Chief's masked men lead the kidnapped Edwin Stanley to their laboratory hideout.

Suddenly U.S. fighter planes appear. Zorka's plane is completely surrounded. He tells Monk that they'll never shoot at the plane while the box with the meteorite is aboard. It would cause a disaster. But Monk is not convinced. He wants to surrender, and he battles with Zorka for control of the plane, which goes into a dive and crashes into the ocean. The resulting explosion "shakes the continent," as Jean's exclusive front-page story proclaims, and Bob gets a medal from a grateful nation.

Jack C. Smith has his wounded arm healed in the miraculous machine invented by evil genius Bela Lugosi and powered by the awesome meteorite,

and tear. Monk, it might be noted, is not your typical henchman. It's obvious he doesn't like Zorka and even revolts a few times, only to be cowed into subservience. "I own you," Zorka tells him. "I will always own you."

The meteor fragment, in its metal box, changes hands often, with each faction getting to possess it several times, no matter how fleetingly. Jean and especially Mallory are kidnapped and rescued, there are fist fights in airplanes, crashes, shootouts and explosions. Bob is nearly crushed by the robot, is trapped in a burning building and, ignoring all warning signs, nearly blasted to death by dynamite.

Eventually Zorka is fleetingly spotted, and it's known that he's alive.

Mallory theorizes that Zorka could have come up with an invisibility device, and starts to work on a neutralizer. Almost by accident, while chasing Zorka, Bob happens upon Jarvis and an accomplice and arrests them, bringing to an end the spy ring.

Mallory comes up with a device that neutralizes Zorka's invisibility machine. Caught in the act, Zorka is forced to flee. His underground laboratory is raided by federal troops. The robot is destroyed. Zorka and Monk flee in a biplane loaded with meteorite bombs. Monk pilots while Zorka, with gleeful abandon, drops bombs on federal buildings, homes, ships and dirigibles (footage of the Hindenberg disaster is shown—so *that's* what caused it).

THE 40s

Flash Gordon Conquers the Universe (Universal-1940)

Directed by Ford Beebe, Ray Taylor. Associate producer: Henry MacRae. Original screenplay: George Plympton, Basil Dickey, Barry Shipman. Photography: Jerome Ash, William Sickner. Supervising editor: Saul Goodkind. Editors: Alvin Todd, Louis Sackin, Joseph Glick. Art director: Harold MacArthur. [2-8-40] Feature titles: *The Peril From Planet Mongo*, *The Purple Death From Outer Space*.

Cast:

Flash Gordon . Larry "Buster" Crabbe
Dale Arden . . . . Carol Hughes
Ming . . . . Charles Middleton
Dr. Zarkov . . . . Frank Shannon

Herbert Rawlinson (left) with Tom Chatterton next to him, and Jac George (2nd from right) and other dignitaries listen with bated breath as John Hamilton gets word from his son Flash, with news from the planet Mongo.

Frank Shannon and Buster Crabbe explore an exotic region of Mongo.

Victor Zimmerman and Anne Gwynne watch Dan Rowan look into a periscope-type tube, while another officer lounges about.

12 Chapters:

82

When the Earth is hit by a deadly epidemic known as the Plague of Purple Death (a purple spot appears on the forehead of all its victims, who abruptly stagger around and drop dead in the street), Flash Gordon, Dale Arden and Dr. Zarkov set out into the stratosphere to investigate. They spot a rocket ship, like the ones used by Ming the Merciless on Mongo, dropping vast amounts of a suspicious dust into Earth's atmosphere.

The other rocket ship, piloted by Torch, one of Ming's officers, sees Zarkov's ship and orders it destroyed, for Ming doesn't want Earth to know the source of the plague. "We'll burn 'em to cinders," Torch boasts. There's a spirited battle, but Zarkov's ship is clearly outgunned. It appears to be hit and goes into a dive. Torch comments that Ming will be happy to hear the news. At the last minute Flash pulls the ship out of the dive (he'd wanted the enemy to think they'd been hit) and the trio proceed on their way.

They head for Mongo and the peaceful region of Arboria, ruled by their friend Prince Barin and his wife Aura, Ming's daughter, who has renounced her father and cast her lot with Barin. They also meet Captain Ronal, with whom Flash had shared previous adventures. The prince and

Aura are delighted to see their old friends, and confirm that Ming is indeed alive "and rules more ruthlessly than ever." They tell him there's a banquet that evening in honor of the visiting Queen Fria, the Queen of Frigia, the ice kingdom of northern Mongo.

That evening, nattily-plumaged Flash, when introduced to the queen, bows gallantly and kisses her hand, drawing a look of astonishment, then jealousy, from Dale. Fria wants Barin's help in rescuing one of her top officers, General Lupi, who's a prisoner in Ming's dungeon. It seems that one of Ming's scientists has come up with an invention that kills only those with intelligence enough to oppose the would-be master of the universe, and

Your basic Mongo rocket ship.

Lupi is to be the first guinea pig to see if the machine really works. Although Flash has nothing to fear in this regard, he volunteers to help the queen.

Barin knows all this because they've got an ally planted within Ming's palace: Captain Sudan, the com-

mander of Ming's palace guards, is loyal to Barin and serves as a well-placed spy. Acting on information provided by Sudan, Flash leads Dr. Zarkov and Captains Ronal and Roka on a rescue mission.

There are complications: Flash and one of Ming's men in hand-to-hand combat at the edge of a very deep pit with molten lava at the bottom. Of course they fall in. Flash manages to grab a rail on the side of the pit, while the other man falls to his doom, but in the end Flash destroys the deadly intelligence-identifying machine, General Lupi (who shows a tendency to sell out anybody to save his own neck) and a Frigian diplomat are rescued and the entire party board their rocket ship and

That's Anne Gwynne and Frank Shannon (4th and 5th from left) among some Rock men. Carol Hughes (3rd from right) and Lee Powell stand by as Buster Crabbe examines a fallen enemy officer (Victor Zimmerman).

Lee Powell (left), Larry Crabbe (2nd from left) and Roland Drew (right) watch Frank Shannon perform another technological miracle.

head for Arboria.

Ming is furious, but nonetheless insists that Flash, Dale and Zarkov be captured alive. "I have my own way of destroying them," he says loftily, ordering his air force into action. Soon the skies are filled with Ming's rocket ships in pursuit of Flash's fleeing ship, which desperately tries to duck and withstand incoming missiles. The friends escape by employing one of Zarkov's handy inventions—that renders their rocket ship temporarily invisible. They all land safely in Arboria.

In return for Flash's help, Queen Fria allows him to lead an expedition to the most frigid northernmost part of her kingdom where, Zarkov has learned, there are deposits of Polarite, the only known antidote for the Purple Death.

The northland is like a mountainous iceberg and the cold is unbearable to all but native Frigians. Fortunately, the group is warmed by special garments invented by Zarkov. The Polarite is easy to locate because its energy turns the snow above it black.

Worshippers do their thing before the great idol.

One of Ming's spaceships, operated by his most trusted officers, Captains Torch and Thong, and the pert and beautiful-but-deadly Sonja, bombs Flash's location, causing an avalanche that all but buries Flash, Dale and Barin. They fall into a deep crevice and face imminent freezing regardless of their garments, but manage to establish radio contact with Dr. Zarkov, who quickly organizes a rescue party. The party is seen moving through the frigid white land and climbing walls of ice in impressive on-location scenes obviously lifted from another film. Flash and friends are found and rescued.

Ming is bitterly disappointed in the performance of Captains Torch and Thong. "I had big plans for you in my subjugation of the universe," he tells

Can there be any doubt that Charles Middleton is the Supreme Commander of the Universe?

them.

They have one last chance to redeem themselves (this is just one of many occasions when Ming tells them that one more failure on their part means death, always finding an excuse to give them another chance): they must return to the Frigian north in a rocket ship loaded with "annihilants"—exploding robots—remote controlled by Torch from the safety of his ship. These "walking bombs" succeed in capturing Dale and Zarkov despite Flash's valiant efforts. Although Flash's first inclination is to try to rescue Zarkov and Dale immediately, he realizes he has a greater responsibility: on Earth millions of lives are at stake, so he returns to Earth with the Polarite, leaves

it atop of Mt. McKinley while radioing the location to his dad, who broadcasts the news to a grateful world.

(In all fairness it must be admitted that Flash is not the lunkhead he was in the original *Flash Gordon*. He's a lot more thoughtful, even reflective, and less likely to fight with someone without knowing if his opponent is friend or foe.)

Zarkov is given a choice by Ming: reveal the formula for the anti-freezing fabric, or face the consequences. Ming tells him to think it over before deciding, and assigns him to the laboratory, where he meets Professor Karm, another scientist held prisoner. The two immediately conspire to develop a means for destroying Ming's empire.

Along with Ronal and Roka, Flash heads back to Mongo, gains access to the palace and arrives in time to see Zarkov (who has refused to reveal the formula for his anti-freezing fabric) strapped between two pillars and about to be zapped by a "destroyer ray." In trying to free Zarkov, Flash is almost destroyed by the ray, and only the arrival of Roka, who blasts the ray timer, saves the day. But Zarkov refuses to be rescued because he and Prof. Karm are on the verge of an invention which will forever destroy Ming's power. He'll stay even if it means his life. Flash and his friends have to run for it without Zarkov or Dale.

Ming, who has been smitten with Dale since the day he set eyes on her,

Below: Charles Middleton lets Princess Shirley Deane know who's boss, as Don Rowan holds onto Anne Gwynne.

Welcome to the land of the Rock Men. Guests Lee Powell (3rd from left), Frank Shannon, Buster Crabbe and Carol Hughes observe the rock formations. The skin rugs add a homey touch.

concocts a plan to marry her. "Now that I have deprived you of your loved one," he tells her, thinking Flash is dead, "it is only fitting that I should take his place." He is as frustrated as ever when Flash and Roka infiltrate the palace and rescue her. And Karm convinces Zarkov that he can carry on alone and gives him a disguise he had constructed for his own escape (a monk's robe) which Zarkov puts on and uses to simply walk out of the castle.

(Dale, too, is a changed person. She is one feisty, tough babe. At one point she hauls off and whacks an abusive Mongoan maid in the face, and a few times hits and tries to scratch the eyes out of Ming.)

There are many rocket ship battles throughout this adventure—among the tackiest ever filmed (as always, the rocket ships have to get within a few feet of each other before firing, and even then the blasts have little effect), and more insidious weapons that must be destroyed before they can be misused by Ming: projectiles made of Zotronillium (which burns with the heat of the sun), solarite (a powerful explosive), and the Nullitron, a deadly weapon with what would seem to be limited use, for, as Zarkov explains, "in launching its neutralizing cartridge the gun destroys itself and the explosion releases a poisonous gas that will destroy all life over a wide area."

Arboria is the target of Ming's first Zotronillium attack, and Flash has to go to the bomb sites and plant a "thermal control" device—another of Zarkov's inventions, which puts out the fires. Before launching the attack, Ming had Aura kidnapped and brought back to his kingdom—bad as he is, he won't kill his own daughter. She uses the opportunity to scold him and assure him that Flash will rescue her and defeat him "just as he did last time." Dale and Sonja get to fight with each other, most spiritedly, a few times. The friends are captured and rescued regularly, have to overcome explosions, rocket crashes, electrocution, floods, falls, flames, earthquakes and death rays, and visit the Land of the Dead, wherein live "a race of Rock Men who long ago passed into oblivion."

87

A rare view of Ming's ceremonial chamber.

Flash and his friends, as well as Torch, Thong and Sonja are captured by this strange underground race who at first believe the Earthlings are enemies but who become their allies when Flash saves the life of the Rock Men's king. The Land of the Dead is also populated by "iguanants," giant lizard-like creatures who battle furiously (and actually succeed in killing one of Ming's troopers) in footage lifted from Chapter 1 of the original *Flash Gordon*. The Rock Men speak an almost undecipherable language (a sound track run backwards). Fortunately Dr, Zarkov is quite fluent in Rock and can translate for his friends. The friends take off from the Land of the Dead in Barin's rocket ship. Torch, Thong and Sonja are brought back as prisoners.

Flash, Barin and Captain Roka,

Below: A platoon of annihilators—walking bombs—guards a rocket ship.

Carol Hughes and Buster Crabbe, ready for whatever.

after a false start, gain access to the palace through underground caverns in which they're discovered by Ming's troops and nearly drowned when water is released into the tunnels. When it's over, Dale and Ronal have been captured by Ming, Thong and Sonja have escaped and Captain Torch is Flash's prisoner.

Craftily, Ming arranges a flat-out trade: Dale and Ronal for Torch. He lets Dr. Zarkov select the meeting site. Each side's rocket ships show up at the prearranged time. Dale and Ronal are released and Flash lets Torch go. Torch is quickly urged into his ship, which takes off and is gone. It now becomes obvious that Dale has been drugged. She falls into a deep coma and is near

death. A message from Ming advises them that Dale will die unless she's given an antidote which only he possesses. To save Dale's life, Zarkov must deliver her to Ming. Flash and Zarkov agree, there's no other choice.

Dale is given the antidote, recovers, and is brought to the same room in which Aura has been held captive. Aura assures Ming that Flash will rescue them. He thinks not. He points to the rug in front of the door. "That rug will be charged with four thousand volts of electricity the moment that I go through that door. If you touch that rug after I leave this room, you will be instantly killed." He starts to leave, but pauses. "Remember, I have warned you," he says, and exits. Dale tosses a metal

object onto the rug. It explodes and sizzles.

Flash , Barin and Roka, utilizing a secret entrance known only to Barin, manage to get into Ming's palace and find the room the women are imprisoned in. Flash steps on the rug but is warned at the last second by Aura, and escapes with only mild burns. They find their way to the laboratory and are reunited with Zarkov, who introduces them to Professor Drog, another prisoner-scientist who hates Ming. Professor Karm, alas, was executed by Ming for conspiring with the Earthmen, but had secretly passed his knowledge on to Drog. Now Zarkov has discovered the source of Ming's power—energy obtained from the sun, and knows how to counter it. They lock themselves in the laboratory.

Communicating with his foes via television, Ming demands their immediate surrender. Zarkov tells him that he has already developed a means for rendering Ming helpless, and that their mission is to save the universe. "The universe?," Ming retorts. "*I* am the universe." He gives them an hour to surrender, tells Zarkov he has another source of power, and that with it he will destroy the Earth.

He commands that a rocketship be loaded with solarite, for bombing Earth's cities. Flash sneaks into the launching site, seizes the rocketship and takes off. Ming, followed by his underlings, rushes to his control tower, where he can see what's happening. What he sees is the rocket make a u-turn and head straight for his tower as Flash parachutes to safety. It is, presumably, the last thing Ming sees before the rocket hits and destroys the tower in a spectacular explosion.

In Arboria, as everyone celebrates, Dr. Zarkov proclaims that since Ming considered himself the universe, and Flash conquered him, it could be truly said that "Flash Gordon conquers the universe."

Mysterious Doctor Satan

(Republic Studios-1940) Directed by William Witney, John English. Original screen play by; Franklyn Adreon, Ronald Davidson, Norman S. Hall, Joseph Poland, Sol Shor. Production manager, Al Wilson. Unit manager, Mack D'Agostino. Photographed by William Nobles. Editors: Edward Todd, William Thompson. Musical score: Cy Feuer. Associate producer, Hiram Brown. [12-13-40]

Cast:

Doctor Satan . . . . . Edward Ciannelli
Bob Wayne . . . . Robert Wilcox
Speed Martin . . . . . . William Newell
Thomas Scott . . . C. Montague Shaw
Lois Scott . . . . Ella Neal
Alice Brent . . . . Dorothy Herbert
Gov. Bronson . . . Charles Trowbridge
Chief of Police Rand . . . Jack Mulhall
Col. Bevans . . . . Edwin Stanley
Stoner . . . . Walter McGrail
Gort . . . . Joe McGuinn
Hallett . . . . Bud Geary
The Stranger . . . . Paul Marion
Airport announcer . . Archie Twitchell
Scarlett . . . . Lynton Brent
Corwin . . . . Kenneth Terrell
Joe . . . . Al Taylor
Brock . . . . William Stahl
Duke . . . . Duke Green
Wells . . . . Tristram Coffin
Lathrop . . . . Kenneth Harlan
Davis . . . . Harry Strang
Fallon . . . . Bert LeBaron
Barton . . . . Edward Cassidy
Panamint Pete . . . . . . Frank Brownlee
Palmer . . . . Wally West
Red . . . . Alan Gregg
Smith . . . . Hal Price
Gray . . . . John Bagni

15 Chapters:

1. Return of the Copperhead
2. Thirteen Steps   3. Undersea Tomb
4. The Human Bomb   5. Dr. Satan's Man of Steel   6. Double Cross
7. The Monster Strikes   8. Highway of Death   9. Double Jeopardy
10. Bridge of Peril   11. Death Closes In   12. Crack Up   13. Disguised
14. The Flaming Coffin   15. Dr. Satan Strikes

Bob Wayne arrives at the State Building to keep an appointment with his guardian, Governor Bronson. The

WHO IS THE COPPERHEAD?

WHAT IS HIS MYSTERIOUS ASSIGNMENT?

You'll THRILL to his action-packed adventures as he plays a fearless hand in the game of death dealt by a power-crazed madman who threatens to crush a nation!

MYSTERIOUS DOCTOR SATAN

with...

EDWARD CIANNELLI
ROBERT WILCOX · WILLIAM NEWELL
C. MONTAGUE SHAW · ELLA NEAL
DOROTHY HERBERT

A REPUBLIC SERIAL IN 15 CHAPTERS

governor is concerned. A master criminal, Doctor Satan, plans to terrorize and dominate the nation. He has been killing the people assigned to investigate him. Bronson himself has been threatened. "For the first time in my life I'm really worried," he admits. Not just for himself, but because there are certain things he wants to accomplish. "I sent for you because there's something I want you to hear from me, rather than read in a will after I'm dead," he tells Bob.

First he reminisces a bit. He reminds Bob he wasn't born in the state but was born and raised on a cattle ranch in Arizona. "The best friend I ever had was a young puncher who came out of Texas to ride for my father.

For the moment we'll call him Smith." Bronson paces about his spacious office as he speaks.

He and Smith were inseparable, until word spread that Smith was riding with a wild bunch. He quit the ranch and soon after a series of raids began, by an unknown masked rider called the Copperhead. "Was he your friend Smith?," Bob asks. "Yes. He was called the Copperhead because he always wore this copper mask." Bronson shows Bob a copper mail mask, and a copper miniature coiled snake. "Whenever he made a raid, or had to kill a man, one of these copper serpents was always found at the scene."

Bob studies the items and asks

what they have to do with him. "The Copperhead was your father," Bronson says gravely. "Your father died a few months after you were born and your mother died the next winter. I started then to look after your affairs, and you've been with me ever since." He tells the Bob that his father was not a criminal, but someone who operated outside the law "to right wrongs badly in need of righting. That's the plain simple truth, and never forget it."

Bob thanks the governor for the news, takes the mask and serpent and prepares to leave. Bronson tells him not to feel anything but pride in his father. "He was the most courageous man I've ever known. Why, if the Copperhead were alive today he'd run this Doctor Satan to earth before he

could strike another blow." They agree to meet the next morning. As he leaves the building, Bob pauses and studies the mask. He recalls the governor's words, reflects, seems to come to a decision, turns around and reenters the building.

Bronson is working at his desk when a sinister figure in a wide-brim hat and wide-lapel jacket enters. The man comes closer. Bronson buzzes Welles, his secretary, but Welles is dead at his desk. The stranger delivers a final warning note (which quickly self-destructs) from Dr. Satan, draws a pistol and shoots Bronson. Bob enters, takes in the scene and leaps across the room onto the intruder. A lively battle follows, which ends with the beaten murderer delivered to police headquarters.

Bob, police chief Rand, reporter

Lois Scott and police photographer Speed Martin listen to the murderer's confession. "I didn't want to do it," he says. "Dr. Satan made me. If I refused to kill the governor Dr. Satan would kill me." Yet he claims that he's never seen Dr. Satan, and doesn't know who he is. Chief Rand asks how he gets his orders. "Through this," he replies, unbuttoning his shirt and revealing what appears to be a speaker strapped to his chest.

Dr. Satan, a sinister foreigner with a slight European accent, is in his laboratory working on a giant mechanical man when an aide rushes in to report that their man, Corbay, has been captured by the police and is being questioned. The doctor walks to a radio-like contraption and turns a few dials. Just above the device, on a wall television

The Copperhead has the remote control unit in one hand and a pistol in the other as he holds Dr. Satan's men—Bud Geary (2nd from left), Walter McGrail (2nd from right)—at bay.

screen, the people facing Corbay appear. Corbay is telling them that Dr. Satan is after a remote control device invented by Thomas Scott. "That's my father," exclaims Lois. Suddenly, a voice is heard from the speaker on Corbay's chest. It's Dr. Satan, who declares there's no protection from him and that Corbay knows the penalty for betrayal. He flips a switch and Corbay is instantly electrocuted. Dr. Satan tells Stoner, his assistant, that once he gets control of Scott's device his power will be limitless.

Bob and Speed know that Scott is on a train heading for the city. They decide to intercept it and provide protection for the scientist. But Dr. Satan already has a room on the train and, with his cohort Hallett, has no trouble

Robert Wilcox gets into the diving bell.

rendering Scott unconscious. When Bob boards the train and gets to Scott's room, he finds himself looking into the barrel of a pistol which is, Dr. Satan informs him, noiseless and loaded with a hypodermic needle containing a deadly poison. "You'll be dead before we leave this room." He fires at Bob, who falls to the ground. But the plans for the device are not on Scott. Satan guesses they're in Scott's briefcase in the luggage car.

Bob gets up and checks his inner breast pocket. He withdraws the Copperhead mask. The needle had gotten tangled in the mail, unable to penetrate it. The mask had saved his life. Bob puts on the mask and the Copperhead is reborn. He exits through a window, climbs to the roof of the train

Below: Eduardo Ciannelli checks the pulse of drugged William Newell, as henchmen Joe McGuinn and Walter McGrail stand by.

A robot holds the unconscious Copperhead captive, as Eduardo Ciannelli gloats and C. Montague Shaw seems worried.

and heads for the luggage car. There, he finds Hallett, who has found Scott's briefcase. During a fierce struggle both men fall from the train, but it's the Copperhead who winds up with the briefcase.

The next day Hallett tells Dr. Satan about the man in the copper mask who foiled their efforts and left a curious momento: a miniature coiled copperhead. Bob, Lois, Alice Brent—the inventor's secretary, and Dr. Scott are in the latter's home when a messenger delivers Scott's briefcase, complete with the plans to the remote control cell and a note from the Copperhead. Scott mentions that the device is going to be tested that evening. He places the plans in a wall safe, explaining that anyone trying to steal them will set off a device that will electrically shock the thief. They leave to accompany Lois to the

docks, where she'll board a yacht that's part of the test.

That evening Scott returns to his home and finds Dr. Satan waiting for him. The master criminal introduces himself and tells the astonished scientist that he wants a complete set of the remote control cell plans. Scott refuses to cooperate. Satan smiles, and explains that Scott's daughter, Lois, is on board a yacht speeding to the test site. Satan's men have wired the yacht so that when it reaches a speed of 25 knots it will explode. Scott remains unconvinced. Dr. Satan suggests that a little time, with each second bringing Lois closer to death, might cause a change of heart

At that moment, Scott's secretary Alice is bound hand and foot in the Scott estate's barn. She manages to untie her feet and hops to a door, push-

ing against it unsuccessfully. She spies a horse in a stall. Climbing over bales of hay she mounts the horse and, holding the reins with her teeth, gets the steed to a gallop, rides it through a window and races off. What a woman! On the road she meets Bob, who is driving to Lohman Park. He unties her as she tells him that some men came into the house, bound her and left her in the barn. He speeds on to Lohman Park.

As the seconds tick away Scott relents and gives the plans to Dr. Satan. The Copperhead appears, pistol drawn, and seizes them Scott objects, pointing out that Lois' life is at stake. Dr. Satan and the Copperhead strike a deal: Satan will make certain that the yacht gets safely to shore, after which Bob will release him and give him a fifteen-minute start.

The evil doctor reaches for the

93

Stuntman Dave Sharpe, as the Copperhead, leaps the leap on bad guy Kenneth Terrell.

phone but instead pulls the plug on the lights and the room is plunged into darkness. Dr. Satan reaches for the plans and is immediately knocked unconscious by the electrical charge. Scott says it will take several hours to revive him. They try to contact the yacht via radio, with no luck. The Copperhead decides to head for the dock to see if he can intercept the yacht. He'll get there in time to warn the crew and escape with Lois just as the ship explodes.

Dr. Satan awakens to find himself safely back in his suburban headquarters, surrounded by his men. They tell him they rescued him from the police and that the yacht was blown up and sunk. "And Scott's remote control device sunk with it," Satan laments. In Lohman Park Scott decides to hold another demonstration the next morning. "This time," he adds brightly, "I'll use a plane." He tells Bob, Lois, Alice and Speed that the plane will be pilotless, directed completely by remote control. He'll operate under a new frequency, so that Dr. Satan won't be able to track the event.

The next morning the demonstration plane, a neat little single-motor job, is ready for take off. It is watched by Col. Scott, of the army, Lois, Alice and Speed, via a television viewing screen and control device in Scott's home and from which he controls the plane's

movement. Un-beknownst to all, the Copperhead has stowed away on board. Dr. Satan, finding his tracking equipment useless due to the frequency change, instructs two of his men to get a plane, follow the test plane, board it and steal its remote control unit. In case that doesn't work, two other men are to follow the test plane by car, be wherever it lands and then steal the unit. The men involved accept these assignments matter of factly.

Ella Neal and Robert Wilcox discover a transmitter.

The plane makes a run over some target buildings, dropping bombs with great precision. "It's marvelous," the colonel enthuses, "it makes every other form of warfare obsolete." Next is a dive-bombing demonstration. As the plane goes through its gyrations the Copperhead, whose faith in technology is being sorely tested, is bounced around its interior. Dr. Satan's men, in their own aircraft, appear over the test plane. Using a rope ladder, one of the men lowers himself onto it. (All in a day's work, for these guys.)

The Copperhead stays hidden, watching as the man crawls in through a window, locates a key tube and severs it, sending the plane into a dive. *Now* the Copperhead emerges and a fist fight begins. The masked hero tosses the thug out of the plane and manages to land it in a field. Competent beyond belief, Dr. Satan's men are waiting. Imagine their surprise when they discover Bob (who has removed his mask), not their man, in the plane. After finding the remote unit, they bind Bob securely and bring him to their hideout.

In a basement room full of tool boxes and crates, Bob, his hands tied behind him, sits in a straight-back chair. The other men have left the room to

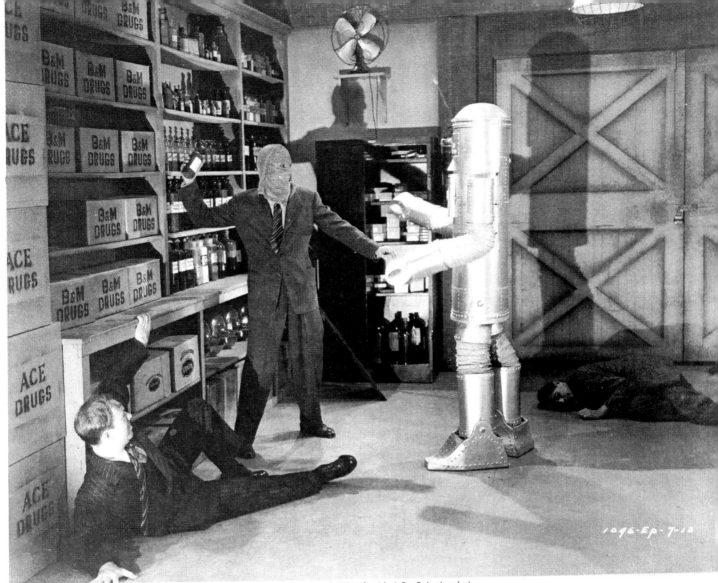

As William Newell cringes on the floor, the Copperhead gets set to toss a bottle of acid at Dr. Satan's robot.

contact Dr. Satan, but one guard is playing solitaire, his pistol in front of him on the table. Bob leans back slightly and rubs his ropes against the rough edge of a crate. Eventually he frees himself and attacks the guard.

Dr. Satan has arrived. His men rush to the basement to get Bob, but discover him gone and their man unconscious. Dr. Satan is not pleased with the news. The guard is reminded of the penalty for failure. He is forced into a small chamber with an ominous metal dome over it. At the flick of a switch the man is electrocuted. The remaining henchmen are told to "get rid of the body." They leave. The evil doctor is working studying the remote control device when the Copperhead enters, gun in hand.

He orders the doctor to put his hands up and takes the remote control device. Dr. Satan's four men return and Bob now has all five of them with their hands up. At the Copperhead's command, they toss their guns on the floor. He announces his intention to call the police, and moves to the phone, which happens to be in the aforementioned domed chamber.

Dr. Satan slowly inches toward the switch as the Copperhead nears the phone. As the receiver is lifted Dr. Satan pulls the switch. But the crime-fighter's reflexes are so sharp that his quick shot hits the switch's control panel before it activates. During this distraction the thugs attack. The remote unit is knocked from the Copperhead's hand and as he flees he steps on it. Dr. Satan checks it out. It's useless.

Pursued by Dr. Satan's men the Copperhead comes to a parked car. Of course, he hides in the trunk, closing it

behind him. Wouldn't you? Dr. Satan and his men gather at that spot, admit that their captive has gotten away, pile into the car and drive "to the warehouse," a large multi-storied commercial building. As the men get out, Bob opens the trunk slightly and hears that "the office is on the twelfth floor." One man is left to guard the car. Bob disposes of him with a single punch.

Bob then walks to the wall of the building and begins to climb it. Utilizing crevices in the stonework he actually climbs several stories straight up along the face of the building. He stops at a parapet to put on his mask, then resumes his climb, presumably to the twelfth floor. From a ledge outside a window he watches and listens as Dr. Satan and his men discuss their plans.

A tube on the remote unit in Dr. Satan's possession had been smashed.

95

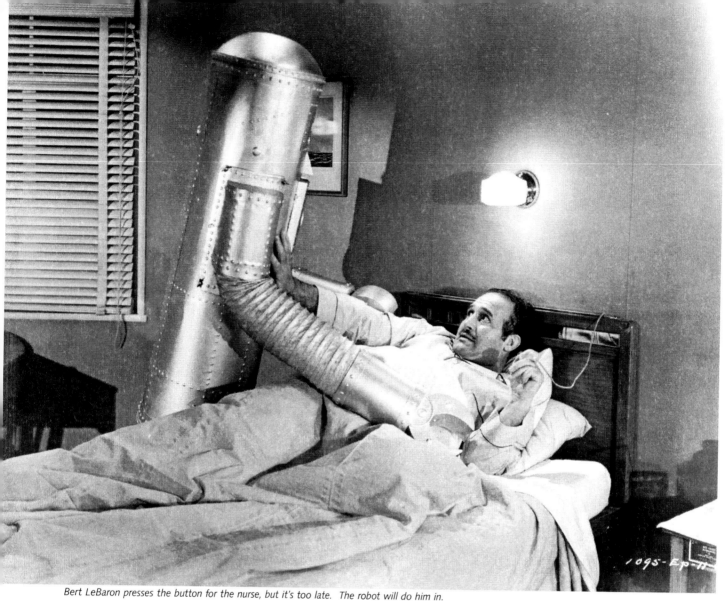

Bert LeBaron presses the button for the nurse, but it's too late. The robot will do him in.

The only other existing tube was on the yacht that sank. On the possibility that the tube itself was undamaged, the doctor intended to have a diver search the yacht the next day. The Copperhead is spotted, but, given his building-climbing abilities, proves hard to catch. He gets to the elevator shaft, slides down the cables and escapes.

The next day, at Lohman Park, in the company of Bob, Lois, Alice and Speed, Scott finds a note from the Copperhead revealing Dr. Satan's plans. Scott tells Bob that by a stroke of good fortune special diving equipment, designed by a fellow scientist, was at the harbor now. In short time they're all on a boat, preparing to lower the diving bell. Bob and Lois get in and are lowered away, as Scott, Alice and Speed handle things on deck. The diving bell looks like a metal barrel with a porthole

and conical ends. It is soon alongside the sunken yacht. For some reason dynamite is lowered into the yacht, with its positioning carefully directed by Bob. That done, he gives the signal to be pulled up. Nothing happens.

Dr. Satan's men have arrived via speedboat and boarded Scott's ship. A lively battle takes place, with Alice climbing a mast and swinging into the thugs, battling them as effectively as any man. During the fray Speed is knocked against a detonator. The resultant explosion on the yacht weakens the wall of the diving bell, which begins to spring leaks. Despite Lois and Bob's efforts at plugging the leaks with their jackets, water rushes in, eventually forming an air pocket, giving the trapped couple a temporary respite.

On deck, Alice has flattened a thug and seized his gun. She stops the fight-

ing and has the thugs line up with hands aloft. But one man grabs Speed and uses him as a shield. All the gangsters hide behind Speed and lower themselves into their boat, getting away with Speed as a hostage. (You must see this scene to believe it.) Scott and Alice quickly bring Lois and Bob to the surface, and describe what happened.

Later, at Scott's Lohman Park estate, a car pulls up and lets Speed out. A camera-speaker system is strapped over his suit. He's brought inside by the Scotts and Alice. Dr. Satan's voice is heard over the speaker. He explains that Speed has been drugged and hypnotized and is in a trance. A powerful bomb is connected to him. The doctor adds that they are all visible to him, and advises them to stay in front of Speed at all times and to move slowly. He instructs them to follow Speed to his

96

headquarters, where, he promises, they will resurrect a remote control unit.

As Dr. Satan is talking the Copperhead enters behind Speed, and signals his friends to stall for time while he calls the police. As Scott deliberately falters and fumbles, the Copperhead calls Chief Rand and tries to convince him to have the city's electricity turned off for thirty seconds. That, he reasons, would shut down Dr. Satan's radio control and provide enough time to relieve Speed of his dangerous vest. At first Rand refuses, citing the possible effects on hospitals, businesses, government, etc. Still, the Copperhead manages to convince him. As the group follows Speed outside, the electricity is turned off and Speed's accouterments are removed and tossed away just seconds before current is resumed and the vest

explodes. Speed, however, is still in a trance, and stands zombie-like as events transpire around him.

Suddenly a car appears and three thugs pile out. Bob, who had rejoined the others, is knocked out. Scott is seized, tossed into the car and driven off. Bob recovers and fires a few shots at the fast-disappearing auto, hitting the gas tank and causing a steady leak. He gets into his own car and follows the trail of gasoline. Speed, still catatonic, is left standing on the street. The thugs, noticing that they're low on gas, stop at a gas station. When they discover the hole they appropriate the only vehicle available, a gas truck—despite its owner's protests. Bob drives up and the station attendant tells him what happened. Bob drives off in pursuit, donning his mask.

Heading uphill, the truck is having difficulty maintaining speed, so the thugs decide to lighten its load. A spout is opened and gasoline pours all over the mountain road. A stray match causes the gasoline to ignite. The thugs notice this and turn off the flow, but the flames continue to race downhill. The Copperhead is driving along, and hasn't noticed that the road he's on is soaked with gasoline. A rapidly approaching wall of flame gains his immediate attention and he leaps from the car just before it's engulfed.

As Dr. Satan speeds to his wharf-area hideout wherein Scott is being held prisoner, the inventor strikes up a conversation with Scarlett, his guard. It seems that Scarlett is a criminal against his will. He must obey Dr. Satan—or die. He shows Scott the now-familiar

Below: As the walls of his cell close in, the Copperhead tries to execute the difficult mirror shot into the control panel operated by Eduardo Ciannelli.

speaker-camera-bomb device strapped to him. Anyone trying to remove it would be instantly electrocuted. Scott says he can hook-up a circuit breaker rather easily that would enable the safe removal of the harness. "If you can do that, doc, I'll help you escape," promises Scarlett.

Scott is a man of his word. In no time he's fabricated a gizmo that, with a puff of smoke, deactivates the bomb and enables Scarlett to remove the deadly vest. Dr. Satan arrives. He gives Scarlett a few orders and is somewhat surprised when his lackey pulls a gun on him and explains the new facts of life. While Scarlett speaks, Dr. Satan, his hands behind him, presses a button on a remote panel on his desk. Behind Scarlett and Scott a wall slides open, and a mechanical man silently moves forward. Its iron claws clutch Scarlett, who is crushed to death.

With a smile, Dr. Satan introduces Scott to his robot. "You'll like it better after you've worked on it," he assures the horrified scientist. "That's why you're here. At present I can only control this robot over a short distance. But with your remote control cell built in I can send this robot and hundreds like it all over the country. With my army of mechanical men I can seize wealth and power beyond limit." Scott protests, but threatened with death, agrees to cooperate. As guards watch, he toys with some electrical equipment.

At Lohman Park, Bob and Lois are in Scott's laboratory when the inventor's voice is suddenly heard coming through a radio speaker. It's Scott, who has unobtrusively activated a microphone. Loudly, he tells his guards he needs a transformer, which can only be gotten from a particular store. Bob jots down the name and address and races to his car. He gets to the supply house in time to see two of Dr. Satan's men leaving. He follows them, putting on his mask.

The thugs arrive at their hideout, a large, ramshackle house next to a dock. The Copperhead approaches cautiously. He enters and in short order knocks out two guards, finds Scott and has his pistol trained on Dr. Satan as they discuss the situation. Smooth as ever, Dr. Satan presses two buttons, one marked "robot," the other "trapdoor." He quickly drops from sight through a trapdoor, while the wall slides open and the robot bears down on the Copperhead.

The mechanical man seizes the masked hero and in its plodding manner carries him to a terrace and holds him over the water. Scott, meanwhile, rush-

The Copperhead (stunt man David Sharpe) leaps onto a hijacked truck.

Robert Wilcox and Ella Neal think the man under the bandages is good Prof. Williams, but he's really the evil Eduardo Ciannelli.

es to the control panel and turns it off, resulting in the robot going limp and the Copperhead being dropped into the sea. Dr. Satan reappears through the trapdoor and reminds Scott that he's still a prisoner. The Copperhead swims to safety. Scott proves intractable, and will not work on the control cell. Dr. Satan injects him with a powerful drug, depriving him of his will power. Scott reveals that the secret behind his cell is the rare mineral tungite. He has an ample supply of it at his estate. Alice is in charge of it.

This sets off a prolonged quest for tungite, kidnappings of Alice (one of which has her tied to a chair which at midnight will move a basket that releases a gas pellet into a pan of acid, the resulting vapor capable of killing her within two minutes), and rescue attempts.

Satan will use Scott's new device to have his robot rob banks and break into tungite storage facilities, but failing in the latter, he'll decide to buy a tungite mine and refine the ore himself. On horseback, Lois and Alice try to locate Satan's tungite mine, get captured by Gort and another henchman and escape when Alice grabs an overhead tree branch, summersaults over it, lands feet first on Gort's chest, knocks him from his horse, mounts it and gallops away, following Lois. Gort fires a shot at her and Alice falls sideways as if hit, but manages to stay in the saddle. When she's out of range she suddenly straightens up and gallops off in earnest, doing some very fancy riding. Hanging from the saddle by one leg and facing backwards, she removes Gort's rifle from its bag, takes aim and hits him in the gun hand, once again knocking him from his

saddle. As he gets up, nursing his wounded hand, he looks at Alice who stops, circles around, and waves an *adieu* before riding off. Terrific!

One of Satan's men, Fallon, is wounded, captured and placed in a hospital, followed by the mandatory attempt to kill him before he talks. The robot is sent to the hospital to do the deed and, despite Fallon's police guard, succeeds. The Copperhead is captured while following Satan's truck, and imprisoned in a basement cell whose far wall starts to close in on him as Satan works control switches.. The Copperhead's cell has a door with a small, barred window. Holding a pocket mirror through the bars, lines up his pistol barrel in the reflection, aims at the switches and fires, stopping the wall's advance. A minute later Speed appears and gets him out of the room.

99

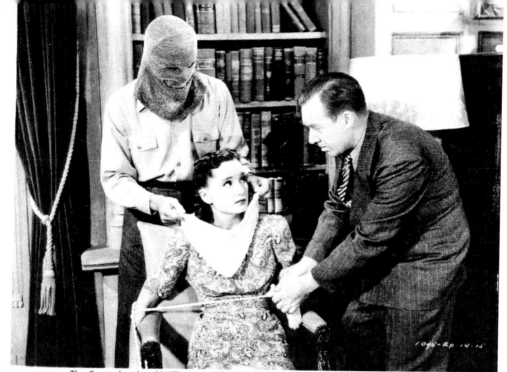

The Copperhead and William Newell rescue Ella Neal.

Later, going through the doctor's papers, it's discovered that his next target is Prof. Williams, a famed scientist, who is flying to Capital City with a formula for a deadly gas. As you can guess, Satan's efforts to get this new formula trigger a chain of events involving Bob and Williams in a plane crash, Williams being kidnapped, Speed taking a photo of Satan's license plate (meaning there will be attempts to destroy this evidence), Satan replacing a head-bandaged Williams, Bob placing himself in a box to be delivered to Dr. Satan, who immediately smells a rat and decides to put the box in a furnace and incinerate it.

During an attempt to rescue Scott, he finds Scott and Dr. Satan together, knocks the villain out and places his mask on Dr. Satan. "Bob," says Scott in surprise, "you are the Copperhead." Bob says he'll explain later, and hides as two thugs approach and ask Scott what happened. He explains that he saw the Copperhead prowling about and "took him by surprise." The two thugs decide to put the Copperhead in the room with the other prisoners "and let the robot take care of him."

Lois is a prisoner in the other room, tied to a chair and menaced by the robot. The henchmen find another chair, set the unconscious Copperhead in it, then run from the room. Stoner

sees the Copperhead sitting there and decides he's higher priority than Lois. The robot grabs the masked man and starts to crush him. Bob and Scott race to the control room and do battle with Stoner and Gort. Dr. Satan has awakened and has ripped off his mask. He screams to Stoner to stop the robot, but both his men are battling for their own lives. The robot carries Dr. Satan to a balcony and keeps going, both robot and doctor falling to their doom.

Later, Bob and Scott reveal to Lois and Speed the Copperhead's true identity. "Aww, I knew it all along," says Speed. The DA rounds up all of Dr. Satan's men and closes down his places of operation. "What a story," Speed enthuses, and Lois promises that her news stories will clear the name of the Copperhead forever.

The Purple Monster Strikes (Republic-1945) Directed by Spencer Bennet, Fred Brannon. Original screenplay: Royal Cole, Albert Demond, Basil Dickey, Lynn Perkins, Joseph F. Poland, Barney Sarecky. Photography: Bud Thackery. Editors: Cliff Bell, Harold Minter. Special effects: Howard Lydecker, Theodore

Lydecker. Unit manager: Roy Wade. Associate producer: Ronald Davidson. [10-6-45]

Cast:

Craig Foster . . . . Dennis Moore
Sheila Layton . . . . Linda Stirling
Purple Monster . . . . . Roy Barcroft
Dr. Cyrus Layton . . . . . James Craven
Hart Garrett . . . . Bud Geary
Marcia . . . . Mary Moore
Emperor of Mars . . . . John Davidson
Stewart . . . . Joe Whitehead
Saunders . . . . Emmett Vogan
Meredith . . . . George Carleton
Mitchell . . . . Kenne Duncan
Helen . . . . Rosemonde James
Harvey. . . . . Monte Hale
Dr. Benjamin . . . . Wheaton Chambers
Crandall . . . . Frederick Howard
Tony . . . . Anthony Warde
Andy . . . . Ken Terrell
Fritz Benham (and others) Tom Steele

15 Chapters:

1. The Man in the Meteor 2. The Time Trap 3. Flaming Avalanche 4. The Lethal Pit 5. Death on the Beam 6. The Demon Killer 7. The Evil Eye 8. Descending Doom 9. The Living Dead 10. House of Horror 11. Menace from Mars 12. Perilous Plunge 13. Fiery Shroud 14. The Fatal Trail 15. Take-Off to Destruction

Dr. Cyrus Layton of the Scientific

Below: Guess who's coming for dinner? An unwelcome visitor from Mars: Roy Barcroft.

It's a permanent good night for James Craven as Roy Barcroft prepares to take over his identity.

Foundation, celebrated astronomer and inventor, notices a strange meteor approaching his observatory. He calls his niece, Sheila Layton, and tells her he's going to follow it to see where it crashes. The object hits the earth, bursts into flames and explodes just as Layton arrives. He sees a metal pod, thrown clear, a door slide open and a mysterious being, dressed in a presumably purple wet suit with a nifty mailed hood-type cowl, belt and cuffs, gets out of it before it, too, bursts into flames and self-destructs. Layton runs over to the stranger, who introduces himself as an inhabitant of Mars sent to talk to the doctor about his inventions, particularly a space ship capable of flying to other planets.

Layton asks how the stranger understands and speaks English. The Martian explains he understands all lan-

guages, that many years ago his people invented the "distance eliminator," a device that enabled him to "see and hear everything that's happened on Earth."

Flattered if not astonished by the high regard of a visitor from outer space, Layton brings the stranger to the observatory and shows him the construction plans for the spacecraft, mentioning that "this is the proudest day of my life." "Unfortunately for you, doctor," remarks the Martian matter of fact-ly, "it is also the last day of your life."

He tells the bewildered astronomer that he is the Purple Monster, the scout of an invasion force from Mars bent on conquering Earth. The invasion has been planned for a long time. The only thing delaying it is the lack of a space ship capable of making round trips from Earth to Mars, and the doctor has con-veniently solved that problem. The

stranger ("my name would mean noth-ing to you") uses toxic fumes to kill Layton, then through a highly-advanced scientific process (involving the inhal-ing of a special gas), the Martian pre-pares to enter the doctor's body and assume his physical characteristics.

He's half-way through this process when Sheila arrives along with Craig Foster, legal counsel for the Scientific Foundation. When no one answers the door, Craig peers through a window and sees what seems to be an oddly-clad person hovering over the unconscious seated Dr. Layton. He crashes through the window and attacks. The Martian is well able to defend himself and knocks Craig out in short order. He then hur-riedly completes the process and is seat-ed in the chair, pretending to be uncon-scious when Sheila comes in and Craig revives.

101

Roy Barcroft gets ready to clobber Robert Wilcox, who's choking Bud Geary.

Naturally enough, they believe him when he says a Martin known as the Purple Monster stole his plans for the space ship. He tells them he'll be busy replacing the plans—it might take months. Craig reminds the doctor that a few weeks ago he'd received a threatening note demanding $50,000. Maybe the note was connected to the Monster. Layton says it's possible, and wishes Craig and Sheila well in their pursuit of the Purple Monster.

As soon as they leave, the Martian (henceforth referred to as Layton) starts going through the doctor's desk. He finds the threatening letter and is reading it when an armed intruder appears. "Who are you?" Layton asks. "I'm the man who sent you that note," the man replies. It turns out he's a gangster

named Hart Garrett who wants in on the money he thinks the Foundation gave to Layton. "Now you come across with that money," he threatens, "or I'll hold you for ransom and make them pay double."

Layton says "Give me a moment," walks over to the chair, sits down, and goes through his transformation procedure, emerging as the Purple Monster before an astounded Garrett, who drops his gun in awe and is very receptive to the Purple Monster's job offer. Garrett's first task is to round up dependable men who'll follow orders.

While Dr. Layton continues to pretend to work on reproducing his stolen plans, as the the Purple Monster he's busy developing the space ship. First he needs the new Mitchell Rocket

Launcher which provides added propulsion and is to be demonstrated to Craig and Sheila that very day. With pistols in hand, the Monster and Garrett barge in on Mitchell as he's preparing the rocket launcher for its test. There's a huge missile in the launching cradle, and the Purple Monster studies the mechanism with interest. "I presume this is the lever that fires the rocket," he says to Mitchell, who replies, "That's right. When the hand on the gauge reaches one hundred, the main rocket fires and the machine takes off."

The Purple Monster suggests they start loading the launcher onto a truck just outside. Mitchell tells them loading will take a while and Foster will be there before they finish. The Monster orders Mitchell to call Craig and tell

102

Martian boss John Davidson is not pleased with Roy Barcroft's progress on Earth.

one hundred thousand dollars is in a nearby bank safe, and he and Garrett make plans to steal it. Viia interplanetary television he reports in to the emperor of Mars, who says he's proud of the Monster's progress. "You'll lead the first wave of the invasion," he tells him. The Purple Monster is honored.

First Layton, under the pretext of withdrawing funds, visits the bank so he can scout out the vault which, he is told by the trusting bank manager, operates on a time lock so that it's automatically locked between 5 P.M. and 9 A.M. the next day. Layton plants a device which speeds up the time lock, then leaves. But Craig, visiting the bank to check things out, notices that the timer is running fast and calculates the safe will automatically open about midnight. He deduces that a robbery attempt will take place and determines to be there when it happens.

When the Purple Monster and Garrett get into the vault room via a ladder stretched horizontally from a window in an adjoining building, Craig is right there, but can't prevent their escape (with the money) and nearly gets killed, being on the ladder as it's pushed free. Luckily, the ladder hooks onto a wire, stopping its fall and enabling

him the demonstration has been cancelled. "One word to betray us," he warns, "and it will be your last." At the Foundation, Craig and Sheila are about to leave when the phone rings. It's Mitchell, and he has to postpone the demonstration until the next day—just a little engine trouble. As he speaks, he taps a code on the receiver with his finger. Craig says fine, he'll see Mitchell tomorrow, and hangs up. He tells Sheila that Mitchell was tapping an SOS signal. They leave in a hurry.

Mitchell is tied securely to a chair, while Garrett brings the truck into the scientist's large shop. The men place the launcher on a ramp and start to push it into the truck. They're pushing away when Craig and Sheila arrive. "That's enough work for today," Craig tells announces, covering them with a pistol. He gets a little too close to Garrett, who knocks the pistol from his hand. A fight ensues. Sheila, who has jumped onto the Purple Monster, is shaken off, bumps her head and is knocked out.

Craig continues the fight, as the lever is pulled and the countdown begins. The three men struggle prodigiously. Sheila recovers, attacks Garrett and is knocked into the missile launcher cradle as the rockets charge up. The gauge approaches the 100

mark. Craig is temporarily stunned and the purple one and Garrett escape. Craig recovers, tries to turn off the launcher, but it's too late. The rocket blasts off, crashes through the roof of the building and explodes. Fortunately, Craig had removed Sheila from the cradle at the very last second.

Now the Purple Monster learns that

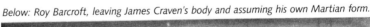

Below: Roy Barcroft, leaving James Craven's body and assuming his own Martian form.

Craig to climb into a window.

To complete the spacecraft the purple one is in constant need of a number of other items being developed by members of the Foundation; like the electro-annihilator invented by Prof. Crandall, who sets up a demonstration for Craig and Dr. Layton. He explains that the annihilator, mounted on a truck, was developed to counter meteors which, he tells them, "are the greatest hazard to space travel." The electro annihilator is able to locate the approaching object and destroy it, and the professor proves it by demolishing a swinging rock. Garrett and an accomplice barge in and, although Craig battles valiantly (and Layton hides behind Crandall), Garrett drives away with the annihilator.

While the annihilator is used to blast Craig and Sheila's cars from the road (they jump out in time), not much else results from the purple one's possession of it: Craig comes up with an annihilator detection device of great accuracy that makes the weapon's use too risky.

Despite the Purple Monster's most imaginative machinations, Craig and Sheila anticipate his needs and, escaping poison darts, acid fumes, a telephone booth with spiked closing walls, drowning and various traps and explosions, constantly thwart his efforts, sometimes even more improbably than others. During one shootout, for example, both parties hide behind oil or chemical drums for protection. Layton, you can bet, gives Craig plenty of false leads and encourages him to walk into traps.

Throughout, the Purple Monster accomplishes his transformations into Dr. Layton (and vice versa) via a set procedure: he sits in a particular chair in the middle of his office, becomes transparent, walks to a preordained spot in the room, inhales fumes from a small cylinder he takes from his belt, and the transformation is completed. This, too, must be said of the Purple Monster: he's not the kind of villain who just gives orders and lets his stooges do the work. No indeed, he is usually right there when the dirty work is being done, fist fights and all—a real hands-on guy.

One Foundation scientist, Dr. Benjamin, is in the process of completing a stabilizer essential to space flight. To aid him in stealing Benjamin's plans the Monster contacts the Emperor of Mars and asks for Marcia, a female Martian scientist-agent, to be sent to assist him. After being briefed, Marcia lands on Earth via the same flaming

Below: Martian Mary Moore arrives on Earth to lend a hand to Roy Barcroft.

Bud Geary settles in behind the control panel of the dread electroannihilator.

missile and self-destructing pod and is greeted by the Purple Monster and Garrett. The Monster tells her his plan. The next day, Marcia enters Dr. Benjamin's laboratory, kills his secretary Helen and takes on her physical characteristics.

Dr. Benjamin arrives back unexpectedly and as he opens the door, overhears Marcia—whose back is to him—talking on the phone with Dr. Layton, telling him she's been successful in taking over Helen's body and ending the conversation with no one knowing that he's the Purple Monster. Benjamin quietly backs out of the room and closes the door. A moment later he re-enters loudly. He asks Helen to find some files in another room, then calls Craig and says he's made an amazing discovery, that the Purple Monster is—

Marcia/Helen, who was listening at the door, shoots him before he can finish the sentence.

When the stabilizing device is completed, Marcia tells her boss, who sends Garrett to steal it. But Craig shows up, captures Garrett and ties his hands behind his back. While Craig is taking him to the authorities Garrett breaks free and, after a brief scuffle, escapes. Craig examines the rope that had bound Garrett and discovers it had been partially cut. He figures out that only Dr. Benjamin's secretary could have cut them and he quickly phones Sheila, who happens to be in the doctor's laboratory, and warns her to keep her eye on the secretary. When she hangs up, Sheila notices a pair of scissors on the desk with several incriminating strands of rope lodged between

the blades.

At that moment the secretary enters and Sheila has no choice but to confront her with the evidence. Marcia replies by knocking Sheila cold, then begins to transform herself back to her normal body. As this transformation is taking place Sheila revives. She sees what is happening but can scarcely believe her eyes. Marcia flees with Sheila in hot pursuit. The chase leads to the edge of a cliff, where the women battle desperately. It's Marcia who finally falls from the cliff, hurtling to her death. When Sheila tells Craig of the amazing phenomenon she witnessed, he realizes that the Purple Monster probably has this same awesome capability and may be any one of the Foundation's scientists.

Following a number of clues, Craig trails Garrett to a phone booth from

Bud Geary (left) is glad to get his hands on the electroannihilator as James Craven describes his latest plan.

which the mobster calls the Monster. Craig is so acute that he determines the number being called by listening to the sound of the dialing. It is with some shock that he realizes it's Dr. Layton's number. After reporting this to Sheila, he prepares a trap. While Layton is away from his desk, Craig plants a movie camera in his office, hoping to catch the transformation on film. He then calls Dr. Layton and tells him he has just learned that a rocket ship is being built somewhere in the observatory and is on his way over with the police.

The ruse works. Dr. Layton quickly transforms himself into his true Martian identity, complete with stylish outfit, and prepares to leave for Mars in the just-completed space ship. The ship blasts off just as Craig discovers the secret rocket room. As the space ship

106

rockets through the atmosphere Craig grabs the electroannihilator, carelessly left behind, and puts it to good use. He aims carefully and destroys the spacecraft and the Purple Monster with one well-directed shot.

The Monster and the Ape

(Columbia-1945) Directed by Howard Bretherton. Screenplay: Sherman Lowe, Royal K. Cole. Assistant director: Leonard J. Shapiro. Photography: L. W. O'Connell. Music: Lee Zahler. Editors: Dwight Caldwell, Earl Turner. Art director: John Datu. Producer: Rudolph C. Flothow.

Cast:

Ken Morgan . . . . Robert Lowery
Prof. Ernst . . . . George Macready

Prof. Arnold . . . . Ralph Morgan
Babs Arnold . . . . Carole Mathews
Flash . . . . Willie Best
Nordik . . . . Jack Ingram
Flint . . . . Anthony Warde
Butler . . . . Ted Mapes
Blake . . . . Eddie Parker
Mead . . . . Stanley Price
Rescuing policeman . . . Charles King
Prof. Ames . . . . George Eldredge
Draper . . . . Henry Hall
Prof. Shaw . . . . Forbes Murray
Carson . . . . Lee Shumway
Prof. Marsten . . . . John Elliott
Insp. Hamilton . . Kenneth MacDonald

15 Chapters:

1. The Mechanical Terror   2. The Edge of Doom   3. Flames of Fate   4. The Fatal Search   5. Rocks of Doom   6. A Fiend in Disguise   7. A Scream in the Night   8. Death in the Dark   9. The Secret Tunnel   10. Forty

Thousand Volts   11. The Mad Professor   12. Shadows of Destiny   13. The Gorilla at Large   14. His Last Flight   15. Justice Triumphs

Headlines tell the story: "Scientists Complete Mechanical Man," "Automaton to get First Test," "Inventors Claim Robot Strong Enough to do the Work of Fifty Men," "Nation's Notables to Attend Robot Demonstration Today." The notables are gathered in the prestigious offices of the Bainbridge Laboratories "to witness one of the strangest experiments yet attempted by man."

Five white-coated scientists attend to the "Metalogen Man," a metal, dour-faced, seven-foot robot, as members of the press and scientific community watch them. Professor Arnold, the head of the scientific team, addresses the group. He tells them that two years of intensive experiments have produced "a mechanical creature sensitive to the impulses of electronic energy. This robot represents harnessed power undreamed of by mortal man." He promises a new era of scientific advancement.

He operates a small table-top control unit complete with a screen that shows things through the Metalogen Man's camera eyes, and the robot comes to life. It walks to a one-ton block of cement bound by a chain and lifts it with one hand. There's applause from the audience, and the robot takes a few bows. Next, still controlled by Arnold, it walks to a locked metal door and, with very little effort, rips it from the wall. There is more applause.

Later that day a news announcer reports the robot was a huge success. Its inventors are given full credit: Professors Arnold, Ernst, Ames, Marsten and Shaw. Ames and Marsten happen to be driving along a mountain road when a voice interrupts a radio broadcast and tells them "you and your co-workers are usurping the glory and the credit for an invention that is rightfully mine. For that reason I am forced to destroy you." "That man is mad," Ames says. Marsten agrees. Suddenly a giant ape rises from the back of the car and strangles both of them. As the car

screeches to a halt the ape gets out and lumbers away.

That evening, seated in his spacious study, Professor Shaw receives a call telling him he's been slated for execution. He has one minute to live. He hears a sound outside the room and goes to see what it is. He's attacked and killed by the giant ape, who again shuffles off into the night. A radio announcement soon lists Shaw among three inventors who have been mysteriously murdered. The police are baffled.

The two remaining inventors, Arnold and Ernst, meet in Arnold's home. "I wish you two had never become involved with this invention," says Babs Arnold, the professor's daughter. Flash, the Arnolds' chauffeur, agrees. Ernst suggests they take precautions to protect the invention. Arnold tells him the Brady Manufacturing Company, who will be producing the Metalogen Man, is going to pick up the robot and keep it in their laboratory. The company's engineer, Ken Morgan, is on his way to supervise the transfer. Babs and Prof. Arnold are

Prof. Ralph Morgan (left) and Robert Lowery (right) watch as a scientific colleague examines the amazing mechanical man.

going to meet him at the Union Station. Ernst is satisfied.

Aboard the train, Ken Morgan gets a telegram from Arnold telling him to get off at Oakdale, the stop just before Union Station. He's met by two men who tell him they've been sent by Bainbridge Labs to pick him up. They quickly knock him out, dump him in the enclosed back of a small van, and drive off. Meanwhile, at Union Station, Prof. Arnold and Babs can't imagine why Ken wasn't on the train. She suggests he might have gotten off at Oakdale by mistake, and they decide to take a look. They tell Flash not to spare the horses.

The two thugs, Nordik and Flint, radio their boss as they drive. The voice tells Nordik to remove Ken's identity papers and then, pretending to be the engineer, to go to the Bainbridge labs

and pick up the robot. And as for Morgan? "Get rid of him. I don't want any trace of him left." Nordik assures him it's as good as done. They pull over to the side of the road and open the back of the wagon. Ken comes out slugging and there's a spirited fight before he's hit from behind. The thugs get the documents they need, toss Ken off a cliff and drive away.

At the foot of the cliff Ken regains consciousness, brushes himself off, recovers his hat and climbs to the road, just as the professor and Babs arrive. They don't know who he is, but they stop because he looks like he needs help. They're shocked to find that he's the man they're looking for. He explains what happened and urges them to get to the laboratory immediately.

It's too late. The Metalogen Man

has already been picked up. The lab has been wrecked and the robot's control panel stolen. Ken, Arnold and Babs search the lab for clues. Ken picks up a small mechanical device. "It's the metalogen disc," Arnold declares, "the most vital part of the robot. Without it the automaton can't operate." They hide it in a vault. Arnold tells Ernst what's happening.

Upon hearing the news, Ernst is surprisingly calm. He tells Arnold not to call the police. Instead he suggests that Ken might be in league with the robbers—that he had no credentials and was unbruised even though he claimed to have been tossed off a cliff. Arnold, totally confused, concedes it's a possibility. The smooth-talking Ernst says that the "alleged Morgan" even knows where the metalogen disc is, and is

Carole Mathews, Ralph Morgan, Robert Lowery and chauffeur-servant Willie Best discuss the strange goings on.

The evilly-controlled Metalogen man threatens inventor Ralph Morgan and his daughter Carole Mathews.

probably planning to steal it. He suggests that the disc be brought to his house that evening, for safekeeping. Arnold agrees.

The professor keeps his word, showing up at Ernst's with the metalogen disc in a neatly-tied package. He rings the doorbell. Two men (Nordik and Flint) suddenly appear from the shrubbery, punch him in the stomach, seize the package and flee. He's standing, dazed, as Ernst opens the door. He tells Ernst what happened. Ernst suggests they call the police, but once in his study he changes his mind, urges caution instead, and gives the professor a lot of double talk. "I'll admit I don't know what to do or think," Arnold mutters.

In response to seemingly innocent questions Arnold reveals that no one knows he's come to Ernst's house, nor

that he had taken the disc. Seeing a signal (a blinking light in a painting of a lighthouse), Ernst excuses himself and asks Arnold to wait for him. He goes into another room, pushes a lever to open a sliding door in a fireplace, enters it, goes down stone steps into a cave area, then into a laboratory equipped with various electronic gizmos and, standing against a wall, the Metalogen Man, then through a sliding wall into an inner chamber where he meets with Nordik and Flint, who hand over the package. "With this I can put the rest of my plan into operation," he says dramatically.

In the lab, Babs and Ken are wondering where her dad is. She calls home, but he's not there. She's about to call Ernst's home when Ken suggests they drive over. He wants to meet Ernst in person. In Ernst's study Arnold is

enjoying a cigar and looking at books plucked from the bookshelves lining the room. He flicks an ash into an ashtray, then clicks the little button that drops the ash into the tray bowl (some ashtrays used to be like that). When he does, a wall panel slides open, revealing the robot's control panel. (A '40 ashtray has to be the worst possible spot for a secret switch.) In a flash Arnold realizes he's been duped.

Ernst has returned and is watching Arnold. "So you double crossed me. You're the thief," Arnold charges. Ernst doesn't deny it. He hears the sound of a car pulling up in front of the house. Nordik and Flint remove Arnold while Ernst answers the door. It's Babs and Ken, and Ernst invites them in. He tells them that Arnold had been there earlier in the day, but had left hours ago. While Ernst is talking, Ken notices

Robert Lowery, on a catwalk above molten metal, tries to escape the Metalogen Man.

Arnold's monogrammed hat on a table. If Arnold left hours ago, Ken says to Ernst, "then his hat must have blown back in through the window." With a flourish he displays the hat.

Ernst reaches for a gun but is grabbed and disarmed by Ken, who hands the pistol to Babs and tells her to keep an eye on Ernst while he looks around the house. Ken notices the open fireplace and steps through it. In the basement laboratory a generator is giving off dangerous blasts of current and Nordik and Flint are trying to push Arnold against it. Ken arrives just in time and attacks. There is a spirited fist fight. Arnold hits the deck early.

Upstairs, Babs is caught by surprise when Ernst releases a swinging secret closet that encloses her while he

gets away. (Later she'll shoot her way out.) He dashes to the control device and sets it up. Onscreen he sees Ken battling with Nordik and Flint. He activates the robot. Ken has polished off both opponents and is helping Arnold recover when he's grabbed by the automaton, who lifts him into the air with one hand and dumps him into a shallow pit in front of the generator. Sparks rain upon him. Nordik and Flint flee, as does Ernst. Arnold turns off the current and helps Ken, who's all right, out of the pit.

Ernst temporarily sets up shop elsewhere and, still aided by Nordik and Flint, remains doggedly determined to gain control of the Metalogen Man, which, rest assured and despite Ken's best efforts, changes hands several

times, as does the control device, the disc, and metalogen (a required element). "Arnold and Morgan have it all figured out how they're going to make these machines for the benefit of humanity," Ernst tells his henchmen, "but they're thinking without me. If my plan works out, I'll utterly crush their exalted scheme." His precise objective remains unstated.

Thor, the ape, is well trained, and takes his cues from Ernst, Flint and Nordik. Normally, Thor is a resident of the Zoological Gardens. Nordik, when he's not doing dirty deeds for Ernst, is a keeper at the zoo. In fact the bad guys get to one of their hideouts by walking through a metal door in the rear of Thor's cage. (It's hard to imagine a more public secret entrance.) The ape's great strength is useful for smashing through doors, which it does to get into Arnold's laboratory and to carry off the robot. Thor, who often gets dangerously frisky, is usually led around on a leash by Ernst, Nordik or Flint.

In the performance of his duties Ken tumbles down mountains, drives off cliffs, is crushed by the ape, falls into a pit, finds himself trapped between closing walls, lies unconscious as the mine he's in explodes, is tied up in an enclosed garage next a car discharging carbon monoxide, is nearly electrocuted and is involved in fistfights long and short. Babs is almost incinerated in a furnace and is kidnapped on occasion, as is her father. Flash is stereotypically terrified by everything, and consistently forgets to deliver important messages.

It turns out that Thor isn't such a bad ape after all, merely an exploited one who does what he's told. More

Into the fireplace and through the secret passage goes Robert Lowery.

Looks like broken bones for (supposedly) Robert Lowery (but obviously a double) as he's tossed about by Thor, the ape.

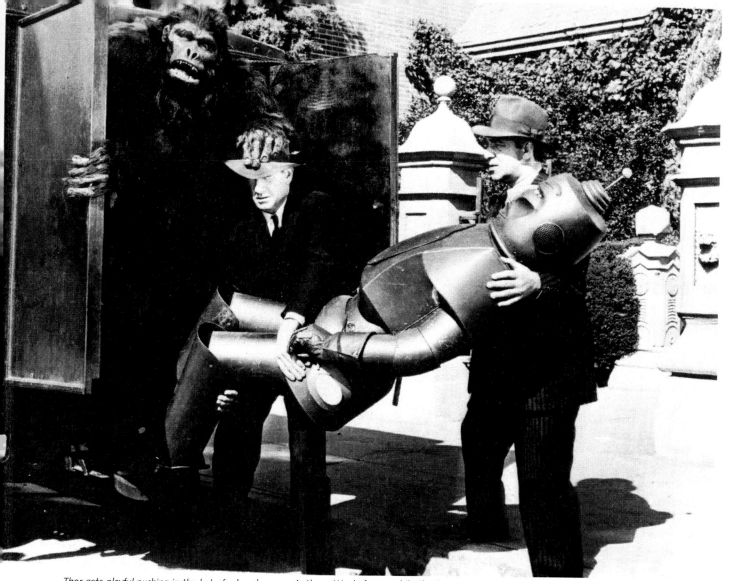

Thor gets playful pushing in the hat of a henchman as Anthony Warde fumes while they're trying to make off with the Metalogen Man.

than once even Ken and a few policemen get to lead him around on his leash (causing some degree of hysteria on the part of passers by). At one point, however, Thor does lose control, attacks Ken and has to be shot by Prof. Arnold, who expresses his sincerest regrets.

The swinging-wall passageway in the back of Thor's spacious cage leads through various caves and mines and is connected to Ernst's former home. Although he's wanted by the police and his home supposedly closed up, Ernst still uses it and especially the tunnels and laboratory beneath it, which remain undetected by the authorities. Ernst remains as determined as ever to get control of the Metalogen Man and the remote control unit, but he has also discovered—he hopes—a meteorite in the mine. The meteorite is rich in metalogen. He picks up a couple of new

112

henchmen, Mead and Taylor.

Mead doesn't turn out to be a very good choice. When he's captured by Ken he makes a deal for a light sentence and leads Ken right to Ernst's hideout. Police are called in from all over the area. With most of his men being apprehended, Ernst packs a fortune in metalogen and flees with it in a van driven by Flint. They're pursued by Ken and a squad of police. The van speeds along winding mountain roads. A detour sign and roadblock appear before them. Unable to stop in time, Flint crashes through the roadblock and off a cliff. He and Ernst die as the van tumbles down a steep incline and sinks into a lake. With all threats out of the way, the Metalogen Man can now be produced for the good of humanity and, more importantly, Ken can spend more time with Babs.

The Crimson Ghost

(Republic-1946) Directed by William Witney, Fred C. Brannon. . Original screenplay: Albert DeMond, Basil Dickey, Jesse Duffy, Sol Shor. Photographed by: Bud Thackery. Film editors: Harold R. Minter, Cliff Bell. Special effects: Howard Lydecker, Theodore Lydecker. Music director: Mort Glickman. Unit manager: Roy Wade. Associate producer: Ronald Davidson. [10-26-46]

Cast:

Duncan Richards . . . Charles Quigley
Diana Farnsworth . . . . Linda Stirling
Louis Ashe . . . . Clayton Moore
Blackton . . . . I. Stanford Jolley
Prof. Chambers . . . . . Kenne Duncan
Prof. Van Wyck . . . . . . Forrest Taylor

12 Chapters:
1. Atomic Peril   2. Thunderbolt
3. The Fatal Sacrifice   4. The Laughing
Skull   5. Flaming Death   6. Mystery
of the Mountain   7. Electrocution
8. The Slave Collar   9. Blazing Fury
10. The Trap that Failed   11. Double
Murder   12. The Invisible Trail

The master criminal known only as the Crimson Ghost, in his abandoned-mansion hideout, tells two henchmen, Ashe and Bain, of his plan to steal a counter-atomic-attack device invented by Doctor Chambers, an internationally prominent physicist. The device, the Cyclotrode, has the power to short-circuit all electric current within the radius of its powerful ray.

In his offices at a university Chambers has just successfully demonstrated Cyclotrode's ability to stop an airplane in mid air. Witnessing the demonstration were his secretary Diana Farnsworth, and four of his academic associates—Professors Van Wyck, Anderson, Maxwell and Parker, one of whom, unknown to the others, is the Crimson Ghost.

They're in the conference room while Chambers, in his office, is confronted by Ashe and another of the Ghost's henchmen, Slim, who demand the device. Instead, Chambers smashes it. At that moment Duncan Richards, a physicist-criminologist and associate of Chambers arrives. (He's also in charge of protecting research secrets.) In the fight that follows Ashe escapes, but Slim is captured and brought into the conference room..

Anderson notices a metal band around Slim's neck. When he tries to remove it there's an electrical flash and Slim slumps to the floor, dead. Prof. Chambers confides that he has another Cyclotrode hidden away for safe-keeping. The Crimson Ghost—a hooded, skull-masked figure with skeletal gloves—must have it. He has his men kidnap Chambers, then injects the professor with a drug that reduces the scientist to a zombie-like state. He reveals the Cyclotrode's hiding place and cooperates in the successful attempt to recover it. (Duncan survives an exploding dashboard and jumps clear as his

Clayton Moore and Fred Graham wait for instructions from their boss, the Crimson Ghost, who's going to get what he wants from Kenne Duncan.

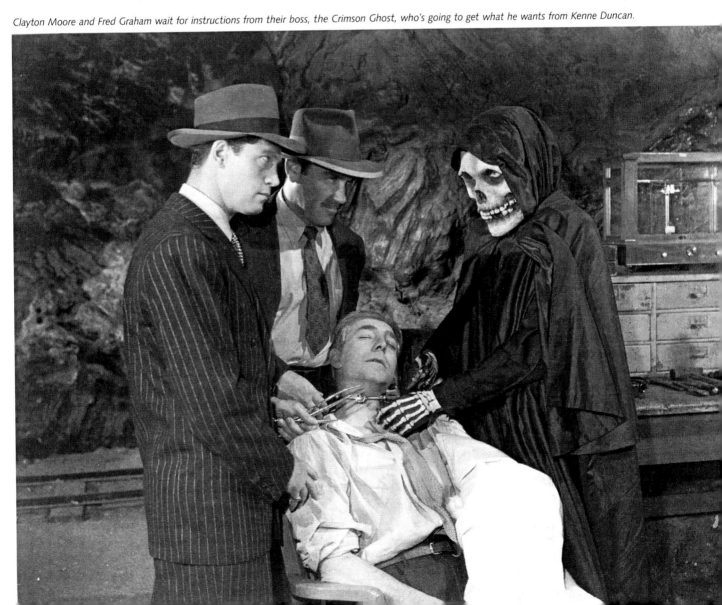

In the Crimson Ghost's secret underground laboratory Fred Graham and Clayton Moore keep their eyes on inventor-captive Kenne Duncan.

car careens into a canyon, as he tries to protect the Cyclotrode.)

In the Ghost's underground workshop, Chambers is forced to wear one of the deadly collars. The Ghost wants him to work on a larger, more powerful Cyclotrode. Although the doctor's mind eventually returns to normal, with the collar around his neck he has little choice except to do what the Ghost orders. He tells the Ghost he needs an X-7 transformer tube, knowing that the tube will have to be stolen from the university and will be a tip off to Duncan. Duncan nearly stops the Ghost's men, Ashe and Milt, from stealing the tube, but they manage to make off with it.

Duncan realizes that the tube is a death-ray component. Using a radium detector, he sets out with Diana to trace Chambers' whereabouts. Meanwhile,

Charles Quigley is startled by a Crimson Ghost loudspeaker as gas seeps into the locked room.

114

the tube is given to Chanbers who quickly installs it. He tells Ashe to get the Ghost, then electrocutes his guard with the death ray and sets a booby trap that he hopes will electrocute Ashe and the Ghost when they step through the door. But it's Duncan who enters and is nearly electrocuted. Chambers recognizes him and jumps in front of the ray, sacrificing himself to save his friend.

With his original plan gone awry, the Crimson Ghost needs a quick infusion of cash to continue his efforts to build the giant Cyclotrode. He uses a working model to execute a successful armored car heist, burning out a patrol car motor along the way. Duncan knows that heavy water is necessary for Cyclotrode development, so he tells the professors that all orders for such water must be authorized by him. A gas-

exuding phonograph record knocks him out and the Ghost's men, Ashe and Fisk, take him to a hotel room where, with some others, they attempt to put a collar on him. He comes to, shoots Fisk, kayos Ashe and runs for it up a flight of stairs and to the roof. He tries to make his way to an adjoining roof by going hand over hand along a wire. Of course the Crimson Ghost emerges just as Duncan is halfway across. Using an acid, the Ghost burns through the wire and Duncan falls toward the ground. Hanging onto the wire he swings to a window and climbs in.

Duncan suspects that someone on the inside is leaking information to the Ghost. He tells the professors he is leaving to pick up a very important message about the Crimson Ghost, and is not surprised when his car is attacked

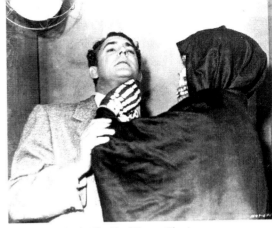

Charles Quigley battles the Crimson Ghost.

on the road, confirming his suspicions.

Next, he and Diana find a dictaphone machine planted in the conference room, talk loudly about placing a bottle of vital heavy water (actually just plain water) in the safe, then surprise Ashe and Prof. Anderson in the act of stealing it. Anderson, who is wearing a collar, is electrocuted when the collar

Below: The Crimson Ghost pays a visit to friendly scientist Rex Bell.

115

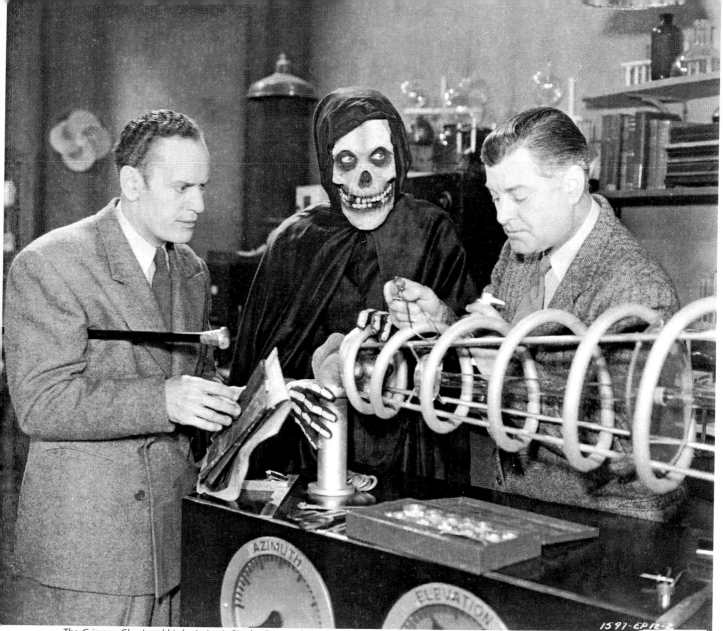

The Crimson Ghost and his brain trust, Stanley Price and Rex Bell, who's puttering with a cyclotrode.

breaks as he struggles. Ashe, with the flask of heavy water, flees with Duncan and Diana in close pursuit. The chase leads to a deserted building where they separate, Duncan finding himself trapped in a room quickly filling with poison gas as the Ghost's maniacal laughter blasts from a skull-shaped wall speaker. Diana rescues him by getting the door open.

Duncan studies the wall speaker and notices a special condenser, which starts him on a tour of radio stores. Pretty much by coincidence he bumps into Ashe (who has come for the still-needed heavy water) in one of the shops, precipitating, in rapid succession, a fist fight, Craig's capture and escape, his pursuit of Ashe to an airfield

where Ashe gives the heavy water to Cole, the pilot of a plane, who starts to take off but is crashed into by Craig's car and is killed in the ensuing explosion. Craig, of course, had leaped from the car.

Diana is captured by Ashe and fitted with a control collar. Helpless, she enables the Ghost to overhear Duncan talking about the isotron, a device that can turn the Cyclotrode back on itself, destroying it. Ashe and Ericson—another accomplice, are sent to Duncan's lab to seize the isotron. Duncan puts up a fight and Ericson is electrocuted when he bumps into one of the electrically-charged dynamos. Diana, obeying the Ghost, tosses a stool at Duncan which seems to knock him

into a dynamo. But it's the stool that triggers the charge, while Duncan remains safe. The Ghost orders Diana to remove her collar, which will kill her instantly. Duncan quickly anesthetizes her while Ashe escapes.

Removing the collar from Diana's neck poses a problem. At a nearby hospital Duncan locates a demagnetization machine which can neutralize the collar, and prepares to remove it. Little does he know that the physician helping him, Dr. Gage, is really Ashe, who waits until the crucial moment before kicking out the machine's plug, causing the collar to blow up in Duncan's face. The collar is already off, and neither Diana nor Duncan is injured. He slugs Ashe, who is turned over to the police.

116

Ashe is allowed to escape, so that his route can be tracked by Diana using a detection device. She radios the route to Duncan, who follows in his car. Ashe leads him to a tunnel laboratory where the Ghost and Zane, another flunky, are processing heavy water. Duncan gets his chance to unmask the Ghost, and he does, only to find it's Ashe behind the mask. The real Crimson Ghost enters and there's a battle. Duncan is left unconscious and the others flee as a broken power cable ignites barrels of fuel and the chamber explodes. Duncan comes to just in time and ducks into an adjoining room seconds before the explosion.

There are more attempts by the Ghost to sabotage Duncan's investigation: when Duncan tries to check the Ghost's fingerprints, he and Diana are gassed, shot at and she has to escape from an out of control truck that crashes through a wall and into the ocean. Another doctor, Fred Cushing, a criminal-psychologist Duncan wants to interview, is replaced by the Ghost's man, Dr. Blackton. Duncan sees through the pretense and Blackton is electrocuted when he tries to remove the control collar he's wearing.

Ashe is sent to the university to steal an isotron model Duncan has developed. He gets the isotron and flees, but Duncan attaches a sponge impregnated with trapper's scent to his car bumper. Using Timmy, a Doberman pinscher to follow the scent, Duncan discovers the Ghost's mansion hideout. In the climactic showdown the Ghost tries to run for it but after a short chase to a wood is caught and pinned down by Timmy. The Ghost's mask is removed and he's revealed to be Professor Parker, who is led away by the police.

Brick Bradford (Columbia-1947) Directed by Spencer Bennet. Screenplay: George H. Plympton, Arthur Hoerl, Lewis Clay. Based on the King Features Syndicate's cartoon strip. Assistant director: R. M. Andrews. Second unit director: Thomas Carr.

Photography: Ira H. Morgan. Music: Mischa Bakaleinikoff. Editor: Earl Turner. Producer: Sam Katzman.
Cast:
Brick Bradford . . . . Kane Richmond
Sandy Sanderson . . . . Rick Vallin
June Salisbury . . . . . . Linda Johnson
Prof. Salisbury . . . . Pierre Watkin
Laydron . . . . Charles Quigley
Albers . . . . Jack Ingram
Black . . . . Fred Graham
Dr. Tymak . . . . John Merton
Eric Byrus . . . . Leonard Penn
Louis Walthar . . . . . Wheeler Oakman

Queen Khana . . . . . . Carol Forman
Creed . . . . Charles King
Dent . . . . John Hart
Carol Preston . . . . Helene Stanley
Prescott . . . . Nelson Leigh
Zuntar . . . . Robert Barron
Meaker . . . . George de Normand
Lulah . . . . Noel Neil
Stevens . . . . Stanley Blystone
Axel . . . . Gene Roth
Rork . . . . Frank Ellis
15 Chapters:
1. Atomic Defense   2. Flight to the Moon   3. Prisoners of the Moon

Intrepid explorer-scientist Kane Richmond.

117

Pierre Watkin and Linda Johnson face the deadly death ray. Charles Quigley (right) points to the timing device as cronies Fred Graham and Jack Ingram observe their boss.

Brick Bradford, the famous adventurer-scientist, receives an urgent visit from Dr. Clarkson, a United Nations representative. Brick introduces him to his long-time friends, Sandy Sanderson, geologist-Professor Salisbury and the professor's daughter June. Clarkson insists on a private conversation with Brick, in the doctor's car, outside. There, he tells Brick that his mission "involves the peace of the world."

Three thugs sneak up on the car and try to overhear what's said.

Clarkson tells Brick of the "interceptor ray" invented by Dr. Tymak, and its enormous potential. Brick suddenly spots one of the thugs and a fight starts, and ends when the interlopers flee in a car. Brick is now convinced of the seriousness of Clarkson's visit. They decide that continuing the conversation inside the house might be safer.

Clarkson tells the group that in a laboratory "located in a remote spot just west of here, Dr. Tymak is perfecting a great weapon for peace." It's a device that can intercept missiles and destroy them before they can reach their target. Unfortunately, this great boon for peace has a drawback: slight modification can change it into "the most devastating weapon of war the world has ever seen." But other forces, who sent the thugs, are after the ray. The UN wants

Brick to find and protect Tymak and help him complete the ray. Brick is happy to do his bit for world peace, and his friends sign-up too. They pile into a station wagon and head for the remote west, where they set up camp. The rest of the journey has to be made on foot. Tymak's lodge is "on the other side of those hills."

Meanwhile, in his lodge, Dr. Tymak is complaining to his two associates, Louis Walthar and Eric Byrus. Work on the ray is proceeding nicely but he's in dire need of Lunarium: the small amount he'd gotten from a meteorite is almost exhausted. "The only other source of supply is on the moon." Fortunately, this is not as big a problem as it seems. He draws a curtain and reveals a glistening "crystal door," a means of "travel into both space and

118

time," which he's perfected, "the entrance to the fifth dimension." It is Tymak's "gateway to the moon. To the far side, which no one has ever seen before."

In a cabin presumably not too far from Tymak's, crime-boss Laydron greets his returning thugs, one of whom says he has "the layout to Tymak's place" and reports that although there are no guards "there's an invisible electric current that surrounds the lab. Touch that and that's all brother." He mentions that Brick Bradford and friends have set up a camp nearby "Bradford can ruin everything," Laydron decides, and assigns two men to get rid of him.

Brick is showing June how to clean pots when one is shot from his hands by Laydron's men, firing rifles from the surrounding hills. Everyone ducks for cover and the attackers are driven off by Brick and Sandy. In Tymak's lodge, Walthar enters—from a wall bookcase that swings open—and reports that "the Lunarium count is less than ten milligrams." Tymak says he'll have to go to the moon soon. Laydron and his men, meanwhile, are sneaking up on the lodge. One of them deliberately sets off the electric fence. When it's turned off momentarily, they all rush through and as Walthar, carrying a rifle, comes to investigate, he's captured.

Laydron confronts Dr. Tymak and

says he wants the interceptor ray plans. Walthar suddenly makes a break for it, causing a commotion. Tymak ducks through the swinging bookcase and shuts it. He dashes into the crystal door. By the time Laydron and his men restrain Walthar and figure out how to open the bookcase, they find Tymak behind the door, in a black limbo. "Follow me to the moon," he laughs as he vanishes, traveling through time and space. "It's just a trick way of getting out of here," Laydron tells Meeker, one of his men, as they search the lodge.

Dr. Tymak exits a large silver pod on the moon, a barren, rocky place. He yells for help. but hears only his echo. He wanders about and is eventually

Linda Johnson and Kane Richmond (foreground) chat while (from left) Pierre Watkin, Leonard Penn, Rick Vallin and Wheeler Oakman stand by.

119

spotted by a Lunarian patrol led by Axel. Tymak's attempts to communicate result in him being zapped unconscious by a ray gun and being brought to the Lunarian palace where he meets Queen Khana and her adviser, Zuntar. They don't believe his claim that he came from Earth. "The man is mocking us," the queen declares. Tymak asks how they came to speak English, but receives no reply. He's tossed into a dungeon. Zuntar says it's possible he did come from Earth, "although no one else has for the past fifty years."

Laydron is still in Tymak's lodge, going over Tymak's papers and checking out the equipment. Told that Brick and Sandy were approaching, he comes up with a bold plan. "I'm going to be Dr. Tymak," he says, and introduces himself as such when Brick and Sandy arrive. Tymak seems younger than expected, which puts Brick on his guard. The erstwhile doctor takes them behind the bookcase, shows them around his lab and says he'll demonstrate one of his rays. He asks them "to step against the wall, out of danger." He turns on the machine, directing it at a section of wall which rapidly disintegrates, then aims it at Brick and Sandy. When they duck under a desk and escape harm, he claims the machine got out of control. Still skeptical, Brick accepts the excuse.

On the moon, Tymak is again brought before Queen Khana and Zuntar and learns he's been sentenced to death. They're sure he's one of "the learneds," a banished group of exiles who have formed a resistance movement. Tymak is shown the fate that awaits him; an air-tight chamber which releases a gas that will freeze him solid forever. There's a sudden report from the prisoner's examiner. Tymak's effects prove indisputably that he is indeed from Earth. The queen orders him released. He tells her how he got to the moon. She orders him held under guard.

Back on Earth, Laydron, still masquerading as Tymak, is providing a very convincing tour of the lodge laboratory for Brick and Prof. Salisbury. He seems totally familiar with all the equipment. Still, Brick is troubled. When Laydron

Kane Richmond (right) cautions his party, including Pierre Watkin (3rd from right) and some Lunarian troops.

120

Gene Roth (left) and Kane Richmond watch as Pierre Watkin tells his story to queen Carol Forman and her adviser Robert Barron. Inventor-genius John Merton (right) listens interestedly.

temporarily leaves to gather some materials, Brick asks the doctor what he thinks. "Would you say he's seventy years old?" Salisbury asks. "He couldn't be," Brick answers—Laydron appears to be in his early forties. Salisbury says that when he'd first heard about him, Tymak was fifty years old—and that was twenty years ago.

They decide to play along with the imitation until they can determine just who the faker is. During all this time, Tymak's assistants, Walthar and Byrus are being held prisoner by the gang. They're tortured constantly by Creeder, who's trying to get them to tell where Tymak is. He doesn't believe their "to the moon" answer. While investigating a cabin and after a fist fight with guards, Sandy and Brick stumble onto Walthar and Byrus, who tell them what happened and where Tymak is, despite Brick's disbelief.

Laydron figures out that Brick knows, and he and his gang clear out before they can be captured. But before they leave they tie Prof. Salisbury and June to chairs, facing a death ray that's set to go off in ten minutes. Brick, Sandy and the two scientists arrive in time to turn the machine off "with seconds to spare," as Brick reassuringly tells June.

Walthar and Byrus show Brick the crystal door and explain how it works. "With the proper controls you can be transported anywhere—if there is a corresponding door on the other end." And there is one on the moon, "propelled there by a guided space ship." Brick still finds it hard to believe. Prof. Salisbury says he'd like to go to through the crystal door and join Tymak. "So would I," says Brick. June and Sandy want to go, too, but Brick wants them to stay and guard the laboratory.

Walthar works the controls and soon Brick and Salisbury are traveling through time and space. They emerge on the moon, are quickly trapped by Lunarian guards and nearly burned to death. They're saved only when Queen Khana—encouraged by Tymak—orders them spared. Zuntar is certain that they, too, are exiles, and wants them dead, but Khana overrules him. The new guests are relegated to "the dungeon," where they meet another prisoner, Carol Preston, one of the exiles, who she describes as "a democratic faction forced by the dictator, Zuntar, to live in the wasteland".

Tymak finds them and the four

121

Kane Richmond points the way to Linda Johnson as they step out of the Time Top

escape. They head for the wasteland, where they meet Carol's father, Edward Preston, who explains that many years ago he and a few other Earth scientists discovered a way to reach the moon, where they established advanced methods of agriculture and production, creating a utopian civilization. But one member, Zuntar, wanted it all for himself, gathered the "worst elements and by treachery and stealth they trapped the rest of us who believe in the democratic way." Queen Khana is simply his puppet. Brick, Salisbury and Tymak pledge to help the exiles, who provide the location of the much-desired Lunarium.

June and Sandy convince Walthar to send them to the moon, confident that he and Byrus can hold the fort back home. They no sooner land than they're taken prisoner by Zuntar—which requires a rescue by Brick—while on Earth Laydron and his men invade the lodge and demand to know where Brick, Salisbury and the others are. A weary "here we go again" expression crosses Walthar's face as he answers "the moon." And indeed, Laydron's man Albers is about to pummel him when Laydron decides maybe he's telling the truth. He and Albers go through the crystal door (Creeder and a few others are left behind to keep an eye on things) and they are soon negotiating with Zuntar, striking a deal to provide him with weapons that can wipe out the exiles.

The weapons are used and Zuntar's forces are demolished. When they see the tide turning, Laydron and Albers quickly return to Earth. With the situation seemingly well in hand, Brick, Tymak, Sandy and the Salisburys go through the crystal door and head back home. When they materialize in the lodge, they're confronted by Laydron and his men. There's a spirited battle, which winds up with Tymak held pris-

Kane Richmond helps while John Merton blasts away with his Interceptor Ray gun.

oner by the fleeing criminals.

Searching Tymak's papers, Brick comes across a strange radio-like device that can be strapped to the wearer's chest. It harnesses "Z rays" and results in the wearer becoming invisible—a handy gizmo that Brick uses to rescue Tymak and at various other times throughout the remaining action.

Tymak discovers that to continue his work he needs a formula developed by an eighteenth-century Englishman and hidden in Central America. (That he even knows of this formula is testament to his brilliance.) Fortunately, Brick and Sandy are able to hop into the Time Top, another of Tymak's inventions, a top-shaped craft that can travel back and forth in time. To obtain the formula the two adventurers go back to

Central America in the the 1700s, where they encounter hostile natives, the beautiful-but-untrustworthy sarong-clad Lulah, and bandit buccaneers (who become allies and who help find the treasure chest and are amazed and delighted when Brick only wants a piece of paper and leaves all the fabulous jewels for them). Brick and Sandy return safely back to their time, where Laydron continues to harass them.

During their many adventures Brick and friends are threatened by sulphuric acid, nearly burned at the stake and narrowly escape explosions, falls, gassings and freezing to death. Byrus decides he'd like to free-lance and makes a deal with Laydron, promising to show Laydron how to use the devices he's been stealing. (The deal doesn't

work: neither Laydron nor Byrus can trust each other.) Laydron keeps trying to steal the never-ending stream of parts and fuels for the Interceptor Ray. When one such part, the activator, is used as a lure by Brick, Laydron is finally trapped. He flees and after a life-or-death battle with Brick, is knocked down a mountain to his doom.

Brick now turns his attention to matters more pressing, like using the Z-Ray kit to make himself and June invisible so they can have a few private moments together.

123

Jack Armstrong
(Columbia-1947) Directed by Wallace Fox. Story treatment: George H. Plympton. Screenplay: Arthur Hoerl, Lewis Clay, Royal Cole, Leslie Swabacher. Adapted from the radio feature "Jack Armstrong, the All-American Boy." Assistant directors: Mike Eason, Leonard Shapiro. Associate producer: Mel DeLay. Photography: Ira Morgan. Special effects: Ray Mercer. Music: Lee Zahler. Editor: Earl Turner. Art director: Paul Palmentola. Producer: Sam Katzman.

Cast:

Jack Armstrong . . . . John Hart
Betty . . . . Rosemary La Planche
Princess Alura . . . . Claire James
Billy . . . . Joe Brown
Jim Fairfield . . . . Pierre Watkin
Jason Grood . . . . Charles Middleton
Prof. Zorn . . . . Wheeler Oakman
Blair . . . . Jack Ingram
Slade . . . . Eddie Parker
Vic Hardy . . . . Hugh Prosser
Gregory Pierce . . . . John Merton
Naga . . . . Frank Marlo
Umala . . . . Russ Vincent
Jacklin . . . . Terry Frost
Dr. Albour . . . . Robert Barron
Marlin . . . . Stanley Blystone
Lessups . . . . Lane Bradford
Bovard/Lobard . . . . Frank Ellis

15 Chapters:

1. Mystery of the Cosmic Ray   2. The Far World   3. Island of Deception   4. Into the Chasm   5. The Space Ship   6. Tunnels of Treachery   7. Cavern of Chance   8. The Secret Room   9. Human Targets   10. Battle of the Warriors   11. Cosmic Annihilator   12. The Grotto of Greed   13. Wheels of Fate   14. Journey into Space   15. Retribution

Reassuringly, the serial starts with the familiar radio voiceover, "Jack Armstrong. Jack Armstrong. Jack Armstrong. The all-American boy." Sadly, the old "Hudson High" theme song is gone.

In the yard of the Fairfield Aviation Company, Jack Armstrong and his buddy Billy are tinkering with the engine of a streamlined futuristic automobile, "fifty miles an hour faster than any other car." Billy's sister, Betty, joins them. Jack gets to show off the car's speed when outside the company

RADIO'S ALL-AMERICAN BOY IN AN ALL-THRILL, ALL-TIME HIGH IN SERIAL ADVENTURE!

BLASTING A MADMAN BENT ON WORLD DESTRUCTION!

JACK ARMSTRONG
THE ALL-AMERICAN BOY
Adapted from the radio feature

with
JOHN HART as Jack   ROSEMARY LaPLANCHE as Betty   JOE BROWN as Billy
PIERRE WATKIN as Uncle Jim
Screenplay by Arthur Hoerl, Lewis Clay, Royal Cole and Leslie Swabacker
Directed by WALLACE FOX   Produced by SAM KATZMAN
A COLUMBIA SERIAL

gate a blind man trying to cross the street is knocked down by a speeding car whose driver notices, but doesn't bother to stop. Jack and Billy hop into their car, catch up to the hit-and-runner, force him to stop, and have him beaten into submission by the time the police arrive.

At the Fairfield plant, founder and president Jim Fairfield tells his gatemen to keep a close watch on a crate of valuable equipment that's to be picked up for Gregory Pierce. Jack and Bill return and Jim invites them, along with Betty, to see "something new on atomic power for planes." As they enter the plant a truck from the "Pierce Exporting Company" pulls up. The drivers are led to the crate.

Jim takes Jack, Billy and Betty into a laboratory and explains that while the atomic-powered plane hasn't been developed yet, "the experts all agree it's a definite possibility." One of the company's scientists, Vic Hardy, has spent weeks on research and has prepared a

Right: Rosemarie LaPlanche, John Hart (third from left), Pierre Watkin (seated) and Joe Brown (right) are interested in dark-suited John Merton's order for advanced research devices.

Below: Prodded by spears, John Hart and Rosemarie LaPlanche are encouraged to walk the plank—into the chasm and to certain death.

TRAPPED IN THE GROTTO OF DEATH!

INTO THE CHASM

CHAPTER 4
JACK ARMSTRONG
The All-American Boy

Adapted from the radio feature

JOHN HART as Jack · ROSEMARY LaPLANCHE as Betty
JOE BROWN as Billy · PIERRE WATKIN as Uncle Jim
Screenplay by Arthur Hoerl, Lewis Clay, Royal Cole
and Leslie Swabacker
Directed by WALLACE FOX · Produced by SAM KATZMAN
A COLUMBIA SERIAL

comprehensive report. They're interrupted by a knock on the door. It's Gregory Pierce, who has the specifications for a new piece of equipment he wants Fairfield to build for him. Jim introduces him to his nephew and niece, and "a very special friend of the family," Jack. (We know instantly Pierce is a bad guy because he smokes.) Vic Hardy enters from an adjoining room. He tells Jim that "those strange radiations are coming in again—I think you'd better have a look."

Jim tells Pierce this is a special matter that can't include outsiders— "I'm sure you'll understand." Pierce understands completely, and excuses himself as the others go into the back room, except for Jack, who lingers to make sure Pierce leaves and closes the door behind him. But Pierce has noticed Jack's scrutiny, and has slipped a matchbook between the doorlock and jamb. He reenters and eavesdrops at the door to the back room.

Vic shows the group the radiation clearly indicated on a video screen. He tells them it's "an emanation of deadly cosmic rays" and that he believes they're controlled by humans. If they can track the source of the rays, which may have travelled half-way around the world, they'll solve the problem. Jack suggests calling the government, but Jim says there's no point in raising false fears without proof, and Vic agrees.

Pierce sneaks away to his car and drives to a warehouse-type building where, after giving a secret knock, he meets with four tough-looking characters, two of whom, Blair and Slade, were the delivery-truck drivers. He tells them Hardy must be stopped before he learns too much, but wants him captured alive—his scientific knowledge might prove valuable.

Blair and Slade appear at the Fairfield gate. Allowed in, they knock out the guard and head for the lab, barging in on Vic as he's talking on the phone with Jim. They knock Vic out and carry him to their truck. Jim tells Jack, Billy and Betty of his abrupt conversation with Vic. They rush to the lab and find it empty. Searching the room, Jack finds the match book, which had fallen to the floor. It's from the Remo Restaurant. Jack guesses it's unlikely that one of Fairfield's customers would patronize a waterfront dive like the Remo, but that kidnappers might. "Let's get going," Betty suggests.

They spot the delivery truck in front of the Remo, and recognize the drivers as the ones who picked up the crate. Billy gets a terrific idea: he'll jump into the back of the truck while Jack and Betty follow it, hopefully to where Vic is being held prisoner. Jack thinks that's a swell idea. Before you know it Billy's in the truck, which takes off with Jack and Betty following. But all this has been observed by a supposed food peddler, who sends a telegraph message from a transmitter in his van. The message is received by Blair and Slade, who pull off the road, go around to the back and order Billy to come on out. He does—swinging, and is doing just fine, when Jack arrives and assists him in pummeling Blair while Slade gets away in the truck. Blair is taken to the Fairfield Aviation building and tied to a chair in a room, then left alone as the others go to call the police.

Blair manages to untie his bonds, slip out of the building and into the street. Which is just what Jim and Jack wanted him to do. Now they can follow him to his hideout. Blair hops into the back of a passing truck. Jack, Jim and Billy, in an auto, follow him. As the truck passes through a certain neighborhood, Blair jumps off and walks into an alley and around a corner. Jack has seen all, pulls up in front of the alley and the three men start to look around. Blair opens a door and closes it behind him. Jim is searching the area when Blair pops out, knocks him unconscious hides him behind a crate and takes off.

Jack and Billy wonder where Jim is. They see a door and decide to investigate. Inside, Blair and three tough guys, playing cards, hear Jack and Bobby approaching. They hide as the two enter—and see Vic Hardy tied up in a corner of the room. Blair and the others reveal themselves and a battle starts. As Jack and Billy take on the four thugs, a wild shot hits a vat of fuel, which starts to leak prodigiously. As

1000 MILES ALOFT!

THE SPACE SHIP

CHAPTER 5
JACK ARMSTRONG
The All-American Boy

Adapted from the radio feature

JOHN HART as Jack · ROSEMARY LaPLANCHE as Betty
JOE BROWN as Billy · PIERRE WATKIN as Uncle Jim
Screenplay by Arthur Hoerl, Lewis Clay, Royal Cole
and Leslie Swabacker
Directed by WALLACE FOX
Produced by SAM KATZMAN
A COLUMBIA SERIAL

the fisticuffs continue a lantern is knocked to the floor, which bursts into flames. Jack and Billy are knocked out and left lying on the floor as the thugs grab Vic and exit in a hurry, locking the door behind them.

Jack and Billy regain consciousness but, try as they might, they can't open the door. They're banging on it desperately when the flames reach the fuel tank and there's an explosion. Fortunately, to say the least, the blast blows the door from its hinges and both men are hurled into the street, bruised but not injured.

With Vic a captive, Jim decides the best way to locate him is by finding out where those radioactive impulses were coming from. There's a knock on the door. It's an angry Gregory Pierce, who wants to know why his equipment was

never delivered. Jim is surprised—the shipment had been picked up by a delivery service. Jack surmises that the drivers were phonies who had come primarily to get a line on Vic. They explain the whole situation to Pierce, including their plan to triangulate on the impulses. Billy and Betty are sent to the airport to round up a plane with enough space on board for all their equipment. Pierce volunteers to help in any way, then leaves.

Vic Hardy is brought by seaplane to a tropical island, blindfolded and led by Blair through rock canyons to a cave, past a sliding rock door to a passageway, through another sliding rock door and into a laboratory, where he meets, among others, Professor Zorn. A voice from a hidden speaker addresses Vic. It's "the Ruler," who welcomes

Vic to his domain and tells him he's been selected to assist "one of the world's foremost scientists, Professor Hogarth Zorn," who is perfecting a "cosmic beam annihilator." Vic's knowledge can be a big help.

Vic is given a choice: cooperate or die. He decides to cooperate, begrudgingly. Zorn says that with Vic's help they'll be able to "destroy cities, entire nations." Escape, he warns, is not possible. They're on a volcanic island far from the nearest mainland.

At that very moment, Jim Fairfield is telling Jack, Betty and Billy that the emanations come from an island thousands of miles away. They obtain a plane and despite and because of Pierce's machinations, crash land on the island. They're unhurt, and spotting a trail, follow it. They're observed by the

Below: Captive scientist Hugh Prosser (left) watches helplessly as his friends John Hart and Pierre Watkin are covered by the Ruler's thugs.

Aboard the Aereodrone John Hart tries to abort the mission but is spotted by a technician.

island's natives, who are garbed in plaid skirts and linen blouses.

Further up the trail is the "Island Trading Post, Jason Grood proprietor," where a native tells Grood about the strangers who are under attack by his tribe. Blair is sent out to 'rescue' the strangers and bring them back for questioning, which is what he does, pretending to be an island-visiting good samaritan. At the post they're introduced to Grood, who welcomes them as guests and tells them that aside from visitors he's the only white man on the island. The only contact with the rest of the world is a tramp steamer that visits every three months. Jack and the others retire to their rooms in the Post.

Vic, meanwhile, is told by Zorn that he's been allowed to witness a test

of the Aereodrone, which will act as a space platform for the cosmic annihilator. Zorn elaborates: "By means of rock impulses and gravity control, the Aereodrone will take off from this island. It will proceed to a point in space where the gravity of the sun and that of the Earth neutralize each other. At this great height our electro annihilator can be aimed at any spot on Earth, ready to destroy every country which refuses to obey our ruler." So, from ground level, Vic watches the Aereodrone, which looks like a stubby missile, blast into the atmosphere, immediately causing the natives to fall to their knees in prayer.

A native is stabbed, using "a white man's knife," and Jack is blamed. The shapely, aptly-named Alura (clad in a

two-piece sarong ensemble with vest), tells them that according to native tradition Jack and Betty must go to the Sacred Grotto where the god Exalta will decide if they're innocent. "I don't like this," Jim says to Grood, who advises that it's best to play along with the natives.

At the grotto, after a native woman does a seductive, no doubt sacred dance, the voice of Exalta (which is Grood, at the post, speaking into a microphone) declares that "blood must be washed out in blood," and that "the white people be taken to the pit of ever-lasting fire and hurled into its depths." Jack puts up a fight, which gives Jim and Billy the chance to escape, but Jack and Betty are taken to the pit and dropped in. The "everlasting fire," however, is actually controlled by one of the Ruler's men who is suddenly knocked out by Umala, a native, who shuts the flame machine off and crawls into a small cave hole, emerging in the pit where Jack and Betty are wondering where the flames went. He tells them there's no time to explain and, with them in tow, returns to the outer world.

Alura becomes an ally, threatening her own position with her natives, who are constantly fed lies by Naga, a treacherous tribesman. At various times Jack and Alura are tied to stakes while knives are tossed at them (Uncle Jim and Billy come to the rescue.)

Pierce has come to the island and learns that he's slated for removal by Grood, who feels he's no longer useful. Pierce convinces Marlin, Robards and Slade that Grood will double cross them too, when the time is ripe. He offers them an equal partnership in his scheme to capture the beam gun and "take over the whole works, including Grood." They like the deal and join forces with Pierce.

The prized weapon is used by Grood to ward off an attack, but although it allegedly discharges "the heat of the sun," all it does is set the grass on fire, causing Jack and the natives to temporarily retreat. The beam gun is captured by Jack and Billy, then taken by Pierce and his crew. Not that it matters—Uncle Jim has the "activator tube" without which the weapon is useless. Jim also figures out that Pierce is an enemy and that Grood is the mastermind behind him.

There are gun fights, car chases, fistfights, explosions and near misses by various death rays. Pierce meets a horrible death when he steps into a booby-trapped area and is electrocuted. A speeding, driverless truck carrying a smoking box of explosives is abandoned by Jack, Blair and others. It rolls down a mountainside but eventually comes to an ignominious stop (an actual explosion being beyond the limits of a Katzman budget).

The cosmic beam annihilator is reclaimed by Grood and prepared for use. Now that it's ready, he tells Zorn, "we'll be masters of the world within twenty-four hours " Vic Hardy, still a captive, listens to these plans with dismay. Once the beam has proved its effectiveness, Grood will radio his ultimatum to the world: "'Surrender or be destroyed.' We'll have such power as the Earth has never known."

The annihilator beam must be fired from the Aereodrone far up in the stratosphere. Grood and Zorn hurry off to prepare the rocket ship. Vic seizes the opportunity, writes a warning message and gives it to a native for delivery to Jim. As soon as they read it, Jim, Jack and Billy and the now-friendly tribe rush off to the cave laboratory.

Vic has been chosen to accompany Zorn and two assistants on the Aereodrone, and dons a hooded uniform for the occasion. As the four men walk through the caves to the launching chamber, Jack spots them and flattens a straggler—who happens to be Vic. Jack tries to revive him, but he's out cold. Jack gets into his outfit and joins the others aboard the rocket ship. They blast off.

Grood is ecstatic and totally delusional. "The world will bow to me in submission," he crows. When a lackey rushes in and tells him the caves are surrounded by hostile natives, he airily says he'll "fly an army to the island and exterminate them." "How can you do that?" asks the straight-man lackey. "Because I am the absolute ruler of the

universe," Grood replies.

As the rocket ship passes through the stratosphere, Grood's men find Vic, just regaining consciousness in the cave. Grood immediately contacts the Aereodrone and tells Zorn that Hardy is still on Earth. There's a fight, during which Jack shuts off as many systems as possible, causing the Aereodrone to reverse its course and move back toward Earth. As the men battle, the cosmic beam annihilator is set off, but even after knocking out his three opponents Jack is unable to shut it off. He puts on a parachute and bails out.

Grood hears the Aereodrone explode (the explosion happens off screen—the Katzman touch, again) and plans his escape with Blair. But Vic, who has been sitting quietly at his desk during all and sundry, now springs into action. He waves a gun and forces Grood, Blair and Jacklin (one of the gang) to put their guns on the table. Then he produces confessions he's prepared and has his captives sign them.

Meanwhile, Jack is still floating toward Earth. As fate would have it, he is spotted by Uncle Jim and Billy, who are right there when he lands. They all

head for Grood's cave laboratory. And a good thing, too, because Vic has been disarmed and is slugging it out with his three opponents when they arrive. It's three against three as they join the battle, but in the end Grood, Blair and Jacklin get away—with Jack, Uncle Jim and Billy in hot pursuit. Jacklin dies in the effort. It is at this auspicious moment that Grood decides he no longer needs Blair, and shoots his astonished partner down in cold blood.

Grood, in his white suit, has to run for it: the natives, as well as Jack, are on his trail. Jack catches up with him and there's an extensive fist fight, with middle-aged Grood more than holding his own. In fact he knocks Jack cold with a hard right. He races away, then looks back at the groggy Jack. Grood produces a hand grenade, pulls the pin and gets set to throw it at Jack. Uncle Jim has raced to the scene and sees all. He aims his pistol, shoots Grood in the hand, causing the grenade to fall and explode at the evil one's feet. Jason Grood is no more.

Later, Vic reveals he has been on a "confidential mission." He represents "a great organization that desires only

That's Charles Middleton, with the gun and white suit, to the left of the big "R."

129

world peace. They are on guard constantly against power-crazed individuals who attempt to overthrow constitutional governments by force." Uh huh. He tells Alura that beneath the Sacred Grotto is an invaluable deposit of pitchblende, from which radium and uranium can be derived. "You and your people will benefit from this natural wealth," he assures her, but warns her to guard it against "those who would use it for destructive power." Breathlessly, Alura, in the name of her people, promises. The whistle of the tramp steamer signals the departure of Jack, Jim, Vic, Betty and Billy, who is looking forward to a home-cooked meal.

King of the Rocket Men

(Republic-1949) Directed by Fred C. Brannon. Writers: Royal Cole, William Lively, Sol Shor. Photography: Ellis W. Carter. Music: Stanley Wilson. Editors: Cliff Bell, Sam Starr. Special effects: Howard Lydecker, Theodore Lydecker. Art director: Fred Ritter. Set decorations: John McCarthy, Jr., James Redd. Sound: Earl Crain, Sr. Unit manager: Roy Wade. Associate producer: Franklin Adreon. [6-8-49] Feature title: *Lost Planet Airmen*.

Cast:

Jeff King . . . . Tristram Coffin
Glenda Thomas . . . . Mae Clark
Tony Dirken . . . . Don Haggerty
Burt Winslow . . . . . . House Peters, Jr.
Prof. Millard . . . . James Craven
Chairman . . . . Douglas Evans
Martin Conway . . . . Ted Adams
Prof. Bryant . . . . I. Stanford Jolley
Gunther von Strum . . . . Stanley Price
Martin . . . . Dale Van Sickel
Knox (and others) . . . . Tom Steele
Blears (and others) . . . . . David Sharpe
Dr. Graffner . . . . . . Marshall Bradford
Rowan . . . . Eddie Parker
Turk . . . . Michael Ferro
Phillips . . . . Buddy Roosevelt
Clay . . . . Bud Wolfe
Sparks . . . . Carey Loftin
Walter . . . . Jack O'Shea

Morgan . . . . Burt LeBaron

12 Chapters:

1. Dr. Vulcan—Traitor   2. Plunging Death   3. Dangerous Evidence 4. High Peril   5. Fatal Dive 6. Mystery of the Rocket Man 7. Molten Menace   8. Suicide Flight 9. Ten Seconds to Live   10. The Deadly Fog   11. Secret of Dr. Vulcan   12. Wave of Disaster

Through a series of contrived "accidents," diabolical Doctor Vulcan causes the deaths of professors Kenyon, Bennett, Drake and (he thinks) Millard of Science Associates, a privately-operated desert research project in Oasis,

Faster than light!
And they hit the moon! 12 thrilling chapters about the most fascinating men who ever lived!

KING OF THE ROCKET MEN

A RE-RELEASE

featuring
TRISTRAM COFFIN · MAE CLARKE
DON HAGGERTY · HOUSE PETERS, JR.
I. STANFORD JOLLEY
A REPUBLIC SERIAL IN 12 CHAPTERS

The Rocket Man intercepts a hijacking.

New Mexico. The professors, being honest, were a threat to his eventual control of the project, which he maintains as one of the respected members of the company.

The accidents attract the attention of Glenda Thomas, a reporter for Science Data magazine. She visits the project to interview publicity director Burt Winslow, who introduces her to Jeffrey King, a young propulsion expert. She also meets the other project members, professors Conway (an atomic expert), Von Strum (nuclear fission), Bryant (a metallurgist), and Dr. Graffner ("an aeronautical wizard"). At a meeting, the group appoints Jeff to investigate the strange accidents and Millard's oft-stated opinion that one of their members was the mysterious Dr. Vulcan who has been causing their

Right: Mae Clarke and the Rocket Man.

problems.

Later, making certain he's not being followed, Jeff visits a remote cave wherein he's been hiding Prof. Millard, whose life he has saved. Jeff knows that the only hope Millard has of staying alive is if Vulcan thinks he's dead, and so he's set the professor up in a cave laboratory where he can continue his important work. The professor shows him the just-completed rocket-propelled flying suit, which he and Jeff have perfected. The leather suit is equipped with an atomic-powered jet-propulsion backpack and a chest-mounted control unit. Jeff tells Millard he'll be glad to try it out. But first he has to escort the shipment of a prototype rocket to the proving grounds.

During this assigment Jeff and a guard are attacked by Dirken, Blears and Knox, three of Vulcan's henchmen, who make off with the truck carrying the missile. Jeff dons the atomic-powered suit, takes to the air—as Glenda and Burt arrive in time to take pictures—catches up with the truck, jumps into the back and beats the tar out of Blears and Dirken (while Knox drives, at first oblivious to what's going on), but in the process Dirken is knocked against the actuating lever and the rocket is launched into space. Rocket Man has to take to the air in pursuit, and manages to blast the rocket with his sonic pistol before it can slam into a populated area. But Blears, Dirken and Knox get away.

It's with considerable regret that Glenda agrees not to report the "Rocket Man" story, in the name of national security, but is gratified when Jeff tells her she can help him track down Vulcan. What a story that will make! We will see Vulcan many times, but only in silhouette, as he radios messages to his men, usually Dirken, who does most of the dirty work. And what a henchman Dirken is. Anything Vulcan requests, no matter how dangerous and implausible, is eagerly pursued without a word of complaint.

After a number of his plans have been foiled, Dr. Vulcan guesses that Jeff is the Rocket Man and arranges to have him kidnapped. As Jeff is preparing to transport a new detection device called the Sonutron he's captured by Dirken and a henchman. The capture is interrupted by the arrival of Rocket Man, who flies in guns blazing. Totally confused, Dirken flees. Jeff returns to the cave with his rescuer, Prof. Millard, to

House Peters, Jr., Mae Clarke (both seated) and James Craven (in lab coat) are the prisoners of Dr. Vulcan's goons: Dave Sharpe (left), Don Haggerty, and Tom Steele (right)

It's into the air for the nuclear-fueled Rocket Man.

whom he had managed to send a radio message and who had donned the flying suit for the occasion.

Along the way Millard has also developed a device he calls the Decimator, capable of liquifying rock strata. We watch a small demonstration of its power: a mini-model is able to melt manganese steel. Dirken succeeds in stealing it for Vulcan and at one point Rocket Man, Millard, Glenda and Burt are trapped in a tunnel as the full-scale Decimator, which has jammed, starts to melt a mountain, causing a wave of molten rock to rush toward them. Fortunately, there's another cave they run into and, miraculously, the lava doesn't follow.

Although the Decimator is destroyed in the meltdown, there are enough must-have items to keep Vulcan's men busy as Millard works to rebuild the Decimator while Vulcan and his cronies repeatedly try to steal it. Dr. Von Strum is shot down in cold blood

by one of Vulcan's enforcers and there are attempts to steal the flying suit or the components that make flight possible, like rockets, as well as vitally-needed supplies and new inventions, such as special "Micro-Film 247," ultrasonic firing tubes, a "direction finder," an aerial torpedo, "X-20 relay tubes"—stuff like that. Rocket Man has to survive explosions, car, truck and plane crashes, gas, booby traps, incineration and the like.

Using a detection device Dirken tracks the Decimator to the cave lab, and with Martin easily outwits Jeff and Burt, who leave the cave unguarded while they chase Clay, a decoy. Dirken and Martin get away with the decimator. Vulcan is delighted, but Jeff is still a thorn in his side—and must be gotten rid of.

Jeff is lured into a remote-controlled taxi whose driver leaps out as the cab suddenly fills up with poison gas. The doors are locked and Jeff faces

certain death. On the other side of the road, Burt and Glenda pass the taxi, notice Jeff's plight. and speed after him. Burt leaps onto the cab, opens the door (although we don't see how this is accomplished) and stops the car. Jeff has recognized the gas odor: it's fuminol, a jet propellant which is also a deadly gas. Jeff determines if they can trace an order for fuminol, it will lead to Dr. Vulcan. Vulcan, through one of his extensive video cameras, sees and hears all this.

When Jeff and Burt go to check the invoices, they're met by Dirken and a crony. There's a fight, but when it's over the two thugs get away with the incriminating purchase order, and with Burt as well. Jeff gets a call from Dr. Vulcan. Burt will be freed if Jeff shows up at a certain address. It's obviously a trap, but Jeff figures he'll trick the criminals by getting there early as Rocket Man. He flies to the office building and enters the designated suite through a

Bad guy Dale Van Sickel trains his gun on Rocket Man, as bound-and-gagged House Peters, Jr., watches helplessly.

window, surprising Dirken, who has Burt tied in a chair.

Vulcan is no fool—he comes in from another room (along with Blears and another thug, Miller), pistol in hand—revealing himself to be Prof. Bryant, and orders Rocket Man to back into a doorway electrically charged to sizzle anything that enters. Burt manages to kick Miller into the doorway, and it's he who is burned to a crisp. In the confusion that follows, Bryant and his men get away.

From his offshore hideout on Fisherman's Island, three hundred miles from New York Harbor, Vulcan sends an ultimatum to the mayor of New York. The mayor happens to be discussing the situation with Jeff, Glenda and Burt when the message arrives. Vulcan demands one billion dollars by two o'clock that day or he will destroy

Left: Rocket Man comes in for a landing.

the city. Jeff warns that Vulcan is dangerous and that the mayor should "offer to compromise," but the mayor refuses to submit "the greatest city in the world" to extortion by a maniac. He orders the police, the reserves and volunteers to "comb every neighborhood, every building, every room in this city." It's a little before noon.

The Decimator's range is two hundred miles. Dirken asks Bryant how the weapon can be used against New York. Bryant shows him a map, and points out that mid way between Fisherman's Island and New York Harbor, "lies the Great Amsterdam Fault, a volcanic fissure" which reaches into "the subterranean fires miles below the city of New York." He plans to blast through the fault and "bring about the worst earthquake and tidal wave in the history of America."

At two o'clock, with no word from the mayor, Bryant has the Decimator turned on and aimed at the fault. In the mayor's office, Jeff and Millard are speculating that since their detection device, with a range of two hundred and fifty miles, didn't pick up any sign of the decimator, there's little danger of "serious damage." Their sanguinity is disturbed when the naval observatory reports that "sudden giant waves" are moving in. There's a loud air tremor.

Jeff studies some instrument readings and concludes that the Amsterdam Fault is being blasted from somewhere on Fisherman's Island.

The mayor issues a quick radio message, asking everyone to evacuate the city immediately. The Air Force is ordered to "blast Fisherman's Island right off the map," but Jeff isn't certain the bombers can get there fast enough. He dons the Rocket Man outfit and blasts off. Huge tidal waves hit New York. The Statue of Liberty is washed away. Buildings collapse under the force of the onslaught. Skyscrapers crash to the ground. People are crushed or drowned. The city skyline vanishes.

Below: The Rocket Man takes on Vulcan's men as the Decimator's deadly beam comes dangerously close.

From what we see, New York City, for all intents and purposes, is history.

Rocket Man flies directly into the hideout (a modest, white clapboard, house), destroys the infernal machine with one blast of a sonic ray gun then takes on Bryant and Dirken. During the fray Bryant attempts to shoot Rocket Man but kills Dirken. Still, Bryant puts up a terrific battle against his metal-helmeted opponent, using everything at his disposal—clubs, chairs, whatever.

The air force arrives and it's 'bombs away.' Rocket Man manages to fly off just as the bombs land. A direct hit totally destroys the house, the Decimator and Dr. Vulcan. More bombs level the rest of the island. And it's possible that things in New York are not as bad as they seemed. The mayor's office seems to be intact, the view from his skyscraper window seems just as before and everyone is jovial as the mayor congratulates them and (mostly) himself for getting rid of Dr. Vulcan. Jeff, Zelda and Burt are hopelessly bored as he drones on about how "this fine administration" will rebuild New York "into the greatest city the world has ever known."

THE 50s

Atom Man vs. Superman

(Columbia-1950) Directed by Spencer Bennet. Screenplay: George H. Plympton, Joseph F. Poland, David Mathews. Based on the Superman Adventure Feature appearing in the magazines "Superman" and "Action Comics." Adapted from the Superman radio program. Assistant director: R. M. Andrews. Second unit director: Derwin Abrahams. Photography: Ira H. Morgan. Editor: Earl Turner. Musical director: Mischa Bakaleinikoff. Producer: Sam Katzman. [6-19-50]

Cast:

Clark Kent . . . . Kirk Alyn
Lois Lane. . . . . Noel Neill
Luthor . . . . Lyle Talbot
Jimmy Olson . . . . Tommy Bond
Perry White . . . . Pierre Watkin
Foster . . . . Jack Ingram
Albert . . . . Don Harvey
Carl . . . . Rusty Wescoatt
Beer . . . . Terry Frost
Dorr . . . . Wally West
Lawson . . . . Paul Strader
Earl . . . . George Robotham

15 Chapters:
1. Superman Flies Again 2. Atom Man Appears! 3. A Blaze in the Sky! 4. Super-man Meets Atom Man 5. Atom Man Tricks Superman 6. Atom Man's Challenge 7. At the Mercy of Atom Man 8. Into the Empty Doom 9. Superman Crashes Through! 10. Atom Man's Heat Ray 11. Luthor's Strategy 12. Atom Man Strikes! 13. Atom Man's Flying Saucer 14. Rocket of Vengeance 15. Superman Saves the Universe

Luthor, Superman's archenemy, is in jail, but that doesn't stop his illegal activities. The criminal wizard comes up with a way (a "disintegrating machine") to teleport himself from his cell to his secret laboratory. He puts on a metallic mask [recycled from the robot in *The Monster and the Ape*] so no one will recognize him, and calls himself Atom Man. As Atom Man, he blackmails Metropolis by threatening to destroy the entire city. Perry White, editor of the *Daily Planet*, assigns Lois Lane, Jimmy Olson and Clark Kent to cover the story.

The ingenious Luthor invents an impressive variety of deadly devices in

Kirk Alyn in Atom Man's underground laboratory.

As astonished passengers look on, Kirk Alyn apprehends disguised villain Jack Ingram.

Lyle Talbot, aka Rex Luthor, aka Atom Man, a tricky customer regardless of name.

addition to the disintegrating machine which can reduce people to their basic atom structure and then reassemble them in any given spot. He uses it to transport Jimmy Olson to his headquarters, just to give him a braggadocio challenge to deliver to Superman. Jimmy innocently picks up what he thinks is a coin and puts it in his pocket. Unwittingly he's picked up the power battery without which the disintegrator is useless. This causes its share of confusion and danger, for Luthor thinks that Lois has it.

Because of his "good behavior" Luthor is granted a parole despite the protests of right-minded citizens. He opens a television station and assures everyone he's an honest man. Fact is, once he's alone he transports himself to his secret cave laboratory, from which he can direct his evil empire. Superman is kept busy: saving Lois from a car headed over a cliff, and Lois and Jimmy from being asphyxiated in a garage.

Since kryptonite can rob Superman of his power, it eventually occurs to Luthor to invent a synthetic kryptonite and, with this in mind, the evil scientist goes about obtaining the necessary ingredients: plutonium, radium, etc. Luthor announces he now has the required elements to make kryptonite and stop the Man of Steel. He plants the kryptonite at the launching of a big ship with Superman in attendance. Superman is exposed to the toxic element and passes out. An ambulance pulls up and he's placed inside, right into Luthor's hands.

Additional synthetic kryptonite is held close to the helpless superhero, and he grows even weaker. He's put into the transportation machine, a lever is

Kirk Alyn stops a getaway car.

Kirk Alyn rescues Noel Neill from a safe, as a relieved bank executive looks on.

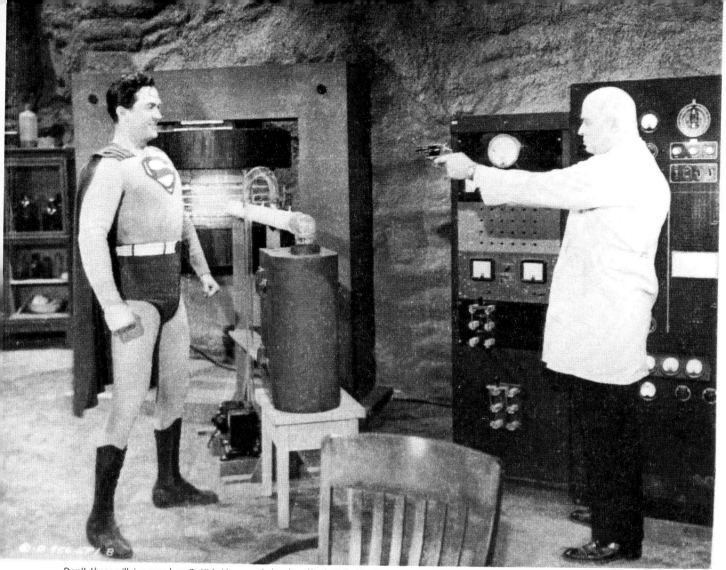

Don't these villains ever learn? Kirk Alyn merely laughs off Lyle Talbot's attempts to shoot him.

pulled and the Man of Steel vanishes into "the Empty Doom," disappearing into thin air. We see an almost transparent Superman trying to stop a crime but unable to do so—he's invisible and has no effect on solid objects. He places himself in front of a fleeing car, but it goes right through him. He tries to grab a sheet of paper from Lois's typewriter, but can't even do that. (Perry White has noticed that Clark has vanished along with Superman, and has assigned Lois to write a story, "Is Clark Kent Superman?") Finally, using all his remaining mental strength, Superman manages to type out a message on Lois's typewriter, which Perry White rejects as a phony. A subsequent message, saying Clark is in grave danger, convinces him. One day, Lois and Jimmy get a typed message from Superman stating he'll return, as good as new, that night. Luthor reads the

Luthor, in his Atom Man disguise.

140

It's Kirk Alyn to the rescue, saving Tommy Bond and Noel Neill from electrocution.

Jack Ingram raises an arm to protect himself as Kirk Alyn gets set to bash his brains out with a motor block.

Kirk Alyn soars above Metropolis.

message and is worried. What he doesn't know is that the effect of the synthetic kryptonite was temporary and has worn off. The Man of Steel returns and proceeds to foil Atom Man's plans.

Luthor's last scheme is to wreck Metropolis with another of his inventions, a sonic vibrator, and then to leave Earth in his spaceship, taking Lois along as his prisoner. Havoc and destruction are inflicted upon the city. Superman is busy rescuing victims everywhere. Luthor and Lois are launched in the spaceship and Superman flies off in search of them. Since he's merely dealing with the space between Earth and Mars he quickly spots the ship, crashes through its hull and flies back to Earth carrying Lois and Luthor. The evil genius is imprisoned once again and Lois fails in an attempt to prove that Clark Kent is Superman. In the end, she laughs at the notion that the meek, mild and somewhat incompetent Clark could be the Man of Steel.

Flying Disc Man from Mars

(Republic-1950) Directed by Fred C. Brannon. Writer: Ronald Davidson. Cinematography: Walter Strenge. Music: Stanley Wilson. Art director: Fred Ritter. Special effects: Howard Lydecker, Theodore Lydecker. Editors: Clifford Bell, Sr., Sam Starr. Sound: Earl Crain, Sr. Associate producer: Franklin Adreon. [10-25-50] Feature title: *Missile Monsters*.

Cast:

Kent Fowler . . . . Walter Reed
Helen Hull . . . . Lois Collier
Mota . . . . Gregory Gay
Dr. Bryant . . . . James Craven
Drake . . . . Harry Lauter
Ryan . . . . Richard Irving
Steve . . . . Sandy Sanders
Trent . . . . Michael Carr
Watchman . . . . Dale Van Sickel
Taylor . . . . Tom Steele
Gateman . . . . George Sherwood
Grady . . . . Jimmy O'Gatty
Crane . . . . Lester Dorr
Louis Ashe . . . . Clayton Moore
Curtis . . . . John DeSimone
Kirk . . . . Dick Cogan
Graves . . . . Ken Terrell
Hagen . . . . Carey Loftin

12 Chapters:

1. Menace from Mars   2. The Volcano's Secret   3. Death Rides the Stratosphere   4. Execution by Fire 5. The Living Projectile   6. Perilous Mission   7. Descending Doom 8. Suicidal Sacrifice   9. The Funeral Pyre   10. Weapons of Hate 11. Disaster on the Highway 12. Volcanic Vengeance

Doctor Bryant, a brilliant scientist and builder of experimental planes, notices a mysterious aircraft hovering over his factories every night. He hires Kent Fowler, a young aviator who operates Fowler Air Patrol, to investigate. Kent shoots down the mysterious craft and when it crash lands Dr. Bryant is right there. A man clad in tights and a mailed hood gets out of the craft, introduces himself as Mota, from Mars, and

James Craven (right) aims the radar-controlled atomic gun while two underlings take notes.

claims he's familiar with the doctor.

Dr. Bryant is bug-eyed. "This is astonishing," he says. Mota promises to tell more in a safer place, "and dressed as an earth man." Bryant takes Mota to his laboratory and gets him some clothes, then calls Kent, who's still flying around, and reports the plane he shot down "exploded when it hit and there's practically nothing left." He tells Kent he'll call him when he has another assignment.

Mota says his being shot down wasn't much of a disruption—he had planned to land anyway to visit Bryant. He says that ever since Earth began developing atomic power the Martians had been watching closely in "large atomic-powered patrol ships, perma-nently stationed just outside your field of gravity. We make our closer inspec-tions in small flying discs, such as the one you shot down." Bryant is amazed and speculates that Mars must be far beyond Earth technologically. Mota admits they've had atomic power for over a century, and now that Earth was ready, he had been sent "to guide you." "That's certainly very generous of you," Bryant says.

There is, of course, a catch. "I am here to see," Mota adds, "that your world is put under control of a supreme dictator of the universe." And he has sought Bryant specifically, because it had been noticed that "during the last World War you were so sympathetic to the idea of world dictatorship that you did everything possible to help Hitler and his plan for world conquest." Now Bryant is *really* bug eyed. "You can't prove that," he shouts. Mota smiles. "I can," he says, "but I don't think it will be necessary. Hitler failed because he had to depend on relatively crude equipment and large armies of men." He leans toward Bryant and continues. "The atomic weapons I'll show you how to make are so powerful we can subdue the world with a mere handful of assistants. How would you like to rule planet Earth under our guidance, Dr. Bryant?"

Bryant obviously loves the idea. "How do we get started?" he asks. Mota suggests finding a "few intelligent criminals" to acquire the supplies need-

Walter Reed (left) discusses strange goings on with James Craven (right).

Gregory Gay (right), in Earth garb, barks orders to Michael Carr, who's atop a semi-disc in their secret hideout.

ed, and using Bryant's factory to produce the weapons. Bryant recruits two hoodlums, Drake and Ryan, and sends them to steal uranium from the Argosy Refining Plant. Coincidentally, Kent has been hired to guard that plant and, as the thugs steal a bag of uranium he catches them in the act. After a brief battle the two crooks flee in their car, with Kent in close pursuit.

They drive to a meadow outside the city, where a plane is waiting. They hand the bag to the pilot who starts to take off. Drake fires a few shots at Kent's car as he approaches. The shot shatters Kent's windshield and he crashes into the plane, both plane and car blowing up spectacularly. Fortunately, Kent leaps from the car a second before it hits. Drake and Ryan drive off and Kent starts the long walk back to town.

This is only the first of many life-threatening adventures experienced by Kent, his secretary Helen and his assistant Steve in their encounters with the interplanetary enemy. They notice that uranium is always the objective and decide to double their watch on all plants that make or store the element. Mota and Bryant, too, have reached a decision: in order to keep their operation a secret they must find a safer place in which to work. "And there is one," Mota declares, "which our scouts from Mars once used as an outpost. It is already partially equipped. It's in the crater of the Altamount volcano."

"But that volcano is still partially active," Bryant comments. "How do we get into the crater?" "Not with any Earth device," Mota answers, "but this atomic semi disc we are building, crude as it is by Martian standards, will easily

transport the supplies we need to set up a laboratory." Bryant likes the idea. "You can build the atomic units there," he says, "while I can work safely here on the heavier construction." "Exactly," Mota agrees.

Soon the semi-disc ship is completed. Mota gets into it and instructs Trent, the pilot. "The controls are similar to those on conventional planes," he explains, "except there are also jets on the other side. The plane can rise or descend vertically." It can even hover motionless in space. The semi-disc proceeds to take off in an amazingly small space, rising straight up before proceeding horizontally.

Kent, who's flying around in one of his patrol planes, sees the disc and radios Steve that he's going to follow it. Mota spots Kent's plane and, taking over the disc's controls, executes some

Mota and his minions pile into a semi-disc ship (recycled from *King of the Mounties*) as government agents attack.

fancy maneuvers and shoots it down. Kent bails out, lands safely and starts the long walk back to town. The semi disc reaches Altamount Volcano and drops vertically into the crater, past the flames, and makes a right-angle turn into a cave, where it lands. Mota gets out and goes about setting up shop.

The need for uranium is never-ending and Mota's attempts to get it at all costs necessitate the blowing up of factories, trains and dams; Kent is grenaded, time-bombed, shot down several times and presumed dead by Mota and Bryant, only to reappear to foil their plans. There are car chases and crashes, attempted incinerations and kidnappings, with Helen used as bait to draw Kent into traps. The semi-disc ship is used to transport the stolen uranium to the volcano laboratory, and Bryant finishes work on an "atomic gun" and an

"aerial torpedo," which Mota hopes will serve "as a demonstration of the effectiveness of Martian weapons."

Bryant's connection to Drake and Ryan is noticed by Kent and Steve, who had already confronted the doctor and been told to by him to stay out of his factories. "Those two crooks go in and out of Bryant's plant like they're on the payroll," Steve comments. "They probably are," Kent agrees, but points out that since they can't get into the plants, they'll have to work from the outside. Realizing that the saboteurs are most vulnerable when they're loading swag into the semi disc, Kent patrols constantly and catches Mota's men often, but they always escape.

Mota is fed up. "We have delayed our campaign long enough," he declares. "It's time to bring this planet Earth under the control of our supreme

dictator on Mars." He is certain that he can use the semi-disc plane to drop small atomic bombs that will bring the U. S. to its knees. "I merely wish to prove to the government how helpless it is against the scientific weapons of Mars," he declares. "Then we can demand the surrender or whatever equipment we need, under the threat of destroying the whole national economy." Bryant isn't so sure. "The American people don't scare easily. I hope it works," he says.

Mota leaves on a bombing mission and succeeds in blowing up factories, dams, railroads, tunnels, and bridges. At the Fowler Air Patrol office, Helen and Steve are discussing the situation when Kent bursts in with big news. He's been deputized by the district attorney and given a warrant to search Bryant's plant. He and Steve leave for

146

the plant immediately. Confronted by them, Bryant and his men put up a fight. During the battle Bryant and Drake slip away, get into a delivery truck and speed off. Kent gets into his car and gives chase, not aware that a remaining thug has hopped onto the back of his car.

Bryant is tossing hand grenades behind him, causing Kent to swerve sharply and to keep a sharp eye on the road, even as the thug in the back removes the gas tank cap, stuffs some paper in and lights it, creating a mobile Molotov cocktail. He leaps from the car, rolls a few times and watches as it explodes. Fortunately, Kent, too, had noticed the flames and jumped just before the explosion. He heads for the road and starts the long walk to town.

Bryant and Drake call Mota and tell him what's happened. Bryant mentions that he had to leave his files behind. "Were the plans for the radar-controlled atomic gun in those files?" Mota asks. Bryant admits they were, and is ordered to recover them, for that is the one weapon that is effective against Martian stratosphere ships. Bryant says he'll do his best, and agrees to meet Mota and the semi disc a little while later in the canyon field.

Helen is working alone in the Air Patrol office when Bryant and Drake enter. "Where are the plans for my radar-controlled atomic gun?," Bryant asks. She's mum. Drake pulls out a gun. "It's in the safe," she says. "Open it," Bryant orders. With a swift move Helen sets off an alarm. "That'll bring

every cop in town," Drake says. They flee, but they take Helen with them, piling into a car and riding off. They're seen by Kent and Steve, who follow.

Helen is taken directly to the canyon field, where Mota waits with the semi-disc ship. He agrees that she will make a valuable hostage. Helen, Bryant and Mota get into the ship just as Kent and Steve arrive, guns blazing. Mota takes off, leaving Drake and Ryan behind. A bullet from Steve kills Ryan and, when he runs out of ammunition, Drake gives up. "Looks like your pals walked out on you," Kent tells him. "Maybe you'd better change sides." Drake does just that, cooperating in a plan in exchange for clemency.

The disc ship flies into Mota's volcano hideout just in time for him to

Aboard the semi disc, Walter Reed (left) struggles with Gregory Gay while Michael Carr mans the controls.

receive a phone call from Drake, who reports that Kent is willing to return him and the atomic-gun plans in exchange for Helen. "That's a reasonable trade," Mota concludes. "But it must be handled on my terms. Fowler must give you the plans and let you go. Then you radio us where we are to pick you up. We will leave the girl there." Kent nods yes to Drake. "Fowler says okay," Drake tells Mota. The deal is made.

Later, Drake calls Mota, tells him he has the plans and arranges to get picked up. "You did all right," Kent says to Drake, after the latter hangs up. "Now you'll have to shoot square with me," Drake reminds him. Steve takes Drake to town while Kent waits for the space ship. The semi disc arrives and lands like a rock, dropping straight down before levelling off. Kent hides behind a tree and watches as Trent, the pilot, gets out and looks around. Kent gets the drop on Trent and demands to be taken to where Helen is. With a gun at Trent's back, the ship returns to the volcano.

Getting past the volcano's flames and then landing, Trent climbs out of the disc's roof panel as Mota, Bryant and the captive Helen wait to greet him. Imagine their surprise when Kent emerges also, pistol in hand. He tells Helen to get into the ship. She does. Mota knocks the gun from Kent's hand and a fight begins, with the two-fisted pilot taking on the Martian, Bryant and Trent. During the battle, Trent and a couple of atom bombs are knocked into the volcano, reactivating it. Lava explodes and bubbles ominously. Kent recovers his pistol and shots are exchanged.

Mota and Bryant hide behind rocks and Kent seizes the opportunity to get into the semi disc. He sits at the controls and pilots it out of the volcano. Mota and Bryant are cringing in a corner when the volcano erupts, the atom bombs explode and the Martians' dream of conquest comes to an end. But now the disc is on fire and Kent and Helen

are forced to parachute out. They land safely but the disc explodes in mid air and practically disintegrates, leaving no trace.

The next day, in the Air Patrol office, Kent announces to Helen and Steve that the district attorney has declared the case closed. All of Mota's weaponry was destroyed in the eruption. "Well, it's just as well," says Helen. "Those weapons were too dangerous anyway." Steve isn't so sure. "Maybe," he says, "but I'd sure liked to have tried 'em out." "Do you mean that?," Kent asks, earnestly. "Why sure," Steve replies, "why?" Kent explains. "As a reward for our help in running down Bryant, the air force is taking us back. I'll go in as a colonel." Steve is delighted. "Will I get my wings this time?" Sure, Kent tells him, if he'll accept the job of testing ejector seats for the air force. Kent and Helen laugh, but where this new arrangement leaves her is anyone's guess.

Another unwelcome visitor from outer space, Gregory Gay

Mysterious Island (Columbia-1951)
Directed by Spencer Bennet. Screenplay: Lewis Clay, Royal K. Cole, George H. Plympton. Based on "L'Ile Mysterieuse" by Jules Verne. Assistant director: R. M. Andrews. Photography: Fayte Browne. Editor: Earl Turner. Music director: Mischa Bakaleinikoff. Producer: Sam Katzman.

Cast:

Capt. Harding	Richard Crane
Jack Pencroft	Marshall Reed
Rulu	Karen Randle
Bert Brown	Ralph Hodges
Captain Shard	Gene Roth
Gideon Spilett	Hugh Prosser
Capt. Nemo	Leonard Penn
Ayrton	Terry Frost
Moley	Rusty Wescoatt
Neb	Bernard Hamilton

15 Chapters:
1. Lost in Space   2. Sinister Savages   3. Savage Justice   4. Wild Man at Large   5. Trail of the Mystery Man   6. The Pirates Attack   7. Menace of the Mercurians   8. Between Two Fires   9. Shrine of the Silver Bird

Richard Crane holds Top, the dog, Hugh Prosser, Bernard Hamilton, Marshall Reed and Ralph Hodges, get set for lift off.

During the Civil War, in the western territories, Union Captain Harding, a "brilliant engineer" captured and held in Houston as a prisoner of the Confederates, escapes in an enemy observation balloon along with prisoners Gideon Spilett, a war correspondent for the *New York Eagle*, Jack Pencroft, a sailor, late-teener Bert Brown, who's Pencroft's ward, Neb, Harding's servant ("He's been with me as long as I can remember"), and Top, a dog Harding has befriended. They immediately run into a hurricane that sends them off course. For five days the balloon drifts

and eventually begins to drop near an uncharted island. When it looks like the balloon will land on some dangerous coral reefs, Harding leaps overboard (followed by Top) to decrease ballast. He's lost from sight as the balloon crash lands on the island.

As the four castaways gather and lament the loss of Harding, a short distance away a helmeted, black-clad figure emerges from the sea carrying the captain. He gently places the unconscious Harding on the beach, then returns to the sea. Top comes swimming out of the water and stands guard.

Beyond the reefs is a pirate ship, skippered by Captain Shard, who wants to land on the island but finds the conditions too perilous. He tells his crew they'll have to wait till the weather is

better. At the same time two strange top-shaped spacecraft appear in the sky and land on the island. A beautiful woman wearing a silver blouse, short-shorts and leg-hugging slacks gets out of one ship and is joined by two spider-web-hooded assistants from the other space ship. (We'll find out later her name is Rulu.) She tells them they'll head for her "work shop," and they walk off. She leads them to a cave wherein there is a chamber that serves as a laboratory, and they start setting up shop. After she's contacted her leader, we learn that Rulu is from Mercury, sent to the island to find an elusive radioactive element her planet needs so it can mount an invasion of Earth.

The castaways are wandering around looking for water when they

149

notice a smoking volcano in the distance, and a band of natives coming toward them. The natives seem somewhat Asian, wear black uniforms and carry lightning-bolt shaped spears. The castaways flee, pursued by the natives who stop suddenly when the volcano shows signs of erupting and bow down before it. The castaways run toward the caves, but are driven off by blasts from Rulu's ray gun—she just wants to keep them away from her work shop.

Captain Harding wakes up in a cave and finds himself facing the helmeted stranger who demands to know why he's "come to my island." As this is going on a bearded, wild-acting fellow attacks the castaways, runs away from them and then reports their whereabouts to the black-clad natives (known as "the Volcano People"). The Volcano

People attack the castaways but flee in terror when the helmeted figure shows himself from a hill top.

A little while later, the castaways see Harding lying in a field, with Top barking beside him. Before they can get to him they're beaten to it by the Volcano people and the wild man. Gideon and Jack follow them while Bert and Neb are sent back to the beach to set up camp and search for any supplies in the balloon supply bag. Instead, they discover a crate filled with weapons and ammunition. They can't believe their luck and quickly notify Harding and Gideon. Using the weapons (just the sound of gunfire is enough to send the Volcano People running) the castaways rescue Harding.

When they ask Harding what happened, he's not sure. He remembers a

helmeted figure, but that's about all. They tell him about the strange girl they've seen. "She has the appearance of one from another planet," says Jack. They search the island and come across a stone, shingle-roofed cabin. It's empty, so they move in. Rulu has been watching them. "Now we know where the Earthmen will live," she tells her two aides.

In the cabin the castaways notice a sliding door, activate it and enter a spacious rock-walled inner chamber where they find more crates filled with food and weapons. The wild man, attacking Jack, is captured and brought to the cabin where the group discovers he can speak English. He claims to have been captured by pirates who abandoned him on the island. He can't remember how long ago. He tells them the pirates built

Below: Karen Randle and two spider-web-hooded assistants, fresh from Mercury, emerge on Earth from their space ships.

Karen Randle gives the earthlings a blast from her ray gun.

the cabin, that they'd stored food on a mountain nearby and leads them to it. The food is piled at the very tip of a mountain peak in a precarious manner —"to keep the animals from getting at it" the wild man explains—and he rushes to it and starts a food-crate landslide that nearly kills the castaways while he scurries away.

The wild man doesn't get far. He's captured by a couple of Captain Shard's seamen who were sent in a rowboat to check out the island. He's brought aboard the pirate ship and taken to Shard. He reminds the captain that he's a former crewman, Ayrton, who had been abandoned. Shard remembers all too well. Ayrton tells him of the armed castaways on the island.

Shard and his men row to the island and use Ayrton as bait to attract Harding

and company. They're beaten off, but in ensuing action Bert is temporarily captured, then rescued by the hard-slugging Harding, then captured by the space aliens. Rulu introduces herself to Bert, explaining that Mercurians have mastered all Earth languages. By waving a wand in front of his face she places him under a spell—he blindly obeys her orders. (The fact is, spell or no, Bert is smitten with Rulu.)

For no apparent reason the Volcano People approach the castaways bearing baskets of food and fruit and offer to share it. Although Gideon is suspicious, Harding accepts the offer. Soon they're all seated in a circle, Volcano People and Americans, enjoying their repast.

The casataways learn that the Volcano People's ancestors had origi-

nally lived underwater in the sunken volcano, but adapted when it arose above the ocean. Shard is not happy when he hears that the two groups have become friendly. United, he fears, the castaways and Volcano People might be able to defeat him. He schemes to divide them, but his efforts backfire, the two groups grow even closer and the Americans frequently visit the thatch hut of the Volcano People's chief.

Still, the castaways continue their search for the missing Bert and are threatened regularly by Shard and his crew as well as by Rulu and her men. Top makes an appearance every so often, either saving the day or causing a disturbance. The friends have to survive booby traps, falls from cliffs, explosions, drowning and the like. Every now and then the helmeted figure

Karen Randle phones home as one of her accomplices stands by.

shows up and either provides supplies or scares away whoever is threatening the castaways. Ayrton continues to run amuck.

As Rulu leaves on one of her missions, she drops her wand. Bert notices it and picks it up. As soon as he touches it he snaps out of the spell, and quickly leaves the cave. But he's ambushed by the loony Ayrton, knocked unconscious and tied up. Ayrton, in turn, is captured by Shard and to save his own skin leads Shard and his gang to Bert.

There's a series of captures and escapes: Rulu, Harding and Bert taking turns. For a while Rulu will be friendly and offer to help Harding get the castaways off the island, other times she'll bewitch the Volcano People chief to incite his people against them. When Shard sees her use her ray gun, he's impressed. He tells his men they must

get the "strange weapon the girl had. With it we'll rule the seas from the Sandwich Isles to the Great Australian Bite." A few setbacks give the ever-practical Shard some second thoughts.

For one thing, while Shard and most of his men are on shore, Harding leads a raid on the ship, first overpowering the sailors guarding the rowboat on the beach, then clambering on board the ship and battling with the few crew members. During the mele, the crazed Ayrton (who came on board with Harding's party) puts the torch to several kegs of dynamite, blowing up a part of the ship, himself included. The others escape.

Shard waves a white flag and at a meeting with the castaways suggests they join forces and work together to repair his ship so they can all sail to a neutral port. Harding says it's a good idea, but they've got something to

attend to first: Bert, once again has been captured by Rulu and put under her spell. They've got to rescue him before they work on the boat. Shard says he'll be glad to help, and he and Harding set out on the mission.

Shard proves his friendship in the fist fights and shootouts that follow, although things wind up with him and Harding trapped against a cave wall as Rulu's hooded goons take aim with their ray guns. To Rulu's utter astonishment, the two trapped men vanish into thin air. They materialize in another cave laboratory, where a white haired man tells them he never intended to have contact with them, "but I could not stand by and see you killed."

He introduces himself as Captain Nemo, a name Harding recognizes. "The great scientist, the commander of the submarine Nautilus," believed to have been lost at sea. Nemo tells them

Leonard Penn explains his latest amazing invention, the radiation neautralizer, to Gene Roth and Richard Crane.

he'd survived, reached this island and "hoped to spend my remaining years in peace. But invaders came from another planet, and now I must fight their plan to destroy the Earth." He explains that Rulu came seeking a mysterious ore that can become the most powerful explosive the world has ever seen.

It so happens, Nemo continues, that he's almost perfected a machine that will thwart Rulu's plans. "It will neutralize their dangerous metal and render it harmless." All he needs is the small glowing metal that Rulu uses in her wand. Harding and Shard say they'll get it. They return to Gideon, Jack, Neb and Shard's seamen, tell them that in addition to finding Bert they've got a new mission: saving the world, and off they march.

They've gone a short distance when they see one of the Mercurian rocket ships approaching for a landing. The ship lands, two hooded pilots get out and leave, first settting a booby trap for any snoopers — who just happen to be Harding and Shard. Shard opens the ship's door and there's an explosion. Shard is killed, Harding just shaken up.

Rulu is in her cave chamber when Bert barges in, ray gun in hand. He tells her he's no longer under her spell, that he "was prepared for you the second time you waved your magic wand." A guard sneaks up behind him and a fight ensues. Pretty soon Bert is taking on four of Rulu's men and doing pretty well. Harding hears the ruckus and joins the fray. Soon all Mercurians are subdued, Bert has the wand and Rulu is tightly bound.

They bring the wand to Nemo, who slips it into his machine, noting that he's using the mysterious element "the world will someday call 'uranium'." His machine repels its rays. They now notice that Rulu has escaped. Nemo decides to use his ray machine, just in case Rulu tries to use one of her weapons. But suddenly the walls of the cave start to shake. They rush outside and see the volcano in violent eruption. "This island is doomed," Nemo proclaims, and warns them to get to the beach immediately. "A ship will come," he predicts. Harding urges him to come with them. "This island is my home, my ship," Nemo declares, "I shall never desert her."

The castaways, joined by Top, race to the beach and are amazed to see a huge sailing ship heading toward them. It's friendly, Harding announces. Pretty soon they're on board, looking back at the island, which sinks beneath the waves, vanishing forever. Gideon, who all along had been making notes for a news story, tosses the pages overboard. "Nobody would believe it," he tells the others.

Captain Video Master of the Stratosphere (Columbia-1951) Directed by Spencer Bennet, Wallace Grissell. Screenplay: Royal K. Cole, Sherman L. Lowe, Joseph F. Poland. Story: George H. Plympton. Assistant director: Charles S. Gould. Photography: Fayte Browne. Music: Mischa Bakaleinikoff. Editor: Earl Turner. Special Effects: Jack Erickson. Producer: Sam Katzman.

Cast:

Capt. Video . . . . Judd Holdren
Ranger . . . . Larry Stewart
Tobor . . . . George Eldredge
Vultura . . . . Gene Roth
Gallagher . . . . Don C. Harvey
Alpha . . . . William Fawcett
Aker . . . . Jack Ingram
Zarol . . . . I. Stanford Jolley
Retner . . . . Skelton Knaggs
Rogers . . . . Jimmy Stark
Beal . . . . Rusty Wescoatt
Elko . . . . Zon Murray
Drock . . . . George Robotham
Prof. Felix Markham . . . Oliver Cross
Prof. Anton Dean . . . . Bill Bailey
J. R. Wade . . . . Selmer Jackson

15 Chapters:

1. Journey into Space   2. Menace to Atoms   3. Captain Video's Peril 4. Entombed in Ice   5. Flames of Atoms   6. Astray in the Atmosphere 7. Blasted by the Atomic Eye 8. Invisible Menace   9. Video Springs a Trap   10. Menace of the Mystery Metal   11. Weapon of Destruction 12. Robot Racket   13. Mystery of Station X   14. Vengeance of Vultura 15. Video vs. Vultura

Unusual atmospheric disturbances from an undetermined source have been causing floods, blizzards and hurricanes on Earth. Using his state-of-the-art technology, famous inter-planetary peace maker Captain Video, of the World Organization's Video Rangers, traces and locates the spot the disturbances are coming from (see *The Lost City* for a similar beginning, or *Flash Gordon* for the intergalactic version): the laboratory of a mysterious scientist—Dr. Tobor. When Captain Video and his sidekick Ranger call on the doctor he denies having anything to do with the catastrophes, but Video isn't convinced.

Tobor reports Video's visit to his boss, Vultura, dictator of the planet Atoma, who orders Tobor to take a

Below: Judd Holdren, Larry Stewart and their rocket ship.

Larry Stewart, Judd Holdren and William Fawcett get another warning message from Vultura

Below: Planet-ruler Gene Roth, up to no good you can bet, sets one of his robots.

rocket to Atoma immediately. Vultura doesn't want snooping earthmen to get wind of his grand plan for interplanetary conquest. Capt. Video, however, detects the rocketship's departure, and he and Ranger rush back to the doctor's lab. They find it deserted, in shambles and Tobor's assistant, Retner, unconscious.

When he comes to, Retner tells them that Tobor was carried off by oddly-clad men. Video notices Tobor's electronic telescope focused on a strange, mobile red planet. Checking with the World Organization, he learns the mobile planet is called Atoma. He and Ranger leave for the planet in their own rocket ship. Throughout their adveturs the Rangers are aided by Gallagher, a World Organization scien-

A robot on the march. Despite their clunky appearance, these guys can move pretty fast.

tist who, with a dazzling variety of hi-tech devices, keeps in touch with the Rangers and on several occasions provides timely, sometimes life-saving, information and assistance.

The trip is not uneventful. Vultura causes comets to collide with Video's ship, destroying it. Fortunately he and Ranger get away in a safety pod, which floats to the surface of another planet. They discover its atmosphere is identical to Earth's, so they get out and look around. They spot a group of people and Ranger runs toward them eagerly. A spear fired by one of the men stops him short. Captain Video blasts the spearman with his ray gun, then he and Ranger take on several aggressive natives, knocking them all cold.

Watching the fray from a short distance is a larger group of natives, dressed in Arab burnoose, led by an elder. Captain Video carries the dead

man to the elder, Alpha, explaining that his "intentions were peaceful until your friends here attacked." "They were our captors," the Alpha corrects him. He tells them they're on Theros, which has recently been invaded by Vultura of Atoma, who claims to be "protecting" them from aggressors with "a so-called War of Liberation." "A familiar trick for a dictatror," Video adds. The Therons can't even defend themselves because they have no weapons. Video asks if they'd fight if they had weapons. "Try us," one replies.

Captain Video and Ranger lead a group of Therons in a raid on an Atoman army weapoms storage base, which can only be reached via underground caverns. Video and Ranger put on the Atoman guard's uniforms, which enables them to overpower the base's sentries and open the gates for the main group of Therons. They quickly find

the storage room where everyone grabs as many ray guns as possible and flees, just as Atoman reinforcements arrive.

As they're retreating, Captain Video and Ranger kind of wander into the laboratory where Tobor is working. They think they're rescuing Tobor, who seems a bit reluctant to be rescued. "Don'tcha want to be rescued?," Video asks, and Tobor has no choice but to play along. But he makes sure he's carrying a detection device, through which Vultura can trace his location.

They return to the rocket ship that delivered them. Captain Video and Tobor get in, but Ranger decides to look around. He's quickly captured by Vultura's soldiers. "He should have been back long ago," a worried Captain Video says to Tobor, and goes out to search for Ranger. As soon as Video departs, Tobor rushes back to his laboratory and contacts Vultura.

156

Captain Video is attacked by Atoman soldiers. He defends himself ably, but a soldier takes aim with his ray gun rifle and is about to fire when a blast from a ray gun disables him. It's Alpha and a band of Therons who have come to the rescue. The Atomans flee. "You've saved my life,' Captain Video tells Alpha. "The boy's life we cannot save," Alpha replies sadly, explaining that Ranger is "a prisoner in the undergound control room." Captain Video is off in a flash.

Eventually Video succeeds in rescuing Ranger despite a rainstorm of toxic cosmic waste unleashed by Vultura, and they rush back to the rocket ship to find it empty. Captain Video radios Earth for a rescue rocket. Tobor has gotten his instructions from Vultura: He's to return to Earth with Captain

Video and figure out a way to kill him. He approaches the rocket ship, supposedly chased by Atoman soldiers, who run away when Captain Video and Ranger rush to the scene. "You came back just in time," Tobor says breathlessly. "The soldiers found the landing craft and chased me into the rocks." The rescue space ship arrives (off screen). They get into it and return to Earth.

Captain Video's interference and escape cause Vultura to change his plans. "The time has come," he declares, to direct all further attacks against the planet Earth." Buildings across Earth suddenly explode, government warehouses collapse, there's flooding and panic. All efforts seem to originate from the American city of Centerport, which is where Video and

Ranger set up operations.

And a new menace threatens the planet. Remote-controlled mechanical men appear, causing mayhem and destruction, and it is Captain Video and Ranger's job to confront them as well as other inventions fielded by the ingenious Vultura. Video manages to dismantle a robot and remove a mechanical brain found inside its chest, and only two men, Professors Felix Markham and Anton Dean, can analyze it. There will, of course, be attempts on the scientists' lives, and they, as well as Video and Ranger, will find themselves being frozen into cakes of ice by another of Vultura's inventions. (Fortuitously, Video's Radionic Directional Beam and his Thermoid Transmitter come to the rescue.)

In the course of Captain Video's

Below: Judd Holdren, in the grip of a robot.

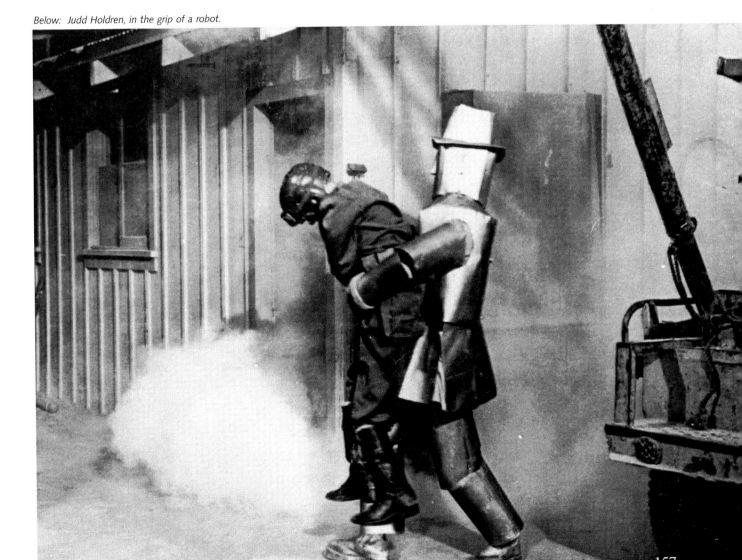

Gene Roth (right) has captured Larry Stewart and Judd Holdren (light outfits) on the planet Atoma.

efforts he and Ranger must return to Theros and pay a visit to Atoma, each trip fraught with danger. They brush with incineration in a polarized furnace, shootouts, electrocution, entrapment in a projectile headed for Earth, explosions, death rays, car crashes and fist fights. And that's the least of it.

Between Captain Video and Vultura there's a veritable cornucopia of hi-tech gadgets and gizmos which either side uses against the other, including Vapo-Projectors (for smothering fires instantly), Static Beams (a sort of death ray), Cosmic Vibrators (for blasting things apart), Gravitational Decelerators (to bring down flying objects), the Atomic Eye (a ray that can disintegrate a human being), Dr. Pauli's Cloak (a cloak that makes one invisible), the Rhombie Materializer (which enables you to see someone who's wearing Dr. Pauli's Cloak), the Whitney Eye (a powerful self-activating lens

158

which enables the viewer to watch every move Vultura makes), platinite (a new and deadly metal), the Jetmobile (Video's small rocket ship), an Anti-Detonator (which nullifies the concussion of a blast), and so on.

As all this is going on, Tobor is pretending to be an ally against Vultura, reporting to the Atoman ruler at every opportunity. But both Video and Gallagher grow suspicious of him and discover his duplicity. Although he appears to be a desk-bound scientist, Tobor turns out to be a tough customer. In a fair fist fight he knocks both Video and Ranger cold, takes them prisoner and gets them aboard a two-prop plane. With a gun trained on them, he has them take over the controls for a flight to a place where Vultura's rocket ship is expected to pick them up. But Vultura has decided he no longer needs Tobor, and releases a "flying disc" to crash into the plane, hoping to kill him, Video and

Ranger together. The saucer makes a pass at the plane but Video evades it. Tobor refuses to believe that Vultura is double crossing him, and remains in the plane as the disc turns around for another pass and Video and Ranger bail out, without parachutes. The plane is blasted out of the sky as Video and Ranger float gently to earth, thanks to quick acting by Gallagher, who has been keeping abreast of events and has activated an anti-gravity device.

Captain Video gets a radio message from Alpha. Theron is under attack again and Video's help is desperately needed, so it's off to Theron for him and Ranger. After leading the Theron forces to victory over Vultura's occupying army, Video and Ranger head for Atoma to deal with the would-be dictator.

In a last desperate effort, Vultura turns a disintegrating ray on the two Earthlings. They're saved when Alpha, watching from his headquarters, activates a ray-reversal device which turns the ray back onto Vultura. He is disintegrated by his own weapon. With peace assured, Video and Ranger return to Earth in their rocket projectile, ready for new adventures.

Radar Men from the Moon

(Republic-1952) Directed by Fred C. Brannon. Screenplay: Ronald Davidson. Unit manager: Roy Wade. Photography: John MacBurnie. Special effects: Howard Lydecker, Theodore Lydecker. Music: Stanley Wilson. Editor: Cliff Bell. Art director: Fred A. Ritter. Sound: Dick Tyler. Set decoration: John McCarthy, Jr., James Redd. Make up: Bob Mark. Producer: Franklin Adreon. [1-9-52]

Cast:

Commando Cody . . . George Wallace
Joan Gilbert . . . . Aline Towne
Retik . . . . Roy Barcroft
Ted Richards . . . . . William Bakewell
Graber . . . . Clayton Moore
Daly . . . . Bob Stevenson
Krog . . . . Peter Brocco
Henderson . . . . Don Walters
Zerg . . . . Tom Steele
Alon. . . . . Dale Van Sickel
Hank . . . . Wilson Wood
Robal . . . . Noel Cravat
Nasor . . . . Baynes Barron
Bream . . . . Paul McGuire
Bartender . . . . Ted Thorpe
Jones . . . . Dick Cogan
Doyle. . . . . Jack O'Shea
Duke. . . . . Billy Dix
Bill . . . . Paul Palmer

12 Chapters:

1. Moon Rocket 2. Molten Terror
3. Bridge of Death 4. Flight to Destruction 5. Murder Car 6. Hills of Death 7. Human Targets 8. The Enemy Planet 9. Battle in the Stratosphere 10. Mass Execution 11. Planned Pursuit 12. Take-Off to Eternity

America's defenses are being sabotaged by a series of mysterious explosions. Oil fields are blown up, transmission lines destroyed and office buildings wrecked. In the office of Cody Laboratories, Commando Cody

and his two assistants, Joan Gilbert and Ted Richards haven't a clue as to what's going on. That's why they're waiting for Mr. Henderson, of the government, to arrive. Perhaps he'll be able to provide some information.

"That guy Henderson wouldn't tell you what time it is," Ted comments. "Just what is his job, anyway?" "He won't tell you that either, Ted, but it's a big one," Cody replies. "He only answers to a few people in this country of ours." Their conversation is interrupted by Henderson's arrival. He reports that the government is very pleased with the top-secret rocket work

Cody Labs has being doing for them, and he's been authorized to tell Cody that his rocket technology will be used to combat the current wave of sabotage and terrorism.

Henderson also mentions that the explosions are of atomic origin. "You mean someone is dropping atomic bombs on us?," Joan asks. Henderson says, no, not bombs, more like a ray, which is exactly what Cody's own investigations indicated. "It's the only possible answer," Henderson says. Cody points out that no one has ever been able to build an atomic ray machine. "You mean no one on Earth

ever has," says Henderson, meaningfully. Government astronomers have noticed "unusual atomic activity on the moon," followed by atomic attacks upon Earth. "The two known facts fit together," Henderson says.

Cody Labs has developed a rocket ship capable of reaching the moon. The government wants him to fly there, find out if it's the source of the explosions and if it is, devise a way to stop the attacks. Cody and his crew can't refuse such an enticing offer. Henderson asks if he still has his flying suit and Cody says yes. Henderson suggests that Cody put it on and see what he can detect from the air. The ray guns causing the damage are being fired from Earth, probably from this area, and if Cody can catch the saboteurs in the

act... Cody says he'll try.

A truck pulls to a stop along a deserted road. Two thugs expose a ray gun in the back, aim at a distant railroad train and blast it from the tracks. As news of the attack reaches Cody Labs, Cody decides it's time to take to the air. He puts on his flying suit, a leather jacket with control knobs strapped in front and rocket tubes strapped in back, and a bullet-shaped metal helmet that covers his head completely. He dashes outside, turns a knob, leaps into the air and flies across the sky.

The saboteurs are at another location, waiting for another train to come by. They're spotted from the air by Cody, who creeps up on them and fires a shot just as one of the thugs is about to blast the train. They return fire. Both

sides fire a multitude of bullets without damage to anyone. The thugs run out of ammo first and instead of driving away, run away, leaving the truck and the ray gun to Cody.

Later, in an elaborate equipment-strewn cave hideout, the two saboteurs, Graber and Daly, report the bad news to their boss, Krog, a Lunarian who wears a dark form-fitting *ensemble* including a peek-a-boo hangman's-type hood. Sort of like a slimmed-down Teletubby. Krog isn't concerned about losing the gun, he's got plenty more. But he doesn't want "the Earth people to learn the secrets of our weapons." He guesses from his men's description that they ran into "Commando Cody and his flying suit," with whom he is evidently familiar. He tells them to go to Cody's labo-

Two lunarian guards step out of their moon tank to search for Cody and Ted, who have made off with a ray gun.

160

Aline Towne, William Bakewell (seated) and George Wallace discuss the strange events taking place. Could this be the work of the Moon men?

ratory and retrieve the "atomic chamber" from the gun.

"That's a large order," complains Graber, who reminds Krog that he was hired only to fire a ray gun. "You were hired to do anything that I may consider necessary to pave the way for our invasion from the moon," Krog says imperiously. "You're being well payed for your work so do as you're ordered!" Chastened, Graber and Daly attend to business and soon are barging into the laboratory where Cody and Ted have been examining the ray gun. There's an enthusiastic fist fight between the four—during which Ted gets kayoed early. Cody does well but is eventually felled from behind. Graber grabs the atomic chamber and both men flee.

On the moon, in what appears to be a run-down ancient Roman city, Retik,

supreme commander of the Moon, receives a radio message from Krog on Earth: a U.S. rocket to the moon would be taking off in five days. Retik is a bit surprised by the advances in rocketry by the Earthmen, but is otherwise unperturbed. He assures Krog he'll be prepared. Retik wears shiny gold robes and colorful hoods.

Five days later Cody, Ted, Joan, and Hank the pilot meet at the rocket ship at an isolated desert location. Cody is reluctant to have a woman along on the trip but Joan assures him he'll change his mind after she's cooked a few meals, and Cody admits that's a possibility. Ted agrees with Joan. "I like to eat, too," he quips. They get into the classically-cigar-shaped ship, sit down and put on their seat belts. They're ready for take off. No plat-

forms, launching pads or boosters for this baby. From a horizontal position she just takes off and is soon zooming on her way to the moon, as the passengers sit back in their little bridge-type chairs and feel a very brief discomfort. In less than a minute they're walking around and going about their duties.

As they approach the moon they spy the Roman-type city in their viewer and decide to land near it. They get back into their flimsy-looking seats, fasten their belts and prepare for landing, which proceeds without incident. They land outside the walled city. Cody puts on his flying suit and exits the rocket ship. Loudspeakers on the great wall direct him to an entrance door. He walks into an elevator which takes him far under ground and brings him face to face with Retik, seated at a desk, who

161

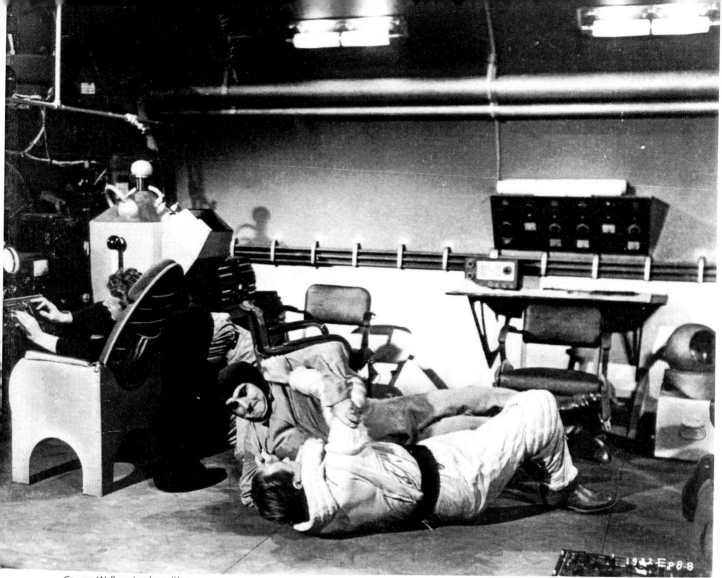

George Wallace tussles with a moon man.

greets him warmly. "Welcome, Commando Cody," he says. "I am Retik, ruler of the Moon."

Cody comments that he seems to have been expected. Retik tells him that radios have kept him informed of events on Earth for years, "and my men there have advised me of your every move." He tells Cody that the attacks are to soften Earth's defenses prior to the Moon's impending invasion which, alas, is necessary "Because the atmosphere on the moon has become so thin and dry it is impossible for us to raise food." They've had to move underground, living in a pressurized city while their old city rots above. Conquering Earth will be easy, Retik says, because of the Moon's superiority in atomic weapons, thanks to lunarium, found only on the moon, an element far superior to uranium as a base for atomic reactions. He's glad to reveal all this

as a reward for Cody's long trip, but unfortunately can't allow him to return to Earth..

Cody replies he may have something to say about that, and pulls out a gun. Retik flicks a switch and the gun flies from Cody's hand, magnetically drawn to the ceiling. Now Retik draws a weapon of his own, a futuristic ray pistol, fires it at Cody—and misses, although the gun produces a lot of smoke. He fires another shot from his futuristic device, misses again and has to reload while his guards battle man to man with Cody, who proceeds to flatten each. Finally Retik reloads, aims and fires and misses yet again. And he has to reload again. While he's doing this, Cody puts on his helmet, gets into the elevator, zips to the surface and flies away.

Back in the rocket ship, Cody tells the others what he learned. He had

noticed an atomic ray gun in Retik's lab. If he could just get hold of that "it would be easy to blast open their pressurized buildings and really put them out of business." But first he must get the gun. It's a dangerous undertaking so Ted volunteers to take a helmet (so he can breathe) and go with him. Cody takes him to a spot near the entrance door where he's to wait while Cody enters. The idea is for Cody to get to the lab, steal the ray gun and get it to the surface, where Ted will help him carry it to the ship.

Cody takes the elevator to the lower level. He empties a pressure canister full of nitrous oxide into the lab's ventilation system, nearly knocking out Retik and his assistant. Nearly, but not quite. As Cody is trying to liberate the ray gun, Retik (who had managed to grab an oxygen mask) revives his man and they attack. There is an extensive

162

battle during which Retik's assistant is knocked out early on. Cody and Retik fight it out, but it's impossible for Retik to hit Cody in the head, it being encased in a metal helmet and all, which limits him to punches to the shoulders and chest. With this advantage Cody eventually knocks out Retik, grabs the ray gun and lugs it to the surface, as planned, where he and Ted start running with it.

A moon security vehicle, looking like a teardrop-shaped tank, speeds into view and after them. They duck into a cave but are spotted by the mooncar drivers. As Cody and Ted retreat into the cave, the car's atomic cannons are trained on the cave entrance and open fire, melting the rock around the entrance and causing lava to flow into

In full regalia, Roy Barcroft as the evil Retik, another would-be conqueror of Earth.

the cave. As the rock melts, more lava rushes in. Cody and Ted abandon the ray gun and race through the cave, a wave of molten lava not far behind them. Things look hopeless, but Cody spies a turnoff passageway and they run into it, escaping the lava which for reasons unknown doesn't enter. Their cavern fortuitously leads them outside.

Looking around, they see the mooncar below them. Cody tosses a hand grenade, which doesn't stop the car from driving off but does warn its drivers that Cody is at large. Cody and Ted hurry back to the rocket ship. The crew agrees they should take off as soon as possible. Hank says he'll need a couple of hours to get the ship ready. Cody uses the time by going off, finding a lunarian guard, disposing of him and

Below: Oh no. Commando Cody has been pushed off the mountainside. How will he get out of this one?

taking his ray pistol. By the time he gets back to the rocket ship it's ready to take off. A mooncar speeds to the scene, guns blazing, but can't stop the rocket ship's quick departure.

Retik radios Krog that Cody and crew are heading back to Earth. He warns that the ship "must be destroyed before anyone can get out of it," by any means possible. The luckless Graber and Daly are given the assignment. They are hiding among bushes and behind rocks on the outskirts of the rocket ship's landing field, which has a police car protecting it. As soon as Cody and the others step from the plane the hirelings open fire and miss, as their targets duck and return fire. When the police join in Graber and Daly (surely two of serialdom's less competent underlings) beat a hasty retreat in their

car and Cody hops into the police car and drives after them.

The chase proceeds along mountain roads. As they cross a bridge Daly tosses a grenade onto the road. Cody's car comes speeding along and reaches the bridge when the grenade goes off. The car plummets from the bridge, tumbles down a mountainside and explodes spectacularly. Fortunately the eagle-eyed Cody had seen the grenade and leaped from the car just seconds before it detonated.

Later, at Cody Laboratories, Cody, Ted and Joan confer with Henderson. Cody reports that against the Moon's awesome firepower the Earth is defenseless, and Henderson agrees. Cody recalls that Retik said he wouldn't attack until his men on Earth had finished softening up the planet's defenses,

so he suggests they concentrate on finding and breaking up Retik's earth-bound operation. Cody says his flying suit gives him a big advantage in checking a sabotage scene and Henderson promises to call him as soon as there's another attack. "In the meantime we'll put every available man on this case," he says.

Krog is having his own problems. He is running out of Earth money and because Graber and Daly keep botching assignments he's having a hard time coming up with any. Graber is ordered to resume his former career as a bank robber, which he does in earnest but with typical Graber skill. The robbery is botched, three of his associates are shot and he has to leap from a speeding car to narrowly escape the police.

When Krog reports the bad news to

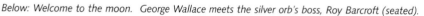

Below: Welcome to the moon. George Wallace meets the silver orb's boss, Roy Barcroft (seated).

Retik, the ruler of the Moon is undisturbed. He has another terrific plan. "From what I hear of activities on Earth," he tells Krog, "kidnapping important persons and holding them for ransom has proved highly profitable." He suggests that Commando Cody is quite valuable and that the government would pay a lot for him. "An excellent idea," says Krog. "We shall carry it out at once." Guess who gets the job. "It'll be safer than robbing another bank," comments Graber as he and Daly get set to leave. "Commando Cody should be worth at least a hundred thousand dollars," Krog says to them as they go.

Graber and Daly pay a visit to Cody Laboratories but find only Ted and Joan. Ted puts up a superb fight, knocking each man down in succession several times, but is eventually overwhelmed and knocked out. The thugs take Joan with them, figuring she'll be good bait for Cody. They leave just as Cody drives up. Ted tells him what's happened. An all-points alert is put out and police scour the area for a car with Joan in it, as Cody dons his flying suit and searches from above.

A good thing, too, for Joan has been transferred to a single-motor plane, piloted by the versatile Graber. Cody sees the plane and flies toward it. Graber draws a pistol and fires a shot. Joan tries to grab Graber's hand and is knocked unconscious. There is a lively pistol battle between Graber in the plane and the flying Commando Cody, with no harm to either party. When Graber runs out of ammunition he does what anyone would do: he puts the plane into a dive, disconnects and tosses out the joystick, and bails out. Joan regains consciousness but can do nothing to control the plane. Cody gets into the craft and tells her to put on the parachute that's laying there—she would never have thought of that herself—and bail out, which she does. Cody flies off just before the ship crashes.

Krog has to report yet another failure to Retik: he couldn't kidnap Cody, he's still out of funds and hasn't got a ray gun to use in their faltering reign of terror. Retik tells him that if his current helpers can't carry out orders he should

That's supposed to be George Wallace under the helmet, proudly displaying his ray gun and the control panel on the chest of his flying suit. Aline Towne is at his side.

fire them and find people who can. Krog gives Graber and Daly one more chance: a relatively simple job, to steal a hotel payroll. But even this penny-ante crime is botched and Graber is wounded and caught. He's placed in a hospital and although the obligatory rescue attempt is successful there are a half-dozen other mishaps that delay the invasion from the Moon.

Eventually Krog gets a ray gun working and happily radios the news to Retik. But Retik has another idea. He tells Krog to set off an atom bomb in the crater of Mount Alta, a dormant volcano. "The present atmospheric conditions on Earth indicate that the eruption would cause torrential rains and the resulting floods would seriously disrupt transportation and defense." And that's when Krog will attack with his ray gun, to completely break down Earth's defenses. Only then could the moon invasion be launched.

An atom bomb is detonated in the crater and the eruption produces the predicted results. There are tremendous lightning and thunder storms with heavy rain, flooding, and all-round calamity. Dams burst, towns are swept away, cities are inundated. "If the moon men did start that eruption," says Joan, "they certainly got results."

Clues lead a non-uniformed Cody and Ted from Al's Cafe (where Cody and Ted fight with Graber and Daly) to a garage (where Cody and Ted fight with Graber and Daly). Ted is captured and escapes, ditto Cody. Here's what happens to Cody during the fight in the garage: taking on two thugs he is punched several times, knocked against a wall and onto a table. He delivers punches right and left. He takes a hard right to the face, delivers a hard right, takes another hard right, falls against a table, leaps upon a fallen foe, is slugged three times in a row by his opponent who breaks a bench on his back, and is eventually beaten unconscious by the two thugs. The point of this description is that at no time during any of the above does Cody lose his snap-brimmed hat.

The ray-gun attacks are devastating Earth's defenses. Henderson and Cody decide the only way for the U.S. to counter the ray guns is to build ray guns of its own, but for that they'll need lunarium. Henderson agrees that Cody and the others should return to the moon and bring back some of the element so that ray-gun production can start. "Anything is better that sitting here like tin ducks in a shooting gallery," says Cody.

Commando Cody trains his pistol on leather-cowled Peter Brocco, while dynamic underworld duo of Clayton Moore (2nd from left) and Bob Stevenson (Graber and Daly) get ready to make their move.

And so it's back to the moon for Cody, Ted, Joan and Hank. Once there, the stealing of lunarium turns out to be a little more complicated than anticipated. Cody has to disguise himself as a moon man to get to the vault where the lunarium is stored, and even when he does he discovers that a box of the element weighs more than he can carry so he must kind of shove it from place to place—somewhat cumbersome when you're trying to steal the stuff. Cody manages to shlep it to the outer wall where he and Ted liberate a moon car, place the lunarium in it, speed to the rocket ship and fly back to the Earth. News of their escape is relayed to Graber and Daly who are there waiting as the crew disembarks. There is a gun battle between parties. Seventeen shots are fired with litle damage to anyone.

In the days that follow Cody faces certain burial in a landslide, his laboratory is gassed, Krog gets to say lines like "I must report to the Moon," and, faced with one failure after another Retik decides that he himself will come to Earth and direct matters. He does, and there is no improvement.

Cody, in his flying suit, follows Graber and Daly's trail to the Moon men's cave hideout. There is a tremendous fist fight with Cody versus Retik, Krog, Graber and Daly. Cody may be a lousy shot but he's one hell of a brawler. During the battle Krog is electrocuted when he falls against a wired section. Eventually Cody falls against the same section and is presumed electrocuted by Retik and the others. They flee, leaving him for dead, but he isn't, and soon recovers.

Graber and Daly, who simply do not learn from experience, show up again at Al's Cafe, and Al tips off Cody. Cody and Ted arrive a few minutes later and another fight starts, which does a good deal of damage to poor Al's Cafe ("No good turn ever goes unpunished." —Dorothy Parker) and spills into a high speed car chase which terminates when Graber and Daly's car goes off a mountain road and explodes spectacularly, a fitting *adios* to one of the more memorable henchman duos.

Eventually Retik is trapped in a cave and there's an extensive shoot out between Cody's forces and Retik's men. Master of the Moon is dressed for the occasion, elegant in presumably purple and gold. A close-fitting purple outfit (with the most darling tights), matching purple mail cowl, and a gold mail collar and belt. An ideal ensemble for a shoot out. Unfortunately his men are quickly wiped out and he retreats into a rocket ship and takes off, destination Moon. Cody and Ted rush to a ray gun, mount it on a truck, aim it carefully at the departing rocket and fire. The rocket ship is blasted to smithereens.

Henderson thanks Cody. Ted, Joan and Hank on behalf of the Earth, and assures them that because of their valiant efforts America would now have time to prepare for an adequate defense, should the Moon men—or anyone—be foolish enough to attempt an attack.

Zombies of the Stratosphere (Republic-1952) Directed by Fred C. Brannon. Screenplay: Ronald Davidson. Based on characters created by Royal K. Cole, William Lively, Sol Shor. Unit manager: Roy Wade. Photography: John MacBurnie. Music: Stanley Wilson. Art director: Fred A. Ritter. Sets: John McCarthy, James Redd. Special effects: Howard Lydecker, Theodore Lydecker. Supervising editor: Murray Seldeen. Editor: Cliff Bell. Makeup: Bob Mark. Sound: Dick Tyler. Producer: Franklin Adreon. [7-16-52] Feature title: *Satan's Satellites.*

Below: It's up and away for Larry Martin, in pursuit of Marex's rocket ship.

Stanley Waxman is caught in his laboratory by gun-toing Judd Holdren.

4. Contraband Cargo   5. The Iron Executioner   6. Murder Mine 7. Death on the Waterfront 8. Hostage for Murder   9. The Human Torpedo 10. Flying Gas Chamber   11. Man vs. Monster   12. Tomb of the Traitors

A rocket from another planet is monitored by Mr. Steele, head of the famous cosmic-policing organization, the Inter-Planetary Patrol. He assigns one of his most dependable executives, Larry Martin, to investigate. With a little help from two friends, Bob Wilson and Sue Davis, he takes off in an amazing invention of his, a flying suit (put it on, turn a knob, and you fly), to locate the strange craft, somewhere in the Marengo Hills.

The invading rocket has brought two dark-eyed, sallow-faced part-human zombies from Mars; Marex and

Cast:

Larry Martin	Judd Holdren	Telegrapher	Dale Van Sickel
Sue Davis	Aline Towne	Lawson	Roy Engel
Bob Wilson	Wilson Wood	Kerr	Jack Harden
Dr. Harding	Stanley Waxman	Kettler	Robert Strange
Mr. Steele	Craig Kelly	Tarner	Norman Willis
Marex	Lane Bradford	Dick	Gayle Kellogg
Narab	Leonard Nimoy	Ross	Clifton Young
Roth	John Crawford	Elah	Robert Garabedian
Shane	Ray Boyle		
Truck Driver	Tom Steele		

12 Chapters:
1. The Zombie Vanguard   2. Battle of the Rockets   3. Undersea Agents

Judd Holdren and Aline Towne are ready for the zombies.

Below: Henchman John Crawford gets his orders from alien Lane Bradford.

Narab, who are met by two Earthmen assistants, Roth and Shane. As they transfer equipment from the rocket to a waiting truck, Larry lands on the truck's roof and plants a direction finder with which the vehicle can be traced.

The equipment is brought to a cave that can only be entered through an underwater passage. Dr. Harding, a renegade scientist, is contacted and persuaded to to help the aliens in a fantastic, possibly lunatic scheme to construct a couple of hydrogen bombs: one to blow Earth out of its orbit, and the other to move the zombies' planet into its place to capitalize on Earth's superior climate. Needless to say there is a

Commando Cody dismantles one of Marex's robots.

Craig Kelly, Judd Holdren and Wilson Wood plan their next move.

considerable amount of advanced technology involved in such a maneuver.

To ward off this impending disaster, Larry, Bob and Sue follow a trail of clues as they try to prevent vital instruments and components from falling into the hands of the zombies, their Earth henchmen, and a robot that Marex has created, a powerful though lumbering iron monster operated by remote control. It would be hard to imagine a more klutzy robot. The friends must face the requisite obstacles, including high-speed chases, car crashes, explosions, and—as the bad guys abandon their rocket-fuel-loaded truck and send it rolling downhill where it crashes into our hero's pursuing car and explodes—sometimes all three at once. Larry is axed, suffocated, gassed, boiled and crushed—or close to it, but comes through each time.

169

Special investigator Wilson Wood, in the grip of Marex's killer robot.

Judd Holdren and his marvelous helmet and flying jacket

While tracking down a stolen shipment of uranium ore the three friends are led to the hideaway cave, where Larry and Bob nearly lose their lives in an underwater battle with the zombies, who can remain submerged longer than Earthmen. In addition to the ever-necessary need for uranium, Marex and his crew engage in various forms of mischief. They attempt to rob the Ferndale National Bank, use a submarine to transport radioactive cargo, intercept the shipment of a radio-activated-detonator assembly Larry needs, and utilize the robot to stalk each of the agents.

Eventually Marex, Narab and Dr. Harding are trapped in the cave. The aliens cold-bloodedly shoot the doctor when he tries to surrender. The zombies have their rocket ship poised in the mountain for a quick getaway. They set a timer which will detonate a hydrogen bomb and push the earth out of orbit, and take off in their rocket. They're met in the air by Larry and the Inter-Planetary Patrol forces. In a furious ray-gun battle the alien ship is shot down and only Narab remains alive, but just barely. He's mortally wounded.

Larry searches through the rocket's wreckage and learns from the dying Narab that the hydrogen bomb in the inner cave is about to destroy Earth. Larry flies to the cave, races through the water tunnel and disconnects the bomb just seconds before it can explode. The Earth is saved, thanks to Larry Martin and the Inter-Planetary Patrol.

The Lost Planet (Columbia-1953) Directed by Spencer G. Bennet. Screenplay: Geo. H. Plympton, Arthur Hoerl. Assistant director: Charles S. Gould. Photography: William Whitley. Editor: Earl Turner. Special effects: Jack Ericson. Set continuity: Moree Herring. Art director: Paul Palmentola. Musical director: Ross DiMaggio. Set decorator: Sidney Clifford. Production

Lane Bradford conspires with accomplices John Crawford and Stanley Waxman.

170

manager: Herbert Leonard. Sound engineer: Josh Westmoreland. Producer: Sam Katzman.

Cast:

Rex Barrow . . . . Judd Holdren
Ella Dorn . . . . Vivian Mason
Tim Johnson . . . . Ted Thorpe
Prof. Edmund Dorn . . . Forrest Taylor
Dr. Grood . . . . Michael Fox
Reckov . . . . Gene Roth
Karlo . . . . Karl Davis
Ken Wolper . . . . Leonard Penn
Hopper . . . . John Cason
Darl . . . . Nick Stuart
Lah . . . . Joseph Mell
Jarva . . . . Jack George
Alden . . . . Frederick Berest
Robot No. 9 . . . . . I. Stanford Jolley
Ned Hilton . . . . Pierre Watkin
Wesley Bren . . . . Lee Roberts

15 Chapters:

1. The Mystery of the Guided Missile
2. Trapped by the Axial Propeller
3. Blasted by the Thermic Disintegrator
4. The Mind-Control Machine   5. The Atomic Plane   6. Disaster in the Stratosphere   7. Snared by the Prysmic Catapult   8. Astray in Space   9. The Hypnotic Ray Machine   10. To Free the Planet People   11. Dr. Grood Defies Gravity   12. Trapped in a Cosmic Jet   13. The Invisible Enemy   14. In the Grip of the De-Thermo Ray   15. Sentenced to Space

"In a primitive Western area but not far from a large city" sits Mt. Vulcan, formerly an active volcano. The rocky, barren surrounding area is "unfit for human use." The mountain is riddled with caves and the area uninhabited, except for a small cabin occupied by a "strange, furtive man" known as 'the hermit," who avoids strangers. The man, in a slouch hat and oversized coat, approaches what seems to be a cave wall and points a pencil-like wand at it. A door appears, slides open and the man enters. He removes his hat, coat and

boots (he's wearing a vest, shirt and tie), puts on a lab coat, presses another button and a bookcase pivots away from the wall and a sliding door rises, revealing a modern laboratory and all sorts of electrical machinery.

His name is Dr. Grood, and his assistant, Jarva, tells him he's gotten a message from Reckov on their home planet Ergro. (From what we see of Ergro, it too is a barren, rocky place.) Using an advanced radio, Grood returns the call and Reckov, splendidly attired in a white uniform (like that of a doorman at a posh Viennese hotel), reports that a captive scientist, Professor Dorn, has "somehow counteracted the effect of your hypnotic ray." Grood tells him that Dorn "must be controlled," and that he will send "the power units" to Ergro so that the ray can be "reactivated." He's going to send the units via cosmojet, and wants some vital ore sent to him the same way.

Below: The malevolent Ergronian Michael Fox and earthmen Judd Holdren and Forrest Taylor in the underground laboratory on the planet Ergro.

Reckov and Jarva load the units into the cosmojet, a large, bullet-shaped missile. Then, to divert the nation so the cosmojet won't be noticed, flying saucers are released into the sky, heading for Washington, D.C. Soon every resource of the government is aimed at tracking and destroying the saucers. The public is agog. While the populace is thus preoccupied the cosmojet is launched and blasts off to Ergro unnoticed. Another flick of a switch and the saucers disappear.

Grood gloats about what the world would think if it knew of his secret metal, with "the power to betray minds, to make things invisible." "They would never believe it," Jarva states. They had their chance, Grood says, but now

"when they learn it will be too late." Using an advanced telescopic device he sees the cosmojet land safely on Ergro.

Directed by Reckov, workmen unload the cosmojet and bring the power units into his laboratory, located in a cave He orders Prof. Dorn be placed in "the hypnotic ray cabinet." White-haired Prof. Dorn, a few feet away, makes a break for it but is quickly grabbed and placed in the glass and metal cabinet. Dorn emerges a few moments later totally hypnotized. Reckov tells him to get back to work, and he does.

The cosmojet returning to Earth with the ore Grood wanted, nears Mt. Vulcan when something goes wrong. Grood and Jarva watch in horror as the

rocket ship crashes into the side of the mountain. The crash is spectacular and draws a lot of attention. The state police cordon off the area

Rex Barrow a reporter, and Tim Johnson, a photographer, are sent to cover the story. Showing press passes they get past the police roadblock, and notice that a pretty woman in a white convertible is let in, too. Rex and Tim snoop around the area for a while before Rex notices a piece of smoking metal on the ground and goes to investigate. Grood sees all this on his tv screen, presses a few buttons and the metal self-destructs before Rex's eyes.

Rex and Tim continue to look around. Grood decides they're getting too close to the cave and issues a few

The situation seems hopeless as flames come closer to Judd Holdren and Vivian Mason. They don't know it, but they are about to be saved by one of Dorn's inventions.

172

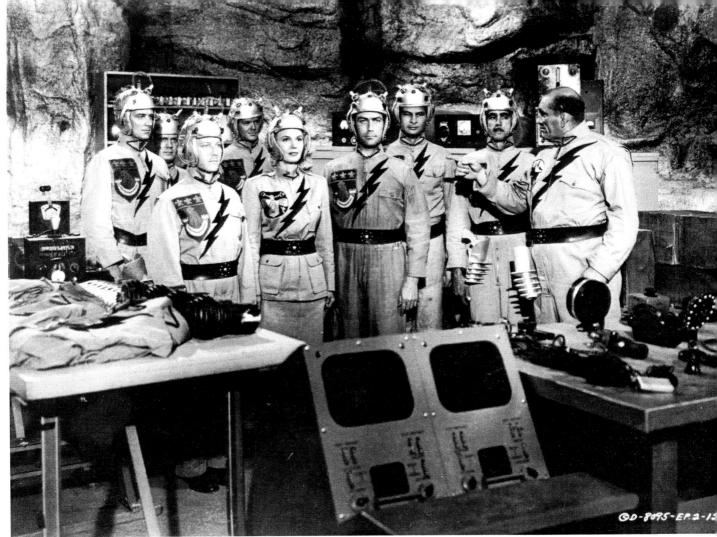

Captured-and-hypnotized Ted Thorpe, Vivian Mason and Judd Holdren (front row; 1st, 2nd and 3rd from left) listen to Karl Davis's (right) orders.

orders to Jarva. A rolling fireball speeds down the mountain toward the two newsmen, who see it and start running. It explodes a short distance from them but neither man is hurt. Rex picks up a smoking piece of metal from the explosion and studies it. In the meantime, Tim bumps into the pretty woman and, after a short conversation, brings her to Rex. She's Ella Dorn. "You probably remember my father," she says. "He disappeared last year, right here on Mt. Vulcan." She asks if she can join their investigation. They love the idea.

They're all quickly captured by Grood, hypnotized, sent to Ergro where, still hypnotized and under Reckov's control, they're forced to mine Ergro's mystery ore, cosmonium. They're all fitted with metallic helmets which reinforce the hypnotism. Secretly aided by Prof. Dorn (who has come up with a

device that unhypnotizes them), the trio manage to escape from the mine and hide in a nearby cave. Grood (who regularly jets back and forth from Earth to Ergro), however, is able to monitor the area using advanced "telopticon" surveillance technology, and he's been watching their flight. He gets his death ray gun and is about to zap the cave when Prof. Dorn, using a cosmic-ray gun, blasts the death ray from his hands. Dorn is quickly subdued by Grood's men, but the death ray is ruined.

Prof. Dorn discovers there is another mystery metal on Ergro: dornite (named after its discoverer). When combined with cosmonium the two ores render their bearer invisible. Rex and Dorn plan to make Rex invisible and get him aboard a cosmojet being used to carry Grood to Earth. Accordingly, he sneaks onto the rocket ship. Once back on Earth Rex visits his boss, newspaper

publisher Ned Hilton, who doesn't believe Rex's ridiculous story of visits to another planet. Rex goes to several government agencies, but no one believes him.

Then it's back to Ergro where: (once again) he's captured, chained to a wall and a "thermic vibrator" turned on him causing the cave he's in to collapse; Ella and Tim, still hypnotized are sent to assassinate Rex with ray guns; Jarva gets to say lines like "for every weapon there is a counter weapon" to Grood; and Dorn tells Rex, "Sometime ago I perfected an atomic propulsion energizer. It counteracts the neutron generators." Grood commands that Dorn, despite his constant escapes and troublemaking, must be taken alive—his knowledge is invaluable.

Another of Dorn's secret inventions is an atomic plane (which looks like a prop-jet), and he plans to have

173

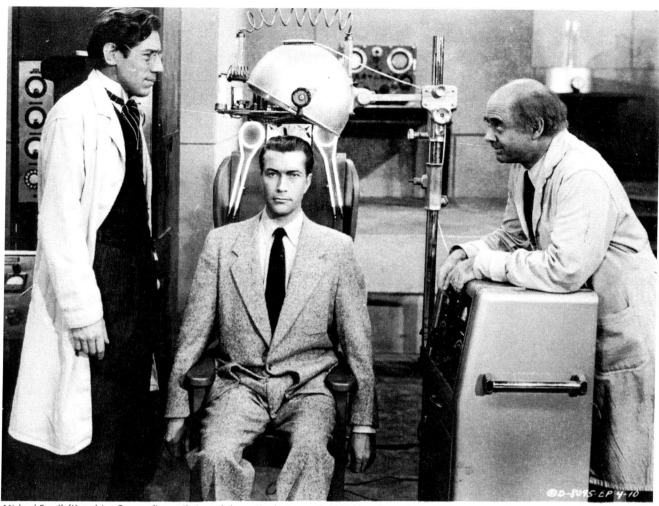

Michael Fox (left) and Jac George discuss their newly-hypnotized prisoner, Judd Holdren (center).

Rex escape to Earth in it. Rex is helped by another prisoner, Wesley Bren, and the two manage to fly the plane to Earth, despite Grood's attempts to shoot them down. Upon landing, Rex tells Bren that after he attends to a few matters he's going to search for the mad scientist operating on Mt. Vulcan. Bren wants to help, and they agree to meet at the foot of the mountain. If they have to return to Ergro it will be easy, because Dorn has outfitted the atomic plane with a "gyro electron and a directional finder that will guide the plane automatically back."

Bren heads straight to his boss, Ken Wolper "the novelty king" (a front for a slot-machine racket) and explains what's happened. Wolper listens incredulously then tells Bren to "figure it was a bad dream." Bren has a better idea: "Suppose you could make the world one big slot machine?" Wolper is

interested. Bren proposes they take over Ergro and Grood and Dorn's ingenious inventions "and everyone on mother Earth pays off—if they want business as usual." Wolper buys it, and assigns Hopper, one of his men, to accompany Bren. What about Rex after he's served their purpose? "Get rid of him," Wolper suggests. Meanwhile, on Ergro, Ella and Tim, continue to work in the mines, supposedly hypnotized, but still really clear-minded, thanks to Dorn's de-hypnotizer, and regularly report in to the professor. What with various defectors and all, Dorn seems to have more control than Reckov over what goes on.

Rex, Bren and Hopper meet at Mt. Vulcan, grab Dr. Grood and force him to take them to the back-room laboratory. Rex is lured to a nook which turns into a trap—he's launched through a crevice into the air and dumped on the

ground at the foot of the mountain. Jarva presses a button and Bren and Hopper are instantly hypnotized. Grood has them put into a Cosmjet and sent to Ergro to join the mine slaves. Rex brushes himself off, finds the atomic plane and blasts off to Ergro.

Ken Wolper is getting impatient; he hasn't heard from Bren and Hopper. He sends trusted assistant Darl and another man to Mt. Vulcan to see what they can find out. Darl is spotted by Grood, captured and placed in a "subconscious mind control" machine that forces him to reveal his mission. Grood is interested and strikes a deal with the now-revived Darl: Wolper will provide men and organization to help Grood protect his control of Ergro (and recapture Rex), in return for Dorn and Grood's technological know-how. (Grood, of course, figures he'll dispose of the Earthmen once they've served his purpose.)

Rex meets the "Planet People," burnoose-wearing folks who are opposed to Grood's rule, but who aren't of much use because they're non-violent and "know nothing of warfare." He also establishes contact with Prof. Dorn and gains regular access to the laboratory. There'll be many more escapes, recaptures and rehypnotisms in the adventures that follow.

Dorn's assistant, Alden, another captive, aids him in his efforts against Grood. And Dorn is certainly productive. Rex, Ellen and Tim are chained to a wall as Grood tries to incinerate them. Flames theaten to engulf them when Rex notices that the flames are cold. The Planet People come and unchain them. "Are you responsible for this?," an enraged Grood asks Dorn. Dorn proudly admits that he "merely reversed the enrgizer on the solar thermal fur-

nace." "There'll be an accounting," Grood warns him. Still, Dorn comes up with a "degravitiser" which "counteracts the force of gravity" and which Rex and Grood get to use with varying degrees of success.

The arrangement between Grood and Darl doesn't work out. Darl becomes aware of Grood's plans to conquer Earth, and switches sides, allying himself, Bren and Hopper with Rex and Dorn. They determine they must shut down Grood's operation on Earth. Rex and Darl volunteer for that mission and blast off in Dorn's atomic plane. While they're gone, the others will succeed in capturing Grood and Reckov and locking them up, only to have Karlo (aka "R-4"), one of Grood's most loyal men, slip them some dornite, enabling them to escape invisibly. Eventually, Bren, Hopper, Tim and (a while later) Dorn wind up imprisoned in a cell along with

some Planet People.

Arriving on Earth, Darl brings Rex to Ken Wolper's office in a dingy warehouse building. Darl fills Wolper in on everything that's happened. Wolper tells them to continue on their mission. Rex and Darl approach the Mt. Vulcan cabin, are spotted by Jarva who turns on the hypnotizing ray. Once more Rex and darl are under Jarva's influence. He contacts Grood, who orders him to capture Ken Wolper, too, and send them to Ergro via cosmojet. Jarva has Darl contact Wolper and lure him to the cabin.

When Wolper shows up he immediately notices that Rex and Darl seem drugged. He pulls a gun on Jarva and forces him to unhypnotize them. Jarva is placed in the mind control cabinet and given a taste of his own medicine. Rex gives Wolper a tour of the laboratory; the radarscope, with which you "can see anything close by, even through

Below: Frederick Berest looks on as Forrest Taylor talks to Judd Holdren, who's holding Karl Davis as Ted Thorpe keeps him covered with a ray gun.

rocks and walls," a gadget "with which Grood can read your subconscious mind," and a "stellarscope—it can reach almost anything in space." Indeed it can, for at that moment Grood is watching them on his stellarscope.

It's decided that Rex and Darl will take off for Ergro in the atomic plane while Ken stays behind to keep an eye on Jarva. Guided by radio by Alden (who's about the only good guy on Egro not in jail), they're able to land undetected. Alden gives them an "emergency kit" prepared by Prof. Dorn. It contains a Dornite box and a dehypnotizer, and that's enough. The three men race to Grood's headquarters, unhypnotizing guards as they go, and free the captives.

Grood, Reckov and Karlo have been monitoring all this and fire "the cosmic cannon" hoping to kill all the escapees, but the cannon misfunctions and blows up, pretty much totalling all the scientific equipment, although Grood, Reckov and Karlo are okay. They rush to the cosmojet launching room. Grood hops in and reminds the others that someone has to stay behind to launch the ship. Reckov pulls rank and forces Karlo to stay behind. At Grood's command, they blast off.

Alden wanders in and sees Karlo at the controls. "You've sent Dr. Grood and Reckov into infinity," he shouts. "I know it," says Karlo, "and I'm gonna make sure they stay there." He decks Alden with one punch, then hits the launching control box with a pipe. It explodes, and Karlo is killed. Alden tells the others that Grood and Reckov will stay in space forever. "A cruel thing, but perhaps a just one," Prof. Dorn concludes.

Rex, Tim, Bren and Darl return to Mt. Vulcan and find Ken searching for Jarva, who has escaped. Jarva's maniacal voice rings out through speakers and warns them that he's going to destroy the place and that they should leave immediately. They take his advice and get out just as the entire cavernous network blows up and is buried under tons of earth.

Index
Boldface indicates photo.

179